BEL MOONEY

a small dog saved my life

A Story of Survival

Collins

Collins,
an imprint of HarperCollins*Publishers*
77–85 Fulham Palace Road
London W6 8JB

www.harpercollins.co.uk

1

First published in 2010 as *Small Dogs Can Save Your Life*
This edition 2011

A catalogue record for this book is available from the British Library.

ISBN: 978-0-00-742721-5

Printed and bound in Great Britain by
Clays Ltd, St Ives plc

For Gaynor and Ernie

(and Bertie too)

I worry.
I have to because nobody else does.
Some strange car comes up the driveway –
They go right on talking. They trust,
I don't. Threat crosses my nose
Twenty times a day.
No wonder I bark and menace,
Who knows who it could be at the door
'Specially in these times.
Arthur Miller, 'Lola's Lament'

How to resist nothingness? What power
Preserves what once was, if memory does not last?
For I remember little. I remember so very little.
Indeed, moments restored would mean the Last Judgement
That is adjourned from day to day, by Mercy perhaps.
Czeslaw Milosz, 'On Parting With My Wife, Janina'

You were never masters, but friends. I was your friend.
I loved you well, and was loved. Deep love endures
To the end and far past the end. If this is my end,
I am not lonely. I am not afraid. I am still yours.
Robinson Jeffers, 'The Housedog's Grave'

CONTENTS

INTRODUCTION

What counts is not necessarily the size of the dog in the fight; it's the size of the fight in the dog.

Dwight D. Eisenhower, Address, Republican National Committee, USA, 31 January 1958

When I look in the mirror I see quite a small person: not tall and quite slight. My skin bruises easily and as I grow older I notice more and more weaknesses, from wrinkles to stiff limbs to hair that is no longer thick and beautiful, as it once was. This is, of course, all inevitable. I can do no more about it than I can change all the experiences, good and ill, which have shaped the mind and spirit within this vulnerable, mortal frame. In this respect I am exactly like you, the über-reader I always imagine as a friend when writing. We can (men and women alike) anoint ourselves with unguents in an attempt to keep time at bay but the most useful exercise for the soul is to square up to your life, no matter how much it terrifies you, and try to make sense of it. That is the true business of self-preservation and it is what I try to do in this book – in the hope that this small, individual journey, one woman's personal experience of love, loss and survival, may (quite simply) be useful. Most of us have endured, or will endure, pain in our lives. If this book has any message it is that recovery and salvation can come from the most unexpected sources, and that largeness of spirit will most equip you for your personal fight.

Working in my study one summer day, writing the journalism which pays the bills but wondering if I would ever return to fiction and slightly desperate for something – anything – to break that block, I flexed a bare left foot which touched my Maltese dog, Bonnie. She sleeps on a small blue bed, patterned with roses, which sits beneath my home-made work surface. All day she waits for attention, rising to follow me wherever I go in the house, longing for the moment when, feeling guilty, I at last suggest a short walk. At which point she leaps up, races up the stairs from the basement and scrabbles wildly at the front door, like a prisoner incarcerated in the Bastille who hears the liberators outside and screams, 'I'm here! Save me!'

On that day in 2008 I suddenly realized how great a part my dog had played in my own salvation, and that I wanted to write about that process. I was encouraged by the experience of an artist I admire very much, David Hockney, whose paintings and drawings of his two dachshunds, Boodgie and Stanley, show the pets curled on cushions, lapping water, rolling on their backs. You don't have to be a lover of small dogs to be delighted by these works, and yet they should not be underestimated, despite their simplicity. What looks like a set of speedily executed images of two faintly absurd, brown sausage dogs adds up to an idiosyncratic statement about love.

In the introduction to *Dog Days* (the 1998 book which collects this work) Hockney writes, 'I make no apologies for the apparent subject matter. These two dear little creatures are my friends. They are intelligent, loving, comical and often bored. They watch me work; I notice the warm shapes they make together, their sadness and their delights.'

What does he mean by 'apparent subject matter'? He's painting his funny tubular dogs, isn't he? End of story. Yet not so. In an online interview the artist explained, 'I think the real reason I did them was as a way of dealing with the recent deaths of a number of my friends ... I was feeling very down. And I started painting the dogs and realized this was a marvellous subject for me at this time, because they were little innocent creatures like us, and they didn't know about much. It was just a marvellous, loving subject.' Asked (mad question!) if the dogs had any sense they were the subject of Hockney portraits, the artist replied, 'The dogs think nothing of them really. They'd just as soon pee on them. They don't care about art since they're simply on to higher things – the source of art, which is love. That's what the paintings are about – love, really.'

So, on an unconscious quest to deal with loss and celebrate love, one of the most popular artists of our time stayed at home and 'saw the nearest things to me, which was two little dogs on cushions'. Similarly, on my own quest to understand how love can survive even an ending, how a marriage can go on reverberating even after divorce and how the process of reinvention in a human life reflects the very movement of the universe and must be embraced, I stayed at home and stroked the nearest thing to me, which was a tiny white dog with a feathery tail who needs me as much as I need her. I had so much to learn from the force of devotion within that minuscule frame.

Dogs are patient with us; they have little choice. They continue with their dogged work of saving our lives, even if we don't know it's happening. Long before my foot reached out to rub her soft white fur that day, my lapdog was asking me to regard her as Muse. She was demanding proper attention, as well as instinctive affection. She was saying, 'I'm here!' And it worked. Since then my 'animal companion' (as the modern phrase insists, implying equality rather than ownership) has inspired my 'Bonnie' series of six books for children, which stars a small white dog from a rescue home who, as the saga progresses, helps to cheer and restore one unsure, unhappy boy and his family.

Now she is the beginning, middle and end of this book's story too – and, like Hockney, 'I make no apologies for the apparent subject matter.' I am writing about what happened to me between 2002 and 2009, using my dog as a way into a painful story, and a way out of it too. During that time my marriage ended and life was turned on its head. What do dogs know about marriage? Probably a lot – because they are in tune to our feelings and it's hard to hide things from your dog. As I get older I want to share more, hide less. That's why I'm willing to invite others to come along on a walk with my pet, in the hope that the activity might act as 'therapy' for them, as it has for me. Dogs are good at therapy – so mine will help me tell this story of a love (affair). Or, rather, a tale of many loves.

It's not easy to embark on anything resembling autobiography, although bookshops are flooded with usually ghosted 'celebrity' tomes and there seems to exist an avid readership for the recollections of (say) a footballer or his wife who are not yet 30. Too often that sort of thing is little more than an extension of newspaper or magazine gossip. What is written will be inevitably full of half-truths and blurred 'fact' as the celebrity dictates the view he or she wishes to present. Even the finest biography will be hampered by unknowing.

If the biographer feels impelled to smooth over instead of flay (and much flaying goes on these days, both in books and column inches, which I doubt adds to the greater good), how much more will the writer of a personal memoir feel the need to evade? As I was working on this book I was entertained (as well as appalled) to read a prominent newspaper diary item about my work in progress which shrieked 'Revelation!' – although not in so few words. The journalist predicted that I would be blowing the lid off relationships within my ex-husband's family, and so on. Now I ask you, why would I want to do that? I agree with the nineteenth-century historian Thomas Carlyle that in writing biography sympathy must be the motivating force. I have no aptitude for slashing and burning, and am glad to say that I shall go happily to my grave never having learnt the arts of war.

A partial life is a slice of reality – a taste which leaves us wanting more. The multifaceted art of memoir suggests that even a few months within a life, when something extraordinary happened, can offer a story of almost mythic power. In the 'new' life writing (a fascinating topic now, especially in the United States) the freedoms of fiction have been introduced into autobiography and obliqueness is allowed. The writer can say, in effect: 'This is what happened that summer, and afterwards. It's not the whole story by any means, because much must remain private. Still, I offer this as an act of mediation. If it happened to you, this might help you survive. This might well stand between you and your nightmare.' That is what I am trying to do in this book – although not without knowledge of the pitfalls.

At the end of 2003 I encountered a successful woman writer who had read in the newspapers about the end of my 35-year-long marriage. 'I hope you're going to write a book about it!' she said with glee. I shook my head. 'But you must!' she went on. 'Tell it like it was! And if you don't want to write it as a true story, just turn it into a novel. People will know it's the truth. You'll do really well.' When I protested that I hated the idea, she asked, 'But why shouldn't you?'

Maybe her counsel made commercial sense, but her avidity drove me further towards reticence. There is enough personal misery swilling around the shelves of bookshops without me adding to the woe, I thought. After all, any celebrity autobiography nowadays is required to take us on a turbulent ride from trouble to trouble – dodgy parents, colon cancer, mental illness, alcohol and drug abuse and the rest. The non-celebrity stories deal in poverty, ill-treatment, sickness and perversion to a degree that would astound even Dickens, who knew about the seamier sides of life. A publishing bandwagon rolls along fuelled by pain and suffering, with the word 'misery' going together with 'memoir' – like 'love and marriage' or 'horse and carriage'. Happy lives, it seems, don't make good 'stories'. But some of the stuff published is not so much gut wrenching as stomach churning.

So this is not a misery memoir. No, this is a happiness memoir, although it deals with unhappiness and recovery. It is just one portion of the narrative of a few years in my life and in the life of one other significant person – the man I married in 1968. Other people close to us have been left out; I do not intend to embarrass either his second wife or my second husband, or indeed to reveal what members of our respective families said, thought or did. Still, since I told that person that I had no intention of writing about the dramatic break-up of my first marriage, things have changed – although my rejection of the notion of 'telling it like it was' is the same. For there is always more than one Truth. Because the experience and its aftermath would not go away, I found myself keeping a 'quarry' notebook for the novel which will remain unwritten, as well as my essential diaries and notebooks, and realized that my own process of learning from them would go on. In the end the impulse to write became like a geyser inside. The aim must always be to find meaning in what happened, for what else can a writer do? I have to agree with the screenwriter Nora Ephron who was taught by her writer parents unapologetically to view her own life as a resource.

So, yes, a memoir of happiness of sorts, because the good times and the bad are indivisible in my memory and roll on forever in the mind's eye like a magic lantern show, or (to be more up-to-date) what Joan Didion calls 'a digital editing system on which … I … show you simultaneously all the frames of memory that come to me now … the marginally different expressions, the variant readings of the same lines'. Writing about the deaths (within days) of her husband, John Gregory Dunne, and her daughter, Quintana, Didion explains (in *The Year of Magical Thinking*) that the book is her attempt to make sense of the period that followed the deaths, which forced her to reconsider so many of her ideas about life, luck, marriage and grief.

Like Joan Didion I was forced to confront not physical death but a different sort of bereavement: the end of a way of life I had thought (somewhat smugly) would continue into a cosy old age. The shattering of that conviction made me confront a myriad of other certainties and set me upon a strange path through the woods – which led, after a while, to the decision to write this book.

'No,' I said to people during that process, 'I'm not writing an autobiography – I'm writing a book about dogs.' The oddness of that statement was enough to stop questions. It came to me one day that all the qualities we associate with dogs, from fidelity to a sense of fun, are ones I admire most in human beings. I also know that small dogs display those qualities in a concentrated form – pure devotion distilled to fill the miniature vessel. Of course, anthropomorphism is dangerous. It pleases us to attribute virtues to canine creatures, who have no moral sense, and when the decision was taken to erect a magnificent monument in central London to all animals killed in war, I remember thinking it feeble-minded to use words like 'loyalty' and 'heroism' and 'courage' about creatures who had no knowledge of such abstracts.

There's a famous Second World War story about an American war dog called Chips who was led ashore by his master, Private John R. Rowell, when his outfit landed at a spot known as Blue Beach, on Sicily's southern coast. They were advancing on the enemy lines in darkness, when they came under machine-gun fire from a pillbox which had been disguised as a peasant's hut. The troops flung themselves to the ground, but the dog charged the machine-gun nest, despite the stream of bullets. Private Rowell said, 'There was an awful lot of noise and the firing stopped. Then I saw one Italian soldier come out of the door with Chips at his throat. I called him off before he could kill the man. Three others followed, holding their hands above their heads.'

I doubt Chips was a titchy Maltese, a Yorkshire terrier or a papillon, although a feisty little Jack Russell might have done some damage, despite his size. Still, the issue is: can you call a dog 'brave'? Was a contemporary writer accurate to assert that 'this American war dog single-handed and at great risk to his own life eliminated an enemy machinegun position and saved the lives of many of his comrades'? Even the most passionate dog lover must admit that the soldier who acts does so in full knowledge of the consequences, carrying within his heart and mind images of parents, wife or girlfriend, children – and risking life despite all. But the dog does not. Men and women act from courage; animals merely act.

Is that true? I do not know – and nowadays I don't really care. In her profound work *Animals and Why They Matter* the philosopher Mary Midgely points out that 'a flood of new and fascinating information about animals' in recent years has educated people who mentally place animal welfare 'at the end of the queue'. She states her belief in 'the vast range of sentient life, of the richness and variety found in even the simplest creatures', and believes it irrelevant that a dog's experience is very different from our own. Philosophers and writers alike have long suggested the idea of the dog as (yes) a moral teacher. This is not fanciful. Anyone who has (for example) studied the psychology of serial killers will recognize the 'flies to wanton boys' argument behind Kant's words: 'He who is cruel to animals becomes hard also in his dealings with men … The more we come into contact with animals, and observe their behaviour, the more we love them, for we see how great is their care of their young.'

Once I was an ignorant young woman who professed dislike of these animals. Now in my sixties, the more I read about dogs and learn what an influence they have had on their owners and the more I love my own small example of the genus, the more I understand Franz Kafka's statement: 'All knowledge, the totality of all questions and answers, is contained within the dog.'

This story asks questions and offers some answers about change and how we can deal with it, in order to survive. It is also about dogs in history, art and literature, dogs as therapy, dogs as everything they can be to humans, helping us in the process of living. The narrative is aided by those diaries and notebooks which were such a catharsis and by a few extracts from my published journalism. I choose to tell this slice of a life discursively, because I have never trodden a straight path and love the side turning which leads to a hidden shrine. During a long career which began in 1970 I have worn many hats – reporter, profile writer, columnist, children's author, commentator on women's issues, travel writer, critic, radio and television presenter, novelist – but it is my latest incarnation which provided the final driving impetus to write this book. In 2005, rebuilding my life, I became – quite by accident, as I will explain – an advice columnist on first one, then another national newspaper. The truth is that, although I have loved all aspects of my working life, I find this the most significantly *useful* role I have ever played, apart from those of wife, mother, daughter and friend.

But the work causes me much sorrow too. So many letters, so much heartbreak, all transferred and carried within me, with none of the safeguards in place for the qualified psychotherapist. This has opened my eyes, in a way impossible before, to the pain caused by the end of love and the destruction of marriage, although the two do not necessarily go together. Oh, I know about the other forms of loss as well. When widows or widowers write to me from their depths of grief and loneliness, it is very hard to know what to say. Death has to be faced, but no such glib statement of the truth of existence is any use to those in mourning. Still, I do my best. I have never been afraid of writing about bereavement. It's easier than addressing vindictiveness, selfishness and despair.

How do you advise people who are dealing with the end of love, or (especially) the 'death' of a long marriage? What resources can be drawn on to cope with the loss of all you were and all you think you might have gone on to be, with that person at your side? How do we make ourselves whole again? The entirely unexpected end of my long marriage confronted me with those questions, and I bring some of the knowledge gained to my job and to this book. Some people will think that all should remain private but I have never been able to shut myself away, and remain unconvinced that battening down the hatches is useful. For one thing, the act of remembering halts the rush of time, as well as being profoundly healing. Seamus Heaney expresses this idea in *Changes*: 'Remember this. It will be good for you to retrace this path when you have grown away and stand at last at the very centre of the empty city.'

Second, I know it is helpful to share stories. My work as an advice columnist has proved to me without doubt that there is valuable consolation for others in telling how it was for you. To hell with privacy, I say – though not with reticence. We *need* each other's stories, all of us, just as I need my small dog. We have to be courageous, just as my dog is brave, no matter how small. We can learn from each other and go on learning, as I have learnt from her. The poet and naturalist David Whyte perfectly encapsulates the motivation behind this evocation of life and dogs:

To be human
Is to become visible
While carrying
What is hidden
As a gift to others.

One

FINDING

There is much to learn from these dogs.
And we must learn these things over and over.
Amy Hempel

I never knew where she came from and will never know. The central mystery will always be there when I look at her, reminding me that my mirror offers a similar puzzle: *who are you?* It is a Zen question, the one Gauguin must have been thinking when he painted *Where Do We Come From? What Are We? Where Are We Going?*, every vibrant brushstroke telling us that the answer can never be known and the central mystery has to be accepted in your journey towards the end. All this I knew. But the coming of my little dog was to herald a deeper awareness: that we cannot know what will happen to us. Not ever.

Yet I have always needed to control things. Spontaneity makes me uneasy. I like to know the history of a house, the provenance of a picture, the origin of a quotation, because such knowledge is a hedge against chaos. I plot and plan. My books are arranged alphabetically or (depending on the subject) chronologically, and my shoes and gloves have to be ordered according to the spectrum. Years ago, having children presented me with a philosophical shock to match the physical and emotional pain, because those outcomes I could not control. A stillborn son and a very sick daughter served only to increase my need for form and structure. Retreating within the four walls of the life I planned was the only security. This was Home. Everything therein could be organized, a perfect bastion created to face down the imperfections in the world outside.

Then, quite unexpectedly, there came from nowhere the smallest dog. She pitter-pattered into my life before I could think but, had I stopped to consider, she certainly would not have been let in. These are the moments when the universe smiles and plays a trick. You get up one morning with no inkling that the day will bring a life-changing moment. The face of a future lover seen across a room, a sudden stumble which leaves you with a black eye, a phone call which will seem to leave your career in tatters, at least for a while. There can be no knowing what will pop out from under the lid of the scary jack-in-a-box – so be ready for it all (I advise people), because then you won't be surprised. But Bonnie surprised me. She slipped in under the radar. My permanent high-alert system must have short-circuited, leaving me wide open. The small dog arrived with the unstoppable force of a Sherman tank, changing things for ever.

You should always share things with the people you love, and make decisions together, but I decided on this tiny creature on impulse. I told no one – not even the most beloved of my heart – that a 'toy' dog, an animal fit only for laps and satin cushions, would come to live on our farm. What did I think when I first saw her – apart from the obvious, '*Ahh*, how can a dog be so small?' As I said, I did not *think* at all. But looking back, with fanciful hindsight, surely I knew she was destined to share my life. *Hers* was the face of the lover seen across a room – the new person, the One. How could I have known that this dog spoke to an urgent need I had not identified, whilst her mixture of vulnerability and toughness would prove an exact match for my own? Bonnie the abandoned creature was to become my saviour during my own time of abandonment; she who was so small taught me most of what I was to learn about largeness of spirit. The lessons carried within the soul of my little dog go on and on. But that is to jump ahead …

This is how it happened.

On 13 June 2002 I drove to Bath's Royal United Hospital for a meeting of the art committee. Our task was to cheer the corridors of the hospital with artworks, and to commission an original work of sculpture with funds from the National Lottery to 'animate the aerial space'. I liked that phrase; it would be a sort of hanging, flying creation in the atrium. It might distract patients afraid of this part of their life journey, reinvigorate families who face so much waiting and generally cheer up everyone who passed that way, from the consultant to the cleaner. My own life is enriched by art every day; naturally I agree that hospitals should be too. So I said I would join the committee, and give time and enthusiasm to the 'unnecessary' decoration of a necessary place.

But I dislike meetings; my claustrophobia kicks in within minutes and I want to leave, do a runner, get the hell out of the 'good works' and go home to a glass of wine and Al Green blasting loudly in the kitchen. I feel a fraud: a 'public' figure who is really somebody disreputable, who wants to hang out and do nothing. Yet the desire to flee fights with my need to give something back – for if you lead a life full of blessings you need to keep them topped up. This is karma: the meals on wheels of a good life. That day it was taking me nearer to my soulmate dog.

The committee met in the hospital's charity office and we were all sitting around waiting to start when the door opened and Lisa (one of the younger committee members) came in, holding something in her hand. Because of the table, I couldn't see properly; she came further into the room and I realized it was a dog lead. With something on the end of it. I craned my head and glimpsed a flurry of white. It was the smallest dog I had ever seen.

Lisa was the head of fundraising for the RSPCA's Bath Cats and Dogs Home. Strangely, J and I had been there for the first time ever, just two days earlier. We went to recover his beautiful Labrador Billie, my fiftieth birthday present to the husband who had everything else and therefore needed a dog. Here I must explain that I was never a dog lover – not as a child when my grandmother got a snappy corgi called Whiskey, nor at any other time in my life. Yet when J and I first met in our second year at University College London and went to visit his mother, I was entranced by his way with the family Labradors, Bill and Ben.

That was the end of 1967; I was 21 and in love and all was new. Everything that the 23-year-old philosophy student did entranced me: the way he hunched his shoulders in his navy pea coat, strode out in his green corduroys and whistled to those sleek black animals, his voice dipping and elongating their names – 'Biiiiill-eee! Bennn-eee!' – with musical authority. I was awkward and nervous as I stroked their velvety ears, making up to the dogs because I wanted to impress *him* – the cleverest, funniest, sexiest, most grown-up man I'd ever met. Those 'real' dogs seemed an extension of his capability. But I was incapable of seeing the point of his mother's precious little dachshund.

Twenty-seven years later, in January 1994, I knew that if I chose to buy him a black Labrador for his July birthday I would have to learn to look after a dog, for the first time in my life. It was a serious decision, for since J was away a lot, the main care would fall to me. And so I, who had resolutely set my face against our son Daniel's pleas for a dog all through his school days, finally capitulated to the reality of dog hairs, dog smells and tins of disgusting mush. I chose Billie (named by me after Billie Holliday. A control freak will even name a man's birthday dog) and liked her, but I didn't know how to love her. Naturally J was delighted by the surprise, and equally happy when, 18 months later, I gave him Sam, a scruffy Border collie, for Christmas. Anyone might think that I had turned myself into a dog lover, but it wasn't true. I liked them, but that's not enough for dogs. They aren't satisfied with being *liked.* I was a dog *minder*, that's all.

This is partly a story of home, for dogs know their place in the pack, and the pack needs its lair, its fastness, its refuge. In 1995 we had moved to our farm, J's dream home, in about 60 rough acres of pasture which we would farm organically. It was a mile down a track, just outside Bath's city boundary, and hung on the edge of a valley like Wuthering Heights, with winter weather to suit.

J briefly employed a girl to exercise his horses and one day, somehow when she was riding with the dogs near the road, Sam came home with her but Billie did not. Nor did she come for supper.

She was missing.

This was June 2002. In the warm night, pierced by the sharp cries of foxes, J roamed the fields with a torch, calling her name, fearing her stolen – for Billie-of-the-velvet-ears was a beautiful bitch. He was in despair. The next day I wrote a round robin letter, got into the car and posted my note through every letter-box within a radius of about half a mile. An hour later the telephone rang and a couple living up on the main road along the top of Lansdown (the ridge which saw one of the decisive battles in the Civil War) told me they had found a collarless black Labrador on the main road and called the dog warden. Billie was safe.

We left the house at a run and went to the RSPCA home to collect her. One of the many glorious things about dogs is that you need no proof of ownership – not *really.* Of course the microchip is a failsafe – but the point is, your dog *knows* you. When she was brought from her holding pen, Billie's face showed relief and joy to match our own. This is something non-doggy people do not understand: the expressiveness of the canine countenance. Dogs' faces change, just like their barks and body language; they may not be as evolved as our primate cousins but human love serves to 'humanize' them in the most expressive way.

Holding tightly to her lead, we saw rows of cages and heard the mournful sounds of dogs wanting to be found homes – a desire of which they could not possibly be cognizant, in the sense that we know, all too painfully sometimes, our own innermost wishes and needs. Nevertheless the desperate wanting was there in those barks and yelps, in the lolling tongues and mournful eyes of the homeless dogs, the pets who were not petted, the working dogs with no jobs. The dogs who wanted to be *known* as much as Billie knew us.

'Let's have a quick look,' I said to J.

We wandered about, but it was too sad.

'Let's go home,' J said.

So we did. Sam welcomed Billie with bounds of joy and lolloping tongue, snuffling his welcome. Even the cats, Django, Ella, Thelonius (Theo for short) and Louis, looked faintly pleased, because cats like the world over which they rule to be complete.

Then, just two days later, Lisa is entering that office with a dog on a lead, but not just any dog. My dog.

'I have never seen such a small dog,' I said. 'What on earth is it?'

'I think she's a shih-tzu', Lisa replied. 'She's in the dogs' home. I'm keeping her with me tonight – that's why she's here, because I'll go home after the meeting. These very small dogs get quite distressed in the home overnight and so if one comes in all of us take turns.'

My first assumption was that the small white dog was lost, as Billie had just been lost, but that was not the case. Lisa explained, 'She was abandoned – left tied to a tree in Henrietta Park.'

Henrietta Park is a pleasant patch of green but very central in the city, and I simply could not believe anyone could abandon such a small dog in a place where – who knows? – drunken oafs might make a football of her.

'Impossible,' I said. 'No way! Somebody must have had to rush off for a dental appointment or something, and forgotten her for a while.'

Lisa explained that it had happened two days before, and nobody had telephoned, and if the dog remained unclaimed in seven days' time, 'We'll be looking for a new home for her.'

By now I had the anonymous shih-tzu on my lap, but she was eager to get off. She wriggled and looked for safety in the person who had brought her, but I was overwhelmed by a need for her to settle down – to *like* me. This was the magical moment of rescue.

'I'll give her a home,' I said.

'Are you sure?'

'Quite sure.'

Looking back, I know that moments of rescue cut two ways.

I gave no thought to the muddy farm (no place for a white lapdog), or the cats (one of which, Django, scourge of rats and rabbits, was certainly bigger than this miniature mutt), or to J, a lover of 'proper' dogs. Real dogs. Big dogs.

Couples should discuss decisions together – I knew that. But in that second of saying '*I'll* give her a home' – that spontaneous, expansive welcoming of the small white dog – I knew instinctively that the personal pronoun was all that mattered. This was to be *my* dog. If I were to mention the idea to my husband, son, daughter, parents or friends they would all shake heads, suck teeth, remind me of hideous yapping tendencies and say it was a Bad Idea. They would talk me out of it, and this small dog would be taken by somebody else, who couldn't possibly (I was sure) give her as good a home as I would. So I would stay silent. This was nobody else's business. I who had never had a dog of my own because I had never wanted a dog of my own was transformed, in that instant, into a lady with a lapdog.

I knew Chekhov's story 'The Lady with the Little Dog', described by Vladimir Nabokov as 'one of the greatest stories ever written'. This tale of an adulterous love affair tells us much about human beings – but once I grew to know and love my dog I felt it showed less insight into women and dogs than I had thought. Before I am accused of trivializing a great work of literature because it lacks dog knowledge, I should point out that the mighty art critic John Ruskin was no different when he wrote, 'My pleasure in the entire *Odyssey* is diminished because Ulysses gives not a word of kindness nor of regret to Argus' – the faithful dog who recognizes him after 20 years.

Chekhov tells how a chance love affair takes possession of two people and changes them against their will. The story closes with them far apart and rarely able to meet. Gurov and Anna are both married. He works in a bank in Moscow, Anna lives in a dead provincial town near St Petersburg. Each has gone on a stolen holiday to Yalta, a fashionable Crimean resort notorious for its casual love affairs. Gurov is an experienced 40-year-old philanderer with a stern wife; Anna is married to a dull provincial civil servant, ten years older than she. The opening sentence of the story dryly establishes the holiday gossip which leads to Gurov's interest: 'People said that a new person had appeared on the sea front: a lady with a little dog.'

The dog is key to Anna's identity; wherever she goes 'a white Pomeranian trotted after her'. The dog is clearly inseparable from his mistress. Gurov's hunting instinct is aroused. One day he sees Anna sitting near him in an open-air restaurant. Her dog growls and he shakes his finger at it. Blushing, she says, 'He doesn't bite.' Gurov asks if he may give the dog a bone ... and so the affair begins.

But here is also where the problems start for the lover of small dogs. A week later Anna and Gurov kiss and make love. *But where is that Pomeranian?* That's what I want to know. The affair goes on – lunches, dinners, carriage drives, evening walks, bedroom intimacy – with no mention of the creature who was so inseparable from his mistress, 'the lady with the little dog'. No dog. For all his great knowledge of human nature Chekhov understands little about ladies and their little dogs, or more specifically, the protective and possessive nature of the Pomeranian tribe. The dog would have been ever present. Those growls would certainly not have ceased, especially when this strange man became intimate with the human being the dog loved. Small dogs do not give themselves as easily as women. Easily bored Gurov would likely have been irritated by the yapping and surely suffered a nip. As a real-life lady with a lapdog, I know this. The dog could not have been written out of the narrative so easily by a man who understood.

Small dogs keep loneliness at bay for women on their own. Small dogs take you out along the promenade, because you must think of your dog, no matter how you are feeling. That Pomeranian would surely have consoled Anna when she reached out a hand in the night to curl her fingers in soft white fur, wondering perhaps if any man was worth so much pain. Or any affair.

Bonnie too was to growl at men. So great was her natural hostility to the faint whiff of testosterone, we speculated that it must have been a man who had tied her to that tree, or an unscrupulous puppy breeder who had decided her back legs were a touch too long for breed 'standard', or an unpleasant son whose elderly mother had succumbed to dementia and couldn't be bothered with her pet. The novelist in me made up stories, but never convincingly, since my imagination quailed at the image of anybody tying this vulnerable young dog to a tree and walking away. I pictured the small creature straining to follow, then being choked back by the lead. Or was it a rope? I never discovered the details.

Men she might not like, yet she was never hostile to J. He was in London on 20 June when I was telephoned by the rescue home and told that nobody had come forward and so the dog could be mine. I should explain that it is policy to make a home visit to be sure that the putative owner is responsible and the place is suitable – but Lisa knew our home, knew us well, and so there was no need. In the time between 'finding' my dog and collecting her I had researched and discovered the 'shih-tzu' was in fact a Maltese, and had already named her Bonnie, after Bonnie Raitt, the singer whose music I always played in my car. This habit of naming animals after musicians (Sam was Sam Cooke, Billie, Billie Holiday) was a foible of mine; it gave cohesion to the menagerie.

I left the house at a run, went to the supermarket for unfamiliar small-dog food and straight to the home to collect her, paying them a goodly sum for the privilege. They estimated her age at six months but, other than saying she was in good condition when found, still knew nothing about where she had come from. Bonnie would never give up her secrets; I looked into her jet-button eyes and wondered who she might be missing, what kind of house she knew, what damage had been done to her. Those who study dog psychology and behaviour know that dogs from rescue homes frequently display separation anxiety – but at the time I didn't know this. Bonnie and I were only just setting out on our journey together.

She was still my secret, not mentioned to anyone – neither daughter and confidante Kitty, nor close family friend Robin, a photographer who rented the cottage next door to our farmhouse (and with whom I occasionally worked on assignment), nor my parents – and certainly not the husband. I knew he would not want this silly scrap of a creature, and therefore need only know the *fait accompli*. But he was out when I called with the news, leaving me to recount my triumph to a disbelieving daughter, who was then living in our London house.

'*You*? *You've* got a little dog? No!'

A day later came J's voice on the phone – cool and faintly accusatory.

'What's this about a little dog? It hasn't got a bow in its hair, has it?'

'Not yet,' I replied.

He did not sound pleased.

Two days later J arrived home after his Sunday political programme on ITV, arriving at the farm after the two-hour drive from London, glad to be home. As always, Billie and Sam raced to meet his car – and right from the beginning Bonnie raced everywhere with the big dogs, who regarded her with puzzled amusement. With no practice, she became part of the welcome committee. Seeing her, J dropped on his knees in his Italian suit and, as the Labrador and collie pranced around their master, held out his arms to the small dog, who covered his face with licks. That, you see, is the point about *true* dog lovers – those in touch with the canine spirit. They can retain no sizeist prejudice when they realize that, although the eyes are tiny and the tail is an apology for a silk whisk, the potential for devotion which characterizes proto-dog abounds in the toy. J adored her – and it took just one week of us attempting to put her to bed in the 'dog room' with the other dogs and the four cats, one week of hearing her jump out through the dog flap into the darkness rich with smells of foxes, badgers, owls, stoats, rats, before she wangled her way on to our bed. And this is where comfort dogs belong.

Do you believe in signs? I do, for Billie going missing and taking us to the RSPCA home was one such. And less than a month before I first saw my small dog I had met two others, who had fascinated me. For some years I had been presenting a yearly series on BBC Radio 4 called *Devout Sceptics*, which took the form of a one-to-one interview about faith and doubt, a searching conversation between me and someone well known in fields of literature, politics, science and ideas. In May 2002, with my producer and friend Malcolm Love, I had been in California, to interview Dr Pamela Connolly in Los Angeles, Amy Tan in San Francisco and Isabel Allende in San Rafael. On 24 May we were up early to fly from LAX to San Francisco. Coming in to land I felt that old lifting of the heart with excitement, not just caused by the eternal promise and threat of travel, but because I love the United States and always feel truly myself there.

We took a cab to the Holiday Inn on Van Ness and California, and checked in, but had no time to change, because our appointment with Amy Tan loomed. I was looking forward to the interview; I loved Tan's novels and anticipated a good conversation about God and destiny. Having looked up our destination, in the smart, leafy Presidio area of the city, Malcolm suggested that on such a fine morning it would be good to walk there. I agreed, but neither of us remembered that San Francisco is up hill and down dale – with the result that when we arrived at the address I was flustered and sweaty, which state seemed to increase as Tan's PA showed us into the huge, elegant condominium, furnished thickly with oriental furniture and fine *objets* which made you afraid to move. There was a crescendo of yapping from one corner; at the sight of us two miniature Yorkshire terriers created a tiny commotion behind a 10-inch barrier which penned them in. I gaped at the dogs – at that time, the smallest I had ever met. But they made me feel better, for when Amy Tan herself glided into the room, astonishingly beautiful in green pleated silk and soft leather ankle boots, I was able to disguise my discomfiture at being less than elegant by fussing over her pets. This much I knew – all people like to have their pets fussed over.

What I did not realize was that Bubba and Lilly were far more than dogs to Amy. We settled down for the interview and Malcolm fitted out microphones, noting with approval how quiet the condo was, the acoustic deadened by thick carpets, drapes and all that furniture. The little Yorkies nestled on her lap and Tan's slim fingers played with their ears as Malcolm took a sound level. Then he stopped.

'Er … Amy … I'm picking up noise from the dogs.'

'Oh really? Doing what?'

'Licking your hands – and snuffling. Er … do you think they could wait in another room while we do this?'

There was one of those moments of silence when the temperature drops a fraction and you know, as an interviewer, that this *faux pas* could spoil things. I caught the corner of Malcolm's gaze, knowing how much he (a man of great sensitivity, especially to women) wished he could recall the impertinent suggestion.

Then Amy Tan said coolly, 'The dogs have to *stay.* The *dogs* are *essential.*'

'Of course they are!' I cried.

Malcolm backtracked. 'Yes, I *absolutely* understand … Uh … but maybe they don't have to lick your hands?'

Pause.

'Sure.'

The novelist kept her hands out of reach of her pets' pink tongues, and the dogs settled down to sleep amidst the folds of her green silk, except for the occasional moment when I would intercept a beady gaze asking me what the hell I was doing there. Or perhaps sourcing that slight odour of perspiration. They yapped once during the next hour, but the interview was going so well by then it didn't matter. And when it was over Tan (more relaxed now) told me how she hates to travel in Europe since she can't take her dogs, how she loathes being in hotel rooms alone and how she dreads the thought of anything happening to her beloved pets. Her words intensified my impression of fragility wrapped in self-contained eccentricity.

As Malcolm and I walked to the restaurant she had recommended for lunch, I delivered myself – solemnly and with a certain degree of patronizing pity – of the opinion that those 'teacup' Yorkies were surrogate children for Amy Tan and her husband, Louis. Oh, statement of the obvious! What did I know? In the same way, years before when we were young, I had found some pathos in the fact that J's elderly aunts, who lived together, posted birthday cards to each other signed from their toy poodles, Lavinia and Amanda-Jane. Later I would shake my head in disbelief on reading, in a magazine profile, that the novelist Jilly Cooper kept a picture of her dead mongrel in a locket. I was smug in my refusal to acknowledge true value in that level of affection for an animal. How fitting it was that hubris would arrive on my horizon shaped as a small dog.

Malcolm was to tease me a few weeks later, when he was editing out those yaps and one or two small dog breaths for the finished programme, and I had already fallen in love with Bonnie. He laughed that the day in San Francisco had turned me into an aspirational copycat who realized that real literary ladies must have dogs. I huffed and puffed at the joke against myself – still resisting the notion that I could be perceived as one of those women with a handbag dog.

What matters is how profoundly I've come to understand what it meant to Amy Tan to have those comforting dogs on her lap as talismans and as inspiration. And now it is I who, with no irony, describe myself as my dog's 'Mummy'. She is as necessary to me now as Amy Tan's two were to her, and just as restricting of the impulse to travel, or even go to restaurants. I send cards from her and expect them back. Just three weeks after the encounter with Amy Tan and her dogs my diary entry reads, '*I adore Bonnie. She has transformed everything.*'

But even then I could not have known that the real transformation would be a work in progress. The dog would make me take myself less seriously – changing me into a foolish woman who would later buy a cushion saying 'Dogs Leave Paw Prints on your Heart' in Minnesota; a *petit point* of a Maltese in Portland, Maine, as well as a lobster-patterned macintosh, lead and collar set; a Navajo jacket and turquoise suede collar and lead complete with silver conchos in Santa Fe; a pink outfit in Brussels; a red set in Cape Town; cool Harley-Davidson accessories in Rapid City, South Dakota; 'bling' sparkles from a shop in Nice; and more. Not to mention purple mock-croc from an internet site for her bridesmaid's outfit ... but that was much later. Small-dog madness, I was to discover, is a worldwide phenomenon.

I concentrate on the trivial deliberately. These are necessarily small steps towards the big jump into that unknown which Bonnie brought with her but which was to drag me, too, into a pit of unknowing.

Smallness, I began to discover, fills some people with an irrational hatred, when they see a chihuahua, a Pekinese, a Yorkshire terrier, a Japanese chin, a shih-tzu, a pug. 'What's *that*?' asked a young man I know when I took Bonnie to his parents' house for lunch. Not to be outdone, his father joined in, suggesting with gentle mockery that Bonnie was 'not a proper dog'.

'Is the wren any less of a bird because he's small?' I demanded, drawing myself up to my full height (without heels) of 5 feet 3 inches.

'Aren't we allowed to tease you over your dog?' he asked, dryly.

I made a measured *so-so* movement with my hand and the subject was dropped.

One day in Bath a pierced and tattooed man in his late twenties said loudly to his big dog, who was pulling menacingly on its string towards Bonnie, 'Leave it! It's not a dog, it's a rat on a lead!' I was filled with a protective fury which took me by surprise. This new feeling was one of many signs that I too had entered into an ancient transaction, known to all owners of small dogs throughout the centuries. What else is this but an example of Darwinian survival? Survival, of course, will gradually unfold as the subject of this book – and so it is fitting to introduce it here, in the destiny of the small dog.

Of course Bonnie, like all canines large and small, is descended from wolves and somewhere – way, way back in her genetic blueprint – a part of her soul is roaming the forests and hills, filling the night with mournful howls to others of her kind. But I admit there is little of that behavioural memory evident in the animated powder puff on my lap. Now *I* am her kind, the leader of her small pack, and it is I to whom she calls, in those unmistakably shrill tones. She knows I will hear, swoop, soothe, hold fast. Out there in the wild the small dog would certainly perish, and therefore it has evolved an effective method of survival: being loveable. The transaction says, 'I will adore you and, in exchange, you – my very own human

– will protect me. Where you go I shall go, when you are full of sorrow I shall comfort you, and in return you will be my shield against the world.'

Or, as Elizabeth Barrett Browning put it when she fell in love with her small spaniel, Flush, who became her consolation and saviour: 'He & I are inseparable companions, and I have vowed him my perpetual society in exchange for his devotion.'

Those who dislike small dogs on principle sometimes ask, 'What are they *for?*' The acutely intelligent Border collie is bred to herd sheep and when not trained to do so it will neurotically round up anything it can, as if to be deprived of your function is to lose identity. Working dogs have a purpose. The veterinarian Bruce Fogle explains that the domestic dog (*Canis familiaris*) has the same number of chromosomes as the wolf, 78, and that over eons different canine cultures emerged. There were hunting dogs, herding dogs, guard dogs and, later, breeds to 'flush, point, corner, retrieve, or sit quietly on satin cushions'.

Later Fogle asserts that the chihuahua 'was bred to act as a hot water bottle', which contains some truth – and yet I suspect that two references to cushions in his book *The Mind of the Dog* indicate a man whose love of dogs grows in proportion to their size. Many men proclaim a dislike of small dogs. Is the opposite of a proper dog a fake dog? Or might it be an 'improper' dog, carrying with it a sense of scented, snuggling, sensual, stroking intimacy, such as would make any man jealous? In the sixteenth century a clergyman named William Harrison included in his *Description of England* a satirical assault on women and lapdogs:

They are little and prettie, proper and fine, and sought out far and neere to satisfie the nice delicacie of daintie dames, and wanton womens willes; instruments of follie to plaie and dallie withal, in trifling away the treasure of time, to withdraw their minds from more commendable exercises, and to content their corrupt concupiscences with vain disport, a sillie poore shift to shun their irksome idleness. These Sybariticall puppies, the smaller they be the better they are accepted, the more pleasure they provoke, as meet plaiefellows for minsing mistresses to beare in their bosoms, to keep companie in their chambers, to succour with sleepe in bed, and nourish with meet at bord, to lie in their laps, and lick their lips as they lie in their wagons and couches.

I wondered, from the tone of this, if the Canon of Windsor's wife had taken up with a toy spaniel. In fact, I find he was plagiarizing a scientific work published seven years earlier by John Caius, MD, court physician to Edward VI, Mary and Elizabeth I and President of the Royal College of Physicians. Our Western concept of breeds was first recorded in his *Short Treatise of English Dogges* in 1570. In this useful work I meet Bonnie:

There is, beside those which wee have already delivered, another sort of gentle dogge in this our Englishe soyle … the Dogges of this kind doth Callimachus call Melitoeos, *of the Island Melita, in the sea of Sicily, (which this day is named* Malta, *an Island in deede famous and reoumed …) where this kind of dogges had their principall beginning.*

He continues, 'These dogges are little, pretty, proper, and fine …' and so on, although the magnificent phrase 'Sybariticall puppies' is the Revd Harrison's own. Dr Caius goes on to make a perceptive point about lapdogs, which I would not have been able to understand in 2002, when Bonnie was so new, as I do now. Criticizing a female tendency to delight in dogs more than in children, he guesses at mitigating circumstances: 'But this abuse peradventure reigneth where there hath bene long lack of issue, or else where barrenness is the best blossom of bewty.' The small dog as child substitute? Of course – for there are many ways to save a life, and this is one to which I shall return.

That summer we took Bonnie to stay on our new boat, a Puget Sound cabin cruiser which was moored at Dittisham, on the river Dart in Devon. J bought the dog a tiny 'pet float' and each morning he would rise early, dress her in her red life jacket and row to the shore so that she could relieve herself. My lack of rowing skills was a good excuse, but in truth, he never once complained. I would stand on deck and watch him, remembering our honeymoon in that very village (so cold in February 1968, while this July gave us the hottest day of the year) and loving the fact that he was so at home on the water which scared me, a non-swimmer. By now he loved my dog; why else would he have agreed that she should come on holiday while Billie and Sam and all the cats remained behind on the farm, taken care of by my father? The dog came everywhere with us and when, after a few days, I developed an inexplicable pain in my right arm, my daughter suggested it must be a repetitive strain injury, caused by clutching Bonnie so tightly. Of course.

Bonnie was sitting between us as J and I heard *Devout Sceptics* broadcast at 9.00 a.m. on Radio 4, Amy Tan's voice filling the cabin as the waves made their soft slapping sound against the blue hull and J listening with his characteristic intensity. I imagined those tiny Yorkies on her knee, her long fingers held carefully out of reach of their tongues, as she talked about her belief that there is a benevolent spirit in the world, larger than any individual. 'That works with the concept of a god,' she said – and went on to link it with the idea of, not so much forgiveness in the Christian sense of the word, but compassion. Her voice was quietly firm as she told me that her aim was to learn about 'this notion of compassion', about empathy with her fellow human beings – which she defined as 'another way of saying Love'.

She added that of course you cannot measure love – it cannot be scientifically proven, no more than the idea of an afterlife. Yet she could say, 'Yes, I believe this,' because she finds 'intuitive emotional truth' in the idea each day of her life and in the writing of her novels.

As I re-read her words today (the interview was printed in my book, *Devout Sceptics*) I realize how much Amy Tan's philosophy informs my own life, and that the meeting with her and her small dogs was significant in more ways than one. Everything that has happened to me since Bonnie arrived from nowhere has at once tested and confirmed it. What's more, the entirely serious lessons my little dog has taught me confirm her optimism. There is no doubt in my mind what small dogs are 'for'.

But it was still so new. My diary entries record the process of dog intoxication – for that is indeed what it was. As the

American genius Amy Hempel wrote in her short story collection *The Dog in the Marriage*, '… you don't just love the dogs, you *fall* in love with them.' In the summer of 2002 I wrote in my diary:

> *27 June – Bonnie has transformed things. She is so sweet I want her to be with me all the time.*
>
> *3 July – I find it hard to concentrate on the novel because I spend too much time fussing over Bonnie.*
>
> *23 July – Bonnie continues to delight me. It is a strange feeling – to love a dog.*

Bonnie fitted easily into the Devon part of our life, although some of the old friends teased the lady with the lapdog. I suppose I can understand, because it was so unexpected to see me in that role; nevertheless we must all allow people to change. And I had changed. Instead of being impatient on the boat and feeling marooned I relaxed, strolling with the dog and gazing at the water, soothed by the ceaseless pinging of rigging in the breeze. Looking back, that summer seems idyllic. Robin had rumbled into the village on his Harley-Davidson, and joined us on the boat. Our son Daniel arrived, tense but liberated at the end of a long relationship. Kitty's boyfriend left early and she was upset. We spent time with the grandparents, I cooked meals in the boat's small galley, J took care of Bonnie's needs … and so family life went. From the time they were babies our children had loved that village, the scene of our many shared family holidays, not to mention our honeymoon.

The weather was hot, but a sudden squall disrupted J's birthday celebrations on the last day of July. No drinks on the boat for family and friends, but dinner in the local café for a pile of us. My diary records, '*The wine flowed and the noise rose and Bonnie sat on my lap and I thought how lucky we are to have all these talented, interesting and deeply kind Devon friends. It was a fabulous night.*' On another evening we joined friends for a beach barbecue. Suddenly fireworks from a celebration up the river filled the sky with falling flowers and stars and '*illuminated the evanescence of it all*'.

The year 2002 marked the jubilee of Her Majesty The Queen. The country which had in March confounded all republicans by mourning the death of Queen Elizabeth the Queen Mother joined in celebration of the fifty-year reign of her daughter. J and I had watched the London procession on television. We are both monarchists: my grandmother cleaned houses for a living and served lunches in a girls' school, yet the Royal Family was part of her sense of identity, like her quiet belief in God and love of her family. She liked to show me pictures of the young Prince Charles and Princess Anne, cutting them out of the *Daily Mirror*. She liked the smart woollen coats with velvet collars and buttons worn by the children of the upper classes.

In contrast, J's father, Richard Dimbleby, was an icon for my grandparents' and parents' generation: the most famous broadcaster the country had ever known, revered by the public first for his fearless war reporting, for his shocking, shattering dispatch as the first journalist into Belsen, and then for his commentaries on great events (the funerals of George VI, Sir

Winston Churchill and John F. Kennedy and the coronation of Elizabeth II) when the poetic dignity of his spoken prose expressed the deepest feelings of the majority of British people. When I first met the philosophy student (two years after his father had died) and told my parents I was dating 'Richard Dimbleby's son' they were awestruck. It was hard for me to believe too.

From different worlds we came, J and I, meeting in the second year of our respective courses and marrying after just three months, so much in love there was nothing else to do. It was just like fireworks – and naturally the years of married life would whoosh, crackle and bang too, sometimes so dangerously. Yet those first flames still had the power to warm, and the showers of stars still hung in the sky, even if sometimes behind clouds.

In 1994 he had published his much-admired biography of the Prince of Wales, a considerable achievement which came not without stress – largely due to the fact that J's simultaneous two-hour documentary about the Prince on ITV had included a short admission of adultery. The world seemed to go mad. J, a political journalist who was initially dubious about taking on the Royal project, knew that he had to ask the Prince about the state of his marriage to Princess Diana and his relationship with the then Camilla Parker-Bowles. He felt that the boil of sleazy gossip and tittle-tattle had to be lanced – and so, under firm but gentle questioning, the Prince revealed to the watching millions that once his marriage to Diana had irretrievably broken down he had started a relationship with Camilla. He would have been damned if he hadn't but was damned for telling the truth. At the same time, many people said that J ought not to have asked the question, although had he not he would have been pilloried for failing to do his journalistic job.

It was an exhausting time. Side by side we faced it all down but, seasoned journalists as we both are, we were unprepared for the tabloid feeding frenzy and the level of vitriol that was unleashed upon the heir to the throne – a much-misunderstood man whom J called in the closing words of his biography 'an individual of singular distinction and virtue'. I recall J standing in our garden or sitting in the library at the farm doing endless interviews with CNN, ABC, Sky, etc. and for a while it seemed as if he was almost the only one who would analyse and interpret not just the Prince of Wales but the British monarchy to the rest of the world. Although he did it with cool insight it was not a role he relished – not at all – but it was to be repeated after that terrible day at the end of August 1997 when Princess Diana died in a car crash in Paris with her lover, Dodi Fayed.

Looking back, the era of his biography and TV documentary seems oddly innocent. It is astonishing to remember that the Prince of Wales had wished to protect his estranged wife by *not* revealing all the detailed information J had in fact discreetly accumulated about Diana and her many problems. A few years later a slurry of cheap, gossipy books, prurient television programmes and mean memoirs by seedy staff would ensure no compassion or respect whatsoever for the dead Princess or for her living sons and ex-husband. Britain was turning into a pit bull of a nation.

The Prince loves dogs and in J's documentary one of his two Jack Russells appeared, jumping about in a Land-Rover as Jack

Russells will, and being told in no uncertain terms, 'Get *down,* Tigger!' Tigger had puppies; one went to Camilla Parker-Bowles and the Prince kept another, which he called Roo but Prince William renamed Pooh. In April 1995 Pooh vanished at Balmoral. This became an instant news story, the animal-loving British public responding with all the interest a beloved lost dog deserves. Jilly Cooper wrote a heartfelt piece about 'poor little Pooh' in the *Daily Mirror*, while the *Daily Mail* ran photos of the dog captioned 'Pooh: loved and lost by a prince'. The Jack Russell had been on a walk with her owner and her mother, when she ran off into the woods. Charles's whistles brought no response, and a three-day search by estate workers was fruitless. Neither an advertisement in the local paper nor the *Daily Mail*'s offer of a good reward brought forth anyone who had seen the dog. As a heartbroken Prince headed back to London on 21 April there was no shortage of theories about Pooh's fate. Some suggested that the dog had become stuck in a rabbit hole, as Jack Russells will, while a psychic asserted that she had 'a very clear picture' of Pooh stuck in a sewer. The *News of the World* gleefully theorized that she was devoured by a feral cat dubbed the Beast of Balmoral.

Such a fuss about a dog. Yet the true dog lover – the person I was metamorphosing into in 2002 – understands it. Once you love a dog you cannot bear the thought of losing your pet and you will torment yourself imagining your dog being kidnapped, or dying. No wonder the Prince of Wales put up a memorial to Tigger at Highgrove, when, in 2002, his beloved dog had to be euthanized because of old age.

That same year, Bonnie accidentally went to Highgrove and met the heir to the throne. For most human beings this would have been exciting, but it was quite an event for a nobody, a dog from nowhere who, just months earlier, had been left tied to a tree – a progression surely worthy of Eliza Doolittle. Yet like Eliza, she took it in her small stride.

Needless to say she had a royal welcome.

For centuries the Royal Family has embraced dogs as their favoured pets. Formal portraits from the seventeenth century onwards show kings, queens and their children happily posing with their beloved animals, from pugs to greyhounds, King Charles spaniels to corgis. Although we associate the British aristocracy with hunting dogs, big dogs with a serious role in life, the Royal Family has always loved smaller hounds too. Some pets have even merited their own portraits, and (as in many households) were considered members of the family. Photographs from the Royal Collection prove how much dogs were valued. A photograph of Queen Victoria's son, the Duke of York, shows him with his pug and is full of a playful humanity we can all recognize. The dog is wrapped in a greatcoat and its royal owner has tied a handkerchief around its head. The dog looks at the camera, the Prince looks down at the dog, full of mirth.

In 1854 the total cost of photographing the dogs in the Royal Kennels and mounting the prints in a special handsome album came to £25 19*s*. – the equivalent of around £1,650 today. When Queen Victoria's beloved collie Noble died at Balmoral in 1887, he was buried in the grounds of the castle and given his own gravestone, which reads:

Noble by name by nature noble too
Faithful companion sympathetic true
His remains are interred here.

A terrier named Caesar belonging to Edward VII was given even greater status when, having outlived the King, he walked behind His Majesty's coffin in the funeral procession.

Elizabeth II favours the corgi. The breed was introduced to the Royal Family by her father, George VI, in 1933, when he bought a corgi called Dookie from a local kennels. The animal proved popular with his daughters, so a second corgi was acquired, called Jane, who had puppies, two of which, Crackers and Carol, were kept. For her eighteenth birthday, the Queen was given a corgi named Susan from whom numerous successive dogs were bred. Some corgis were mated with dachshunds (most notably Pipkin, who belonged to Princess Margaret) to create 'dorgis'. The Queen's corgis travel with her to the Royal residences, and Her Majesty looks after them herself as much as possible. Other members of the Royal Family own dogs of various breeds. The Duchess of Cornwall owns two Jack Russell terriers, Tosca and Rosie.

The day Bonnie went to a Royal residence the country was tossed by storms, with gales of up to 90 mph which screamed around our farm on the hill. Branches cracked from the beech wood and the trees groaned as if in agony. In my diary I wrote, '*I feel overwhelmed by all I have to do, but Bonnie is such a consolation*', but on that day it was hard to walk out with the three dogs and not be blown sideways by the power of the gale. Looking at Bonnie you would have thought she could be blown away, like a tuft of thistledown.

Earlier in the week we had been at the Booker Prize dinner, to see the outsider Yann Martel awarded the plum for *The Life of Pi* and to mingle with peers and swap gossip. When at such events I always feel two people: one at home within the glitz, the literary glamour, but the other detached, wanting to be at home – especially once the Maltese came to stay. The diary captures this feeling, recording, rather than a desire to be in London, '*I want to be home to see Bonnie. The little dog ties me to the farm emotionally more than ever.*' I also wrote, '*Home, home, home*', with no explanation, as if the repetition of what gave me security would fix it for ever. Now I see that scribble as a litany of faith. It was the only faith that possessed me completely.

On Sunday night J and I were due at Highgrove for dinner, and our friend and neighbour Robin offered to drive us. The journey is only 35 minutes' drive from where we lived, yet it would have been less than convivial for J to refuse a glass or three of wine, and even less wise to exit past the policemen having done so. So we left the dogs and barrelled along past fallen trees to arrive at the handsome Georgian house, just outside Tetbury, in Gloucestershire. I loved going there. The house is not overly grand; nor does it have an intimidating atmosphere. From the hats, boots and baskets at the entrance to the comfortable furniture which sometimes bears the marks of dogs (I remember an old chintz that had been shredded and was waiting repair) Highgrove is a genuine home, full of family photographs and treasured mementos.

Camilla was driving herself from her own home, and was late. The Prince fixed us drinks from the trolley, and as always I sensed a hunger within him to talk to someone like J about the issues he cares about: agriculture, the environment, education and so on. As on many previous visits he seemed strangely lonely: a good man marooned in a difficult role, frequently misunderstood and feeling it too keenly for his own good. At last Camilla blew in like a gust from a rather more robust world. My diary observed: '*She is warm and full of mirth – rejoicing that the* Panorama *programme about her is on TV tonight but she doesn't have to watch it because she is with us!*' While the men talked about serious things she and I perched on the leather fender and smoked a cheeky cigarette, puffing the smoke up the chimney as we chatted.

It was a good evening – and when the time came for Robin to pick us up, we were surprised to see Bonnie scamper into the room. With advance warning from the gate the staff had opened the front door and in she went – small dogs do not stand on ceremony. Robin told us later he hadn't had the heart to leave her behind, since she made such a pathetic fuss as he put on his coat. Astonished by her size (very small compared to a Jack Russell) the Prince and Camilla gave her maximum attention and were fascinated by her story of abandonment and rescue. Camilla's elderly, almost-blind terrier smelt the sweet young female and noticeably perked up, chasing her about. Bonnie responded flirtatiously and, vastly entertained, the Prince roared his contagious, bellowing laugh of which Falstaff would have been proud.

On the way home J and I agreed how much we liked 'doggy' people. At last I was including myself in their number.

The Royal Family's traditional affection for dogs might well be an antidote to the fuss that surrounds them. The Prince of Wales is, to his dog, just an owner, a human companion who offers treats and strokes and is always ready to stride out into the indescribably thrilling grass and trees. The dog is always there, always loyal. He will not sell his memoirs; nor will he bite the hand that feeds him. There are no complications; the dog does not have to say 'sir' or bow, and yet he will obey. I can imagine the Prince striding over the countryside he loves and telling a dog everything, knowing that whatever he says will never get back to the newspapers, nor be captured by any paparazzo's telephoto lens.

I would be telling lies if I told you that at this stage in my life I looked at my small white lapdog and saw in her a teacher. Yet I should have done, for the lessons were already beginning. For example, one day I hit her – for the first and last time. It was not a savage blow. The big dogs would not have noticed such a swat and the cats would have easily avoided it. But a padded envelope arrived containing a copy of my latest children's book – the first off the press. It is always an exciting moment for an author – that pause of satisfaction when you hold the fruit of your labour in your hand, look at it, admire your own name and think, I made this. That day I had put the book down on the futon in my study, gone to make coffee and returned to find that the young dog (less than one year old after all) was chewing the corner of my new book. And so I picked it up, swatted her and yelled, 'No!'

I did not know (neophyte that I was) that 'No!' is the cruellest word you can shout at a dog, even if sometimes you must. Nor could I have predicted that she would shrink back, raise just one paw as if for protection and shiver with terror. The lesson I learnt that day, as I cried with remorse and bent to cuddle her, was how quickly she could forgive. She licked me as if to say she was sorry, it was all her fault, it was all right, I shouldn't upset myself any more, all was well. There were no sulks. The tiny creature was bigger than I could have been –

and I was astonished. Much has always been written about the fidelity of the dog, and yet this quality of forgiveness should not be underestimated.

Saturday 12 October was beautiful. The sun glittered on the pond, where water spurted into the air from the spring swollen with autumn rain. The trees in the beech wood had crisped to russet, and the silver birch by the pond was weeping gold, like a metamorphosed princess in myth. J and Robin decided to go logging on our land, ready for winter. The big dogs raced, because they liked nothing else than to be down in the rough fields, smelling rabbits, foxes and badgers and rolling in mud. As always, the cats glided around on the perimeter of the action. But I had to leave the gang and drive the one hour to Cheltenham to take part in a discussion on marriage at the Literature Festival. As I backed my car from the car port I saw J scoop Bonnie up, then turn with her in his arms to tramp down to where the tractor waited in a gilded landscape.

I had contributed to a short book called *Maybe I Do: Marriage and Commitment in Singleton Society,* published by the Institute of Ideas. Over the years, as a prolific journalist, I have written many thousands of words on this subject, and in 1989 I compiled an anthology of poetry and prose about marriage. It had started as a silver wedding present for J, but ended by being published and dedicated to him. We had perfected a double act: reading a selection from the book at festivals and for charity. I liked being married and saw (as I still do) the institution as the bedrock of society – although with no illusions about how difficult it is. 'The greatest test of character any of us will have to face,' was how I described it in my anthology introduction.

Now a group of us were gathering to discuss marriage before a sold-out audience in the Town Hall in Cheltenham: the novelist Fay Weldon, journalist and novelist Yvonne Roberts, radical journalist Jennie Bristow, Claire Fox from the Institute of Ideas (my publisher) and me. It was a good, wide-ranging discussion and as usual I was the most conventional of all the speakers, banging a drum for what I truly believe in: the importance of stable marriage to the upbringing of children. That is, when it works. My chapter in the book was called 'For the Sake of the Children' and ended with these words – which sum up the essence of my platform contribution:

> *Of course marriages go wrong, but I do not believe anybody has the right to put their own needs/feelings/wants before those of their children. Most of us could have skipped out of our marriages at some time or other, in pursuit of romance – by which I mean, fresh sex. 'Staying together for the sake of the children' became a much derided mantra, but I see it as a potential source of good. Who knows – by putting Self on the back burner, many a married couple may find they weather the storms and ease themselves into the best of friendships, to share old age together, in married love.*

Now I regret the trite cynicism of that phrase 'fresh sex' but admit that the last sentence is pure autobiography, not theory. It was where I thought we both were, what I most wanted.

That night we went to a dinner party near Bath. Beautiful converted barn decorated with impeccable taste. Schubert floating through the scented air. Logs roaring in the wood burner. Excellent champagne, cold and biscuity in tall glasses. So many people; we didn't know them all. Such a buzz. Conversation about the arts amongst (mostly) practitioners. Delicious food cooked and served by our perfectionist writer-hostess and free-flowing wine to match its quality. The long, long table, lined with merry faces, as the laughter rose to the ceiling.

How many such evenings had we enjoyed, by the autumn of 2002? How many people had we met, talked to, flirted with, become friends with, forgotten in time? Both social beings, J and I always enjoyed gatherings where conversation was sparkling yet unstuffy – and this one was one of the best. He was sitting at the opposite end of the long table, between our hostess and a blonde woman whom I had not noticed during the pre-dinner drinks. I did not even notice her face in the candlelight; she was too far away. And why indeed would I notice? J and I had come too far together to fret that the person next to one or other of us at dinner might come to mean something.

Yes indeed, the moments do come when the universe smiles and plays a trick. Yes indeed, you get up one morning with no inkling that the day will bring a life-changing moment. The face of a future lover seen across a room, a sudden stumble which leaves you with a black eye ... There can indeed be no knowing what will pop out from under the lid of the scary jack-in-a-box, to shake the foundations of the world you know. As we drove home, exchanging details of conversations and swapping gossip and opinion as we always did, J told me about his neighbour at dinner. He liked her a lot but was, he confessed, slightly bothered because it turned out she was a very well-known opera singer, just making her mark on the international stage, and yet he had not heard of her. Nor had I.

Her name was Susan Chilcott.

Two

LOSING

It is late last night the dog was speaking of you;
The snipe was speaking of you in the deep marsh.
It is you are the lonely bird through the woods;
And that you may be without a mate until you find me.
Lady Gregory, 'Poets and Dreamers'
(translating eighth-century Irish)

Our farm was J's dream from childhood, an echo of his happy family home with its barns and entourage of animals – to which ours bore a strange resemblance. An old, low, sprawling building protected from the worst winds by being tucked into a dip in the land, like the space a dog makes when it turns round and round to scoop out its bed. A house with barns and stables, a settlement whose ancient stones would become imprinted with our story, to add to all those it had known over three centuries. A home that could be created in our own image – the dank inner courtyard brought into the house, glazed and turned into an atrium, its weight supported by Bath stone corbels which we had beautifully carved by an artist-craftsman *in situ* to my master design. They represented the four seasons, four elements, literary themes and so on. We wanted our house to *be* a work of art as well as to contain our collection.

But it needed to be made bigger, for we had moved there (following J's dream of farming organically) from a large rectory in a pretty village a few miles away and the existing farmhouse was too small for our needs. So a long, dilapidated animal shed at right angles to the main house was renovated to form a study for me, a spectacular double-height sitting room with windows on three sides and (best of all) a low, peaceful library with two window seats overlooking the valley. Across from the house was a small building which became a cottage for Robin (when he was around, as he worked a lot abroad) and our son Daniel, and (later) for J's groom and her family. There would be extra rooms for us over there too, and across the yard was the huge barn which would become, in time, a games room. We loved to have a house full of friends and family. At New Year for instance: space was necessary. The place was unusual and extraordinary, with a 145-degree view that was miraculous when the valley was full of mist but the surrounding hills and farms rose above it, like ships on a foaming sea. I find it almost impossible to describe the magical atmosphere of the home J and I created, or its wild beauty.

The summer we moved there (1994) had been the hottest in decades and the whole valley crisped to golden brown. These were the classic dog days of summer, when Sirius burned brightly in the night sky. This is the Dog Star, the faithful creature at the heels of Orion, the brightest star in Canis Major and called Canicula (little dog) by the Romans. Strangely, native American peoples associated it with dogs too – the Cherokee seeing it as a guardian of the 'Path of Souls', the Blackfoot calling it 'Dogface' and the Alaskan Inuit naming it 'Moon Dog'. Yes, it was right that the brightest star in the firmament should hang in the sultry night sky above our new home. But in the *Iliad* Homer describes this frozen firework as 'an evil portent, bringing heat/And fevers to suffering humanity'. That was to prove right.

We celebrated the two stages of the huge building project with parties for the carpenters, stonemasons, electricians and labourers who became as familiar as friends and gained nutty tans working shirtless on the site. But by the end of that first winter we had learned the measure of the place; the wind howled about the house like the ghosts of Cathy and Heathcliff and the north-facing position meant that frost and ice would remain in pockets and corners for weeks. Our flock of Lleyn sheep huddled below the library windows, coughing and grumbling under the ancient stone walls, just a couple of metres from my books. At night the brief, harsh yelps of foxes and screech owls would shatter the bitter air. Upper Langridge Farm justified its reputation as 'the coldest farm for miles around' – as a neighbour had helpfully mentioned while we were moving in and I was wondering what on earth we were doing. I had wept to leave our previous home, where the children had grown up and where the fifteen years had been (for the most part) contented. For a long time I would have a recurring dream of letting myself into the old, beloved rectory, walking through rooms that were empty and just as I had left them, then creeping into the attic to hide – for ever.

J and I were brave with each other, but at times I knew even he wondered if we had done the right thing. We made mistakes with the building, which was cold, cold, cold. The wind howled not just around it but through it. Poet Michael Longley captured both the good and the bad in these lines:

No insulation –
A house full of draughts,
Visitors, friends:
Its warmth escaping –
The snow on our roof
The first to melt.

The unlit yard was slate black. One night, having driven my daughter to a friend's (as the mothers of teenagers must), I stopped halfway down the track to the farm – because nobody was at home and I could not face its dark emptiness. I was starting to cry when, suddenly, I was startled by a flash of white and a muffled thud of paws. A badger charged across the rough track in front of my stationary car, and away into the darkness. Excited, I took it as a positive sign and went home.

The isolation could render your heart speechless in the face of the night and its sounds. This is not a fear of marauders, you must understand – although friends would ask me, 'Don't you get spooked – alone here?' It is the silence that underlies the harsh chatter of rooks in the susurrating stand of trees, as well as the sense of generations of struggle imprinted on the stones of that windy hillside. It is the exposure to such an immensity of sky you cannot but be brought face to face with your own inadequacy. And mortality. The strangest truth was this: in all the years J and I lived at the farm I (who had previously written five novels, many more children's books and liked to paint and make things) found it impossible to *create*. Once the home itself was made, just living there and running our lives took almost all my reserves of energy. Feng shui practitioners would say the *chi* – the energy – could not stay in a house like that because the front door and the back door were exactly aligned. *Whoosh* – it goes, whirling through, and taking a part of your soul with it. Tractors. Hedge planting. Infected sheep. Cows getting out. People coming and going. Black ice matching the hole of the farm finances. Feed delivered by lumbering lorries. Lambing in a May frost. The track so bumpy taxis refused to come down and so it had to be made up properly, at more cost. The troughs frozen. Poisonous ragwort. Fences breaking. Running out of oil. The fox leaving two headless chickens on the track. A kitchen garden carved out of the hillside at great cost. Dead sheep.

Ah, but on summer days, the light would spill over the creamy stone floors of our hall and atrium and the homestead had a Mediterranean air and everybody who came would breathe in the scent of thyme planted in the courtyard, exclaiming with admiration at what we had created for ourselves. There was a meadow called the Aldermoor where grew about twenty varieties of wild flower. The house appeared in magazines. J said it was his favourite place in the whole world and everyone who visited saw why – even if they might not have chosen to live on the windy hill.

You have to allow places to change you, or else you will never settle, let alone be happy. I confess (broken-hearted over the move from *my* dream house, our rectory) that I was puzzled that my husband should become so obsessed with the need to farm, at a time when farming was not in good health. Yet that need was rooted deep in his childhood. Despite myself I understood, even if I lacked sympathy. Not only had he been a champion show-jumper in his teens, but he had studied agriculture, worked on the Royal Farm at Windsor Castle, broken and trained champion horses professionally – and that all before going to University College London to read philosophy where (a brilliant student and student editor who took on the college authorities with late-sixties radicalism) he was to write a dissertation on 'Base and Superstructure in Marx'. There followed a distinguished career during which he reported from all over the world, made history in Ethiopia, risked his life working under cover in Pinochet's Chile, saw terrible sights and interviewed leaders, made countless documentary series (this in the much-lamented golden era of British television), wrote books, did sterling work for various charities ... But through it all he never lost his yearning for a real country life: the deep desire to plant hedges, husband good soil, stride out on land that is your own.

Whenever I welcomed him back home to the farm from London, where he would have been interviewing politicians for his eponymous weekly television programme, he would throw off his suit to pull on old clothes and stride to the sheds to help with the lambing, like a true Renaissance man. When he bought a horse (then two, then three) and was still (in his fifties) able to vault straight up without even putting a foot in the stirrup, I knew that the most accomplished gaucho in Argentina would nod approval at his prowess. Women like men who straddle more than one world.

Gradually I became tougher, although my brother-in-law once said I was the least likely farmer's wife he had ever seen. I bought rubber boots – but rarely wore them. Learned to layer big sweaters over thick skirts. Even once drove the huge, ancient Land-Rover in the snow, because otherwise I would have been marooned. Alone on the farm (as I so often was), I learned independence. Once, with a coat over my nightdress, I even rounded up the escaped cows who were destroying the garden, placing Billie and Sam like troops on the flank and advancing fearlessly, shouting 'Garn!' and thwacking with my stick, driving them up to the barn, so that when the stockman and his wife arrived at last I was in charge. J was immensely (and disbelievingly) proud of me. The story of how the urban writer tamed the herd went up and down the valley. 'Field-cred' I called it.

One spring morning, not a year after we had moved, I experienced the epiphany which leads – in a way I can now see but could not possibly have known then – me back to the subject of this book.

It was late April and I was alone. The light woke me very early and from the window I glimpsed a morning of such limpid perfection it was impossible to remain indoors. I dressed quickly, afraid to miss the glitter of the dew, and released Billie and Sam from the laundry room where they had their beds. No need for leads. Out into the watery gold of the day with the dogs bounding and snapping at the air in exhilaration.

I walked past the well, across the wide circle of gravel, past the handsome barn and thence right into the fields. And then I saw them. The Herefords were crowding near the fence, their chestnut flanks gleaming in the sunlight as they bent their creamy topknots to tug at the grass. There is a sweetness about cows I had never noticed before: their gentle, wary eyes in big white moon faces. That heavy, grassy smell and the rhythmic, chomping sounds they make, between low, faintly protesting moos. Because it was still chilly their breaths came out in little clouds, like ectoplasm hanging in the air – the whispering spirits of their beefy herd. What had they witnessed since the seventeenth century, those pedigree Herefords, what breed memory looked out through those rolling eyes?

They ruminated and inspected me. I leaned on the fence and looked back and we were not afraid of each other. The air waited. And it was with a sudden leap of the spirit that I said aloud, 'Good morning, girls. You're looking so beautiful this morning! *Aren't* you gorgeous?'

To speak to them like that, to acknowledge their presence as I would a fellow human and admire their individual, curly-topped, four-square magnificence, was to put us on a level. To take my part in the wholeness of things. I now realize that it was at that precise point that I allowed myself to be affected by the *genius loci* – the spirit of the place. And it was the animals – rather than the trees or the distant sweep of the land, or the astonishing sense of worship I felt before the first primroses and the swathes of cowslips – which eased my heart finally into love. It was my humility before the universal beauty of which the animals were a part. In making me see the truth of their existence as on a par with my own within the greater Whole they were exerting a *moral* power over me which I had never experienced before.

This is not what you feel when you look at an animal in a zoo, even though you might marvel at the size of the giraffe or the intricacy of the markings on a snake. Nor is it what you feel when you take the lid off a tin and allow dried food to rattle down into your big dog's metal bowl, smiling fondly as he gobbles his supper. You may come near the sensation, though, when you watch your cat unfold its limbs and stretch – and realize that not in any universe could you ever hope to move with such indifferent grace.

I was learning from the cows.

The joy they gave me, in that brief exchange of looks and breaths that crystalline morning, when the brevity of the sunlight, the dew and all our lives, human and animal, made me catch my breath, was something I would never forget. It was as sustainable as J's method of farming. It set me on a journey. Lolloping Billie and Sam were on it too, but it was Bonnie who would – in a future I could not have then predicted – be the truest companion.

One of my favourite writers is Edith Wharton – she who, in late middle age, would so annoy her friends by the fuss she made over 'the damned Pekingese'. Her first biographer, Percy Lubbock, wrote: 'There is always a dog or two about Edith in her home, a small dog of the yapping kind, a still smaller of the fidgeting and whining breed – dogs that had to be called, caressed …' But writing an autobiography in her seventies Edith Wharton recalled the walk with her father in 1865 (when she was four), down Fifth Avenue in Manhatten, when a friend of her father's gave her a spitz-type puppy she called Foxy, the first of her cohorts of little dogs. Near the end of her life, after an unhappy marriage but a brilliant career, when many people she loved had died and many dogs too, Wharton located the beginning of her imaginative awareness: 'The owning of my first dog made me into a conscious, sentient person, fiercely possessive, anxiously watchful, and woke in me that long ache of pity for animals, and for all inarticulate beings, which nothing has ever stilled.'

The first couple of months of 2003 were (as always for J and me) extremely busy. What made us like that – both driving ourselves hard, always taking on extra projects, charity work and so on – and therefore unable to find much peace on our farm? The too-easy psychological answer might be that he was ever striving to emulate a famous father as well as an older brother who was himself a distinguished broadcaster. Yet the Protestant work ethic played an important role, over and above family history. I always thought that the last words of *The Woodlanders* summed J up, Marty South's passionate elegy over the grave of her beloved Giles Winterborne: '... you was a good man, and did good things!' Doing good things demands time and energy.

As for me, I was always striving to prove myself (girl from humble background makes good etc.) yet always worrying that I would be found out: the achievement of a distinguished degree, the marriage, the beautiful homes, the successful journalistic career, the careful glamour, the books, the programmes, the immense jollity of the parties we gave – all of it discounted when I was found out to be a fraud. To keep fear and boredom at bay, to prove myself as a multitasking, perfectionist alpha female, I – like so many women – took on too much. I also had to keep up with my husband. Had I not done so over the years of his success as an international reporter, writer and political journalist, I would have gone under. The key to our marriage was the meeting of minds in friendship. For all the flaws (what union does not have them?) I do not know what better can be said.

The pond was thickly iced, with a dusting of snow on top. In January and February 2003 I was struggling with the book of my radio series, *Devout Sceptics*, re-reading *Daniel Deronda* (because it was time to), brooding over structural problems in my sixth novel, *The Invasion of Sand*, taking on the chairmanship of a £2.2 million appeal to build a new children's theatre in Bath, moving our daughter into her first London flat and supporting her through the intimidating start of her new job at the *London Evening Standard* and arranging all the detail of a 30-minute programme for Radio 4 to mark the 100th anniversary of Harley-Davidson motorcycles. Kitty and I were writing a joint article for the *Daily Mail*, J was off to Iraq to interview the Prime Minister amidst ominous rumblings from the United States and in my diary I wrote, '*The world is such a terrible place at the moment – a cloud over all things.*'

Yet amidst all that, the diary also records consolations:

11 January: Bonnie and I return in the frost-bound midnight to the empty farmhouse. Her companionship is so precious to me, so essential now. Who would have thought that I would become so dependent on a little dog?

13 January: It's good to have J here again – so much cleverer than I could ever be – to sound ideas off. What would I be without him? This afternoon we go to the pet shop with Bonnie for new dog beds and the expedition is fun. We eat sausages, read and doze by the fire.

20 January: ... so good to be home again with Bonnie. She represents home now.

2 February: ... coming back home to be welcomed by an ecstatic, wriggling little dog.

Bonnie always cheered me, always inspired closeness and took both of us away from work.

The day before our thirty-fifth wedding anniversary was a normal Saturday, and so I listened to my husband on the radio, took the three dogs up through our wood for a walk and felt a great surge of happiness in the still, cold air. It was strange, I thought, to be happy when the news was full of the looming war in Iraq, but the sunlight glittered on a hard frost and I took my little dog to be groomed, and picked her up later, a fresh-smelling shorn lamb. How can one suppress natural joy? It was there every day in Bonnie's behaviour: the irrepressible *nowness* of each second, the perpetual readiness for action and adventure, even if that was only chasing a leaf. Each parting would be marked by the reproachful eyes and the drooping tail, even though she had two big dogs to stay with. I would return from shopping, one hour later, to be met with such an effusion of joy, such a frolicsome licking, that there was nothing to do but laugh.

On our anniversary, 23 February, J returned from presenting his usual Sunday television programme and presented me with his gift: a fine, chunky necklace of antique coral, since the thirty-fifth is the coral anniversary. In an imaginative touch he had also entered the bookmakers Joe Coral (for the first ever time) and placed a bet that Liverpool (my home team) would win their next away football match. He handed me the betting slip – and we laughed. That night we went to our favourite restaurant (not the grandest in Bath, but we ate out rarely, preferring to be in our blue and yellow kitchen) and my diary records: '*We ate well and drank better and talked best of all. Perfection. As I say so often, I am so lucky.*'

There it is.

Liverpool did not win.

As I explained in the Introduction, writing a memoir is to offer just a slice of a life, a section of truth – like a sample taken by an archaeologist, full of priceless shards which remain, nevertheless, mere parts, fragments shored against ruin. Sometimes when my dog is snoozing on my knee I trace her ribs with my fingertips, each one in turn, imagining the fragility of her skeleton laid in earth. Yet nowadays the computer can reassemble a whole head from fragments of bone, an image of what once was (a centuries-dead face reconstructed) turning and turning in cyberspace to awe us. So my dog's DNA will lie for ever in earth and so will mine and therefore the essence of what is true is unassailable.

That is how I feel about that last anniversary.

Whatever went before, and no matter what was to come after, what happened that day and is condensed into those few words, remains The Truth.

Yet in the end only he and I know that truth; therefore what is presented to the world remains as shards.

* * *

J was the Chairman of the Bath International Music Festival and worked tirelessly to promote it. It was he who had taken me to my first big classical concert at the Festival Hall in 1968, although in my late teens I did begin a small collection of budget classical LPs. When we met he was rather entertained that I could be so admiring of his piano playing, since I knew so little about technique. When I was 30 a friend took me for the first time to the Royal Opera House, Covent Garden, and my tears at the end of *La Bohème* began a craze for opera which took me to some of the great opera houses of the world and led me to study the famous Kobbé guide so that I knew all the stories. Yet by 2003 I had grown tired of the form, and returned to jazz and blues as my cooking music of choice, as well as classic pop tracks ('Leader of the Pack' etc.), cajun, country, not to mention urban grooves like Fishbelly Black. Our musical tastes had slightly diverged, although we shared a love of chamber music.

I remain unsure of exactly how it came about but this is what I know. Just after our anniversary J had been asked to interview Susan Chilcott where she lived, in a village called Blagdon, not far from Bath and Bristol. The article was to appear in the local evening paper, its purpose to promote the long-established Mid-Somerset Festival, invaluable for its encouragement of young performers each March. Later it was to amaze people that somebody as well known as J should agree to write for a local paper; at the time I hardly knew this was happening because I was planning a trip to Milwaukee as well as starting work on a public lecture at Bath University on the subject of pornography. Still, had it registered on my radar I would have attributed it to his good will. And I do know for certain that there was nothing suspicious about the meeting – on one level. Yet they had liked each other enormously at that dinner party four months before, and she told a mutual friend (I heard later) that she was excited to see him again.

In her case, I should probably have felt the same. Over the years she must have sat next to any number of self-centred men at dinner – you know the ones – who never ask a question yet, puffed up with needy masculine ego, assume you will uncover every achievement and interest in their lives. Sitting next to J she would have dazzled but been enchanted too, since he, the consummate interviewer, would always be sure to find out what made the most humble person tick, let alone a beautiful soprano.

He went to Blagdon that day.

They fell in love.

How can I know what happened? The novelist in me could write the scene and invest it with heady tension. But I never asked how it all came about, and speculation is irrelevant. What's more, in the days following I noticed no change. Our life was hurtling on in its normal way, and I had no inkling of any undercurrent tugging my husband into deeper water. But just as one reads a novel, listens to music or looks at a great painting differently once you know the circumstances of its composition or future, so it is impossible to look back without seeing clouds mass over our farm, our life.

So now I see everything we did after 23 February in the light of what was to come. Evenings with friends in London during which we argued about Iraq; me interviewing Ben Okri at the Bath Literature Festival; our children visiting for weekends to tell us how their jobs were progressing; one special evening when J and I ate caviar (a gift from a friend), blinis and sour cream helped down by shots of bison grass vodka, followed by pot-roasted pheasant and mashed potato with good red wine and then home-made rhubarb crumble and my own ice cream – all by candlelight in front of a crackling dining-room fire. Good times, all – yet now overshadowed.

My own days were made gloomy by work on my lecture for Bath University. Despite the *laisse-faire* attitude of so many of my peers, my attitude to pornography and the insidious 'pornogrification' of society – a subject I'd visited often in journalism – has remained constant over the years: I detested it for reasons that went beyond feminism and perhaps might be called humanist. And now the cruel hydra of internet porn is indestructible. I investigated, read – and became depressed. The dark world I uncovered revolted me even more than I expected. With hindsight it was a mistake to take it on; the task made me withdrawn, and perhaps less observant of what was going on in J's life than I might otherwise have been. A diary entry is very telling:

20 March: The farm is bathed in sunlight but I proceeded to make myself miserable by doing a trawl of porn sites to see what can be accessed freely and easily. It was far, far worse than expected and as I went on I became so overwhelmed by the scale of the horror that my mouth was dry – and at one point I had to walk out into the garden for air. The birds were singing, the crocuses pale gold in sunlight, and sweet little Bonnie rushed about at my feet – all white, all innocence. Yet not even she could make me feel better. That other world was 'in' my computer, 'in' the very air that I had breathed in my study. I felt polluted. Everything spoiled by it. The violence, the hatred against women defies description. This wretched lecture is a terrible black burden pressing down on me.

Meanwhile J was spending much time in London making extra programmes about the war in Iraq and besides writing the lecture I was planning a trip to Kenya for the charity Plan International, to visit my sponsored child and write about the trip for the *London Evening Standard.* I was also unwell; not in pain but afflicted by inconvenient female problems which grew worse and worse. And amidst the repetitive exhaustion of my diary I see one entry, laden now with irony. I went to visit a friend who had recently moved to Bath and wrote: '*What would it be like to be middle aged and alone, your husband having departed? I should realize, perhaps, just how lucky I am.*'

Two months later, I was in the Bath Clinic. My womb had gone, but my room was full of flowers. When the anaesthetist came to see me he admired them and I said, 'Yes, I'm lucky.' He was tall, middle-aged, South African. He smiled and said, 'You make your luck.'

In the silence after his departure I wondered if that was true. I had just learned that my husband was in love with somebody else – and yet that was not the worst thing. During the previous weeks he had seemed so weighed down. It was inevitable that he would have to share it with me – because, after all, we shared almost everything. When, after many years, a married couple become linked symbiotically, they may perhaps live as brother-sisterly best friends and soulmates rather than lovers, yet know what the other is thinking, before the thought has formed. As Judith Thurman puts it (writing about Colette), 'A marriage may be sustained by a deep complicity between two spouses, long after the extinction of desire.' You are attuned to nuances of mood – unless, that is, you allow work and other preoccupations to blind you. The lecture given, the programmes completed, everything else laid aside because of my physical health and the urgency of the hysterectomy, I became aware again, woke up to the real world. And the horizons all around our home filled with his unhappiness.

Dates and details do not matter. The simple truth was this: J and Susan Chilcott had fallen passionately in love, but their affair was not to last long – *as such*. For only about three months later she discovered that the breast cancer for which she had been treated two years earlier had returned, spread to her liver and would not let her live. The beautiful woman of 40, at the very height of her powers (although perhaps not, since opera singers grow in maturity), with a four-year-old son whom she adored and called the light of her life, had been given her sentence. She could expect perhaps another three months. I lay in my room at the clinic, minus my womb, looking at my flowers, full of sorrow for her, brooding hopelessly on the pitiless inevitability of it. Like J, I wondered how people could believe there is a god.

Morphine-induced imaginings chill the soul. I had a dream in that scented room. I am a woman who has lost many children, yet I am outside her, looking on. She goes with my husband to visit a certain church, running through the flowery graveyard as if for refuge. She is drawn to ascend the winding stair into the gallery and her husband follows. Up there is an elaborate monument, covered with dust and spider webs. It is black and grey marble, with skulls beneath. She is looking up and sees that the names of the dead on the tomb are those of her own children, and as she stares in disbelief something is rearing up, a carved figure come to life, arms stretching out towards her. And she is plucked, carried up into the air, then hurled forward over the balustrade, to smash down dead on the floor of the church below. In this short time her husband has been frozen by the stairwell. Now he darts forward to look over the balcony at the corpse lying broken. But even as he looks a form rises by it, a wraith, a personification of malevolence. It looks up; he cannot even cry – struck dumb by what he sees. And then there is a jump cut, as in a movie. A railway station, and a young girl waiting for a train. It chugs in, one of the old-fashioned type with compartments. The girl sees one with a woman in it – with her head shrouded in a scarf – and gets in because she feels safe. Oh no, but I *knew* – even in the dream, the watcher knew. That spirit would kill other people's children. Nowhere was safe.

('*Oh Lord,*' I wrote, '*what was all that about?*')

Our beautiful home awaited me, and it was sunny when I returned. Daniel and Kitty came to visit, as well as my parents – who lived near by. Because of the necessity for post-operative quiet I had no difficulty in keeping what I knew from everybody else. I had been looking forward to this time of rest and reading, with Bonnie on my knee playing the role perfected by Elizabeth Barrett Browning's Flush, 'in his eternal place on my bed'. She would be like the little dogs at the feet of the ladies on medieval tombs, eternally vigilant, devotion incarnate. The point is, at this stage I had no doubt whatsoever that what was happening in J's life would be endured, coped with and survived.

My journal records: '*There is a space inside me, where what we must think of as "womanhood" used to be. The loss of it seems less a source of regret than of celebration. Space in my body. Space in my mind. Space in my life. Vacuums are always filled, aren't they? So we shall wait and see what flows inwards.*'

I did not know that home would never be the same again.

Susan Chilcott sang for the last time in public in June 2003, at a concert in Brussels. She was accompanied by her friend, the pianist and Radio 3 presenter Iain Burnside, and the performance was with the actress Fiona Shaw, reading from Shakespeare. Susan wore white linen. She sang (among other things) the Willow aria from Verdi's *Otello*, when the doomed Desdemona, full of sorrow, remembers a song from her childhood:

The fresh streams ran between the flowery banks,
She moaned in her grief,
In bitter tears which through her eyelids sprang
Her poor heart sought relief.
Willow! Willow! Willow!
Come sing! Come sing!
The green willow shall be my garland.

Later her voice would rise in a crescendo as she begged, '*Ch'io viva ancor, ch'io viva ancor!*' ('Let me live longer, let me live longer!') as death, in the form of her husband Othello, stands over her.

J was in the audience, with other friends. You would need a heart of granite not to see how unbearably poignant it must have been. The word 'heartbreaking' is overused, like 'tragic' and 'hero'. Anyone who watched Susan Chilcott's last performance, knowing that her life was already ebbing away, must surely have felt a breaking inside.

I wrote:

> *I think of her and her son with numbness, because the horror of it is so hard to imagine. As for his feelings … well, my own knowledge of love is so far removed from narrow, tabloid newspaper notions, that I can only empathize. Do we have any choice about these* coups de foudre*? In this case, I don't think so. J is permanently upset – how can he not be? I don't know how he will be able to bear what is coming, but he has made a choice to involve himself and so he has no choice but to endure.*

Stricken, J asked me if I understood that he would want to spend time with Susan in the three months of life she had left. I told him I did understand. Because I *did* – and it makes no difference to me that other women might think me mad. This was not something cheap or clandestine; he was going away from me (and I was regaining strength daily, with enormous reserves of inner fortitude, built up over the years) to take care of somebody very special whose strength was waning. Take care of her son too.

I wrote:

I cannot begrudge a dying woman the love of my husband. Can we choose who we love? To stand in a bookshop is to stand in the midst of a great, tumultuous, seething, writhing, coiling, heaving mass of complex human emotions, and to be deafened by the screams of passion and pain. Who am I to tell them all – all those writers and their creations – that they are wrong? I suppose my sadness is chiefly because I wish J and I could have been all-in-all to each other and yet – after that first intensity of passion – it was never to be. I wonder why? He is still the person I most like to talk to, and whose various roles in life I find the most fascinating. Looking back at us in our youth, falling in love, making a home, doing finals, starting our careers, I marvel at the sheer courage *of it all. Yet that swash-buckling love stepped sideways and lost itself among the alley-ways of other people, other lives, self-indulgence, guilt. And then we never quite managed to find the way back.*

The other day I was pierced by a pang that Dan and Kitty will never again live at home with me. Today this farm feels so empty … and yet, truthfully, I am all right. I will get through this. I know that J would not normally be here today, yet he would be here in spirit – but today he is not even here in spirit. But my little dog is at my feet. I reach forward and stroke her. I hear the fountain – and birds. I must begin to make *again.*

Bovine, I had watched him descend the stairs with a packed bag. What would have happened had I thrown myself down, clung to his leg, begged him not to go? I will never know because I didn't do so. 'I am dumb from human dignity' wrote Yeats, and I know what that means. Yes, I am proud – but perhaps foolish too. Later I began an unfinished novel like this:

She gave her husband away.

It wasn't that she didn't want him any more. Oh no, at that point she wanted him maybe more than she'd ever done before. But perhaps that was contrary of her – acting the child who clutches at an old toy because a friend suddenly wants to play with it, but gives it up all the same, in the end. Maybe if she'd clutched a little more fiercely it wouldn't have turned out as it did.

But I watched as blank passivity slid over her, and the woman who had been so deliciously bad in her past embraced a perverse form of sainthood. She became the kind of person friends described as 'so good', with that slight shake of the head which indicates disquiet, calling into question their own selfishness, but also her common humanity. Good behaviour can sometimes seem intolerable, since we wish others to rage against the dying of the light, as we would ourselves.

I shook my head as she – so generously, so calmly – gave her husband away, and then turned to me as if to ask 'Why did this happen?', those great eyes filling, that generous mouth folded into a moue of sadness. You could strike a woman like that. You could shake her until the teeth rattled, and all her features fell apart, that beauty destroyed forever, with all the rest. But I was her friend and that defined my role – to witness all, to allow all, until the moment they both fell into the pit, at which point I would stretch out my hand to help.

Sometimes it is easier to tell a story in the third person. Yet I find these days I no longer want to make up characters (except for children) when each day, through my work as an advice columnist, I deal with reality and have to try to tell it as it is. When we were both young journalists J used to ask me if I ever thought of writing a novel. He thought it the way I should go. Excited as I was then by filing reports from every corner of Britain for magazines and newspapers, I said I had no wish to. Why would you want to make it up? I asked him. But he was to encourage me, patiently over the years, to write fiction. Without him, I doubt I would ever have done so. Without him, I doubt I will again.

On 20 June my parents came to lunch to celebrate my mother's birthday and the 'official birthday' of Bonnie, who had come to live with us on that day a year earlier. Lunch was outside in the courtyard, under the cream umbrella. I tied ribbons on Mum's chair, on Bonnie's basket, round her neck. J's absence was unremarked because it was unremarkable. He was a busy man. The dog's presence made it all much easier. By focusing on her and the meal I could deflect any anxiety my perceptive mother must have felt, looking at my face.

Here I reach the limit of what I can write about that summer. So much must remain unrecorded, although I will never forget. Too painful to recall the hope we shared that after it was over (it was not possible to utter the brutal words 'After she is dead') we could put it all back together. J and I had been through much in our long marriage but we recognized that this earthquake was truly terrifying, like nothing before. I wondered if, afterwards, we would find we had moved on a ratchet, making it impossible to go back. *Can* you go back? I asked myself if I would be able to live with a perfect ghost – my husband forever haunted by that amazing voice, like a mariner tied to a mast still hearing the fatal sirens' song. I wondered – when I finally told our children and the three of us talked obsessively about the subject, raging over bottles of white wine late into the night as moths slammed at the kitchen window – if I could recover the man I had known.

Susan Chilcott died in J's arms on 4 September. The obituaries were unanimous. The *Independent* noted: 'Her death came three months after she made her operatic debut at the Royal Opera House, in which her "radiant" and "glorious" performance outshone even that of her co-star, Placido Domingo.' The *Guardian* said:

> *Susan Chilcott, who has died of cancer aged 40, was one of the most compelling and intense English operatic stars to emerge in the last decade, with a wonderfully fresh, attractive and open personality and a rare commitment to her work. Her career was so distressingly short that too little of her best work has been captured on DVD or CD. But her singing had a purity and a forceful dramatic impact that made her a formidable operatic actor. Her last role on stage was Jenufa, which she sang in English for Welsh National Opera last March, with Sir Charles Mackerras conducting … Sadly, when the run ended, Chilcott was too ill to record the work with Mackerras, as he had wanted. Her last performance, in Brussels in June, was … with the pianist Iain Burnside and actor Fiona Shaw – and she was singing better than ever. Chilcott made an indelible impression on those who saw and heard her, or worked with her.*

On the day of her funeral at Wells Cathedral hundreds of people gathered to pay their respects. By this stage I had begun to feel enraged that – in the eyes of all those people – J was 'allowed' the role of widower. In fact Susan was married to her manager, although they were not living as man and wife and he was not the father of her son. But what do such details matter? I had packed my own bag, said goodbye to the dogs and cats, felt the (increasing) pang at leaving Bonnie – and was off to Heathrow. At the very hour of her funeral I was high above the Atlantic, en route for my beloved United States. I had work to do, but also needed to escape.

Snapshots in a family photograph album can come unstuck in time – adrift from captions which identify person, time and place. Will future generations know who they were, those faces caught faking smiles? Will *any* of it survive? Knowing all, remembering all, I can still only bear to offer small fragments of what Philip Larkin calls 'a past that now no one can share'.

In Point Reyes, Marin County, somebody has altered a sign on a wall from 'No Parking' to 'No Barking' and my laughter is over the top, hysterical. But when, not long afterwards, I see scrawled on a post overlooking San Francisco, 'I almost died here – but no such luck,' I become ridiculously upset. The view from the Marin Headlands – the Golden Gate Bridge, dwarfed sailboats, white caps on sparkling water – is perfect, and yet I feel my head is crumbling.

I talk obsessively about Bonnie to anyone who will listen (mercifully, Americans like dogs), miss her dreadfully and note, 'Who would have thought I would be so dependent on her?'

Pulling out her photograph to show to our lovely, kind niece, who shares a house with friends in Oakland, I think of Amy Tan and my last visit, when none of this misery could have been dreamt of. The point is, in talking about my love for my dog I'm really talking about my love of home, of J – just as Elizabeth Barrett Browning used Flush as displacement.

Ruefully I notice a hotel called Diva. Everything conspires to remind me. Not far away, just off Geary, in a jazz club called Biscuits and Blues, a guy called R.J. Mischo sings the blues. He reminds me of Snooks Eaglin. The mouth harp moans and the slide swoops and shimmies, mimicking my mood – while the passion he pours into his songs pierces my heart:

I wake up every night around midnight
Cos I just can't sleep no more.

Yes.

You have yourself to blame now baby
For breaking up our happy home.

Yes.

If you don't do right
How you gonna be treated right yourself?

Yes.

I turn up at a reception for the Sacred Dying Foundation, which was founded by a theologian author and deviser-of-ritual called Megory Anderson. One of the many purposes of this trip is a commission from *The Times Magazine*: a feature on the new American way of death – something I'd suggested months before, in a different era. I'd arranged a first meeting with Megory two days earlier but instead of talking about her work I angsted obsessively about my problems, like a skinny Ancient Mariner plucking the sleeve of any kind stranger. To make amends for that self-absorption I decide I must honour her invitation to the reception.

In the elegant house on Vallejo Street I sit on beige velvet under a high, panelled ceiling, determined to engage. There's a bishop here, four other priests over there, and a group of intelligent, lay people, all of whom look as if they have a calling. Their faces are sensitive. I know they would feel sorry for me if they knew what I was feeling. But I do not speak – and a round-room discussion which would normally fascinate me leaves me lost and panicky:

'It is not just our Ministry to the dying but their Ministry to us which matters.'

'The focus is not just on helping people to die with grace, but helping people to survive the death of loved ones with grace.'

'Prayer is placing yourself every day on the threshold of death. Because it is a way of living life to the full.'

No – I can't be doing with this. For years I have been writing articles and broadcasting on the subject of bereavement. I even won an award for this work from the charity Cruse, presented to me by the Queen, as patron. But what do I know? Back in

England my husband is (in his own words) 'broken by a grief that was more dreadful than I had ever imagined any pain could be'. I know he would want to tear down this gracious room and shout that there is no grace attached to dying, not for anybody. He would call these good people dishonest and tell them that to survive the trauma of witnessing a terrible death is beyond such gentle ministrations. He would stamp in fury on kind Megory's 'rituals for embracing the end of life'. In that room, desperate to break free from everything, I realize it is impossible for me to fulfil the bloody assignment.

Afterwards I walk three blocks to Union to meet beloved friends and confidantes, my producer Malcolm and photographer Robin, who have been having fun, cruising those switch-back streets on a rental Harley-Davidson, while I was listening to lofty talk of death. Now they're drinking white wine in a restaurant called Prego. They agree I'm right to ditch the commission and we drink and talk and eat and laugh as if there were no tomorrow. As never before, I sense the Mexican papier-mâché 'Day of the Dead' skulls in my study back home, all gibbering that there *is* no tomorrow. Ha!

Other work to be done, different days – Malcolm and I are making programmes with Armistead Maupin and Professor Jared Diamond. More *Devout Sceptics*, more talk about God, and doubt, and the end of the world. Which is surely at hand. There's a skull in Professor Diamond's office at UCLA and I feel the interviews slipping from my grasp. It's as if I can't do anything any more. My face, in Robin's publicity photographs taken on Maupin's terrace, grins horribly, like a lunatic.

In Grace Cathedral something happens – an epiphany which equals my encounter with the cows that sublime, golden morning. In the soaring miracle of concrete (finished in 1964 when I was just four years off meeting the man I was to share my life with) I find some peace.

In front of the great entrance is a vast carpet labyrinth woven in soft tones of lilac, purple, grey. The labyrinth (I read) is an ancient symbol worldwide. Prehistoric labyrinths served as traps for malevolent spirits, or as paths for ritual dances. In medieval times the labyrinth symbolized a hard path to God with one entrance (birth) leading to the endless winding, looping, puzzling path which leads to one centre (God). When people could not afford to travel on pilgrimages the symbol of the labyrinth substituted; you could walk it with your fingers if you were ill. Later labyrinths as religious symbols faded, to become maze-like entertainments. But now, in the New Age, they are used by people who want to walk in and escape the everyday and by mystics as an aid to meditation. Walking among the turns, passing where you have come and then turning off in a different direction, but always moving onwards, one loses track of direction and of the outside world. The mind is quietened. This (I read) is a form of meditation.

So I place my sandals neatly with the others, and step on the carpet. How strange it is to pace slowly, as if within narrow walls, when there are no partitions. In the stillness of that vast cathedral, I fold my hands behind my back and walk the labyrinth, turning and turning. And I am thinking of Susan Chilcott with such pity it is as if another weight is loosened from my back by invisible hands. I know that J had not intended to hurt me; nothing could have been farther from his mind or will. Yet he was overtaken by a *truth*: an intensity of feeling which could not be denied, or harnessed – not in those circumstances. Why, I think, should she *not* have been his soulmate for that brief period? Who is to know the time or place of a meeting, or what form the soul's pilgrimage will take? Reaching the centre of the carpet labyrinth at last, standing in a beam of light, looking up at nothing, I give thanks for my life. Then, retracing my steps to walk that sinuous track, resisting the temptation to walk straight, I find myself amazed at just how much love there is in this story. Then I arrive back at the beginning, which is the end.

Two days later, at the entrance to the Mission San Carlos Borromeo at Carmel, a woman tries to give me something, pushing at my hand. It's like a playing card, small and laminated, and at first I shake my head, not wanting a religious tract. But she has a gentle face and I don't want to seem churlish, so I say 'Thank you'. Inside the church I look down and see on one side a picture of Father Junipero Serra, the founder of the California Missions in the seventeenth century. On the other side, an image of the Carmel Mission – and the words 'Always go forward and never turn back.' They shimmer. Standing in front of the ornately beautiful Gothic altar, staring at Father Serra's burial place, I wonder in what circumstances he said those words, which are now dancing around in my brain. A devout agnostic, I always light a candle in Catholic churches for the son who was stillborn in 1975. But now, within those adobe walls, I have no choice but to light one for somebody else.

No, for two people.

You may be thinking I have forgotten my small dog. Impossible. To say that I yearned for her, and for home, and the husband, and the old life would be an understatement. In any case Bonnie was fulfilling a very important role back on the farm. J had moved back in my absence, and our daughter was taking care of him. At night, of course, Bonnie slept on the bed with him. 'She is such a *comfort*,' he told me on the telephone.

Thus my small dog fulfilled an ancient destiny, as a 'comforter dog'. Her breed is one of the most ancient in recorded history, about 8,000 years old. Very early on Maltese were believed to have healing powers: place one on the stomach or chest and you would feel better. It isn't hard to see why all lapdogs give comfort. A dog's body temperature is between 100.2 and 102.8°F and therefore, sitting on your lap in a draughty castle (for example), it kept you warm. This is where the vet Bruce Fogle's hot-water bottle idea comes in. Oriental emperors and their courtiers called their pets 'sleeve' dogs; a Pekinese popped in each capacious sleeve must have been invaluable in winter.

Myth has it that Marie Antoinette walked to the guillotine in 1793 clutching her papillon to give her strength. Another doomed queen, Mary Queen of Scots, was also repaid for her lifelong love of dogs by the last service of her faithful pet. Some say it was a Skye terrier, some a Maltese, some a toy spaniel – it doesn't matter. Mary was incarcerated at Fotheringhay Castle, about 80 miles north of London, by her cousin Elizabeth I, who is portrayed in a lovely small work by Marcus Gheeraerts the Elder with a Maltese at her feet, leading one reasonably to assume this was her own dog. Mary Stuart liked to dress her pets in blue velvet collars, and wrote from captivity to the Archbishop of Glasgow, begging for a couple of 'pretty little dogs' from Lyons, and explaining, '... my only pleasure is in all the little animals I can get. They must be sent in baskets, well stored so as to keep them warm.' She embroidered little, leaping dogs amongst flowers and leaves.

On the morning of 8 February 1587 Mary was led into the Great Hall to be executed. After the terrible, bungled hacking was over, an eyewitness records: 'Then one of the executioners noticed her little dog which had hidden under her clothes. Afterwards it would not leave the corpse but came and lay between her head and her shoulders.' The blood-spattered animal lay whimpering, refusing to leave its mistress, until dragged away by force to be washed. But afterwards the small dog pined, refused to eat and did not long survive its mistress.

If I had worn a voluminous gown on top of the multiple petticoats of that time, Bonnie (who sometimes seems tied to my heel by an invisible elastic) could have crept unseen with me to the scaffold. In a sense she did. Summer over, autumn tumbling down into winter, J continued to be absent, staying with friends and unable to shake off his grief, or pull himself back from what seemed like post-traumatic stress disorder. I would watch him on television, listen to him on the radio and marvel that he could still be professional, still be courteous to sometimes mendacious politicians. I thought he would come back, but he did not. Writing much later (in the introduction to his fine book *Russia*, published in 2008) he explained, with simple honesty, 'I was in no condition to repair the damage I had inflicted on my marriage.' So in that dark time, when I existed in a sort of limbo, I would reach out in the night to the space he used to fill – and my fingers would clutch the small, soft shape of my dog.

At this point I was still trying to keep his absence a secret, although close friends knew. For journalists we were both naïve. Susan Chilcott had many, many friends and admirers so it is no surprise their relationship had been the talk of musical London. Inevitably people talk, but I was so wrapped up in my own slow-burning shock that I was unaware how many people knew what was going on. As Chairman of the Children's Theatre Appeal (now flourishing and called The Egg) I had to make public appearances and be as British as possible, keeping a stuff upper lip. But one day I hosted a fundraising reception at the farm and in the middle of my socializing with the generous great and good of Bath, a reporter from the *Mail on Sunday* arrived on the doorstep, wanting to find out the state of my marriage. It happened more than once, and I would utter staccato lies about my own friendship with Susan Chilcott, still trying to conceal what everybody knew. At such moments you dream of a tall high window and the moment when you launch yourself through it into the blue vacancy, surrounded by bright splinters. Falling.

One night I had to go to a similar party, this one hosted by a friend and held at the great house St Catherine's Court, just outside Bath, which was then owned by the actress Jane Seymour. One of our appeal committee collected me at 7.30 p.m., and I remember thinking even then how strange it was that I – the independent and controlling one – was grateful to be looked after. The friend driving me was one of those I reluctantly chose to confide in, only to find he already knew. Of course people like to gossip, but it is not always malicious. The desire to be in the know, and the need to pass on fascinating scraps of information about our fellow men and women, is as old as humanity itself. It is malice that I loathe. Too many newspapers employ columnists whose sole function is to bitch, flinging vitriol around like a maniac on a bus with a bottle of acid, not caring who it burns and scars.

(Incidentally, it is a mystery to me that, for centuries, the term 'bitch' has been derogatory, and the verb 'to bitch' implies the nastiest qualities – traducing the reputation of the female dog. In the opinion of the great scientist Konrad Lorenz (awarded the Nobel prize for medicine and psychology in 1973) a bitch is more faithful than a dog as well as more intelligent. In *Man Meets Dog* (1949) he writes, 'I have known a great many dogs and can say with conviction that of all creatures the one nearest to man in the finest of its perceptions and its capacity to render true friendship, is a bitch. Strange that in English her name has become a term of abuse.')

That night my own little bitch proved her worth. The evening dragged on and I made small talk (as one must) and gazed on the actor Bill Nighy across the room, aware that my old self would have rocked up to meet him, but this new self did not have the mettle. When your marriage is cracking under strain (at that stage I did not yet consider it irretrievably broken) you look at the people around you as aliens, wondering how they can drink and talk and laugh when the world is falling apart. But of course, not *their* world. Yet people in pain subconsciously seek each other out; I met a woman unknown to me who was in a similar situation and we clinked glasses to wish each other strength. At last it was over, and at about 11.30 p.m. another friend drove a long way out of her route to take me home. It was icy and misty, and the half-mile track to the farm seemed longer than ever. As we clunked over the first cattle grid and swung down and round past the path up to the new barn where the cattle were wintering in, my spirits sank even lower, if that were possible. The games barn, the house, the cottage – all were empty. Sue was silent. I knew she didn't want to leave me, for this was something she had been through herself.

I saw the eyes first, chips of emerald in the headlights. There was a very large farm gate which we would close if going out, to keep the dogs enclosed. Bonnie's arrival had necessitated fine chicken wire along the bottom, for she could easily pass beneath. When I left that night at 7.30, climbing into my friend's car beyond the gate, she had been running around with Billie and Sam, all three hating the fact that they were going to be left for the evening. But for big dogs two bowls of food and a cosy bed is a big draw; they know that when they hear the car return they can bust out through the dog flap and set the yard echoing with their commotion. In contrast, small dogs keep watch. Small dogs wait.

'Look!' said Sue.

Bonnie was standing on her hind legs, paws resting on the wood, waiting. Seeing the car, she yapped frantically – and Billie and Sam came out on cue. But when I said goodnight to my friend, and opened the gate to take my dog, squirming rapturously, in my arms, I could tell by the iciness of her paws and the chill of her head that she had not left her vigil by the gate since I had left. Four hours in a bitter wind, 700 feet above sea level.

The American poet (and author of *Dog Years*, one of the best books ever written about the love of dogs) Mark Doty believes that dogs offer a 'cure' for the essential spiritual loneliness of humankind. When J and I had only just fallen in love we agreed one night that the conjoining of human souls is an impossibility: both the head and the body could love in passion and in friendship, yet that love is only possible 'if two keep souls apart' (as I wrote in a love poem to him). Such an idea was probably a product of the zeitgeist: that sixties radicalism which drew so much from Sartre and de Beauvoir (whom we admired) and was fed equally by reforming zeal and existential *angst.* Why did we start out by holding something back? Neither of us had ever been in love in the way we were at the end of 1967, and yet still we clung to something so aridly theoretical as the idea that there is no such thing as a soulmate. It was one of many things (I realize now) that we got wrong. To embrace the idea of the one mate for your soul, to cleave to another, giving and taking in equal measure, is surely the only cure for the loneliness that afflicts you when the umbilical cord is cut. That it is so hard to attain is no reason for not striving. For love, above all, demands great things of the self – including sacrifice.

Mark Doty maintains that animal presences are a door towards feeling and understanding. His account of his love for his dogs Arden and Beau and the agonizing death of his first partner Wally from AIDS demonstrates the profound truth that when you open your heart to such loves, different though they might be, you place yourself permanently on the interface between delight and heartbreak. He writes, 'You can only understand the world through what's at hand.' And if that is the 'intelligence and sensibility … complex of desires and memories, habits and expectations' which is a dog, then why should it not give insight into the human condition too?

The poet had bought the golden retriever Beau to please his partner. Yet generosity and love can bounce right back to reward you, as I too was to discover. Doty writes, 'I thought when I brought Beau home, I was giving a gift to Wally, but in truth the gift was his to me, or mine to myself, or both. If I'd planned it I couldn't have done a better thing to save my life.'

In the same way, Bonnie's vigil by the gate was another stage in my own education. To be adored so much was balm for the wounded spirit; to remain the centre of the world for this single, small breathing creature was solace for the soul. Some days I felt that if all else melted away it would still be me and Bonnie facing up to a universe of missing husbands, dead lovers, gossiping bystanders, curious friends and sorrowful loved ones. In needing me so very much she was throwing me a lifeline – although I did not know it. What's more, a dog (or cat, or horse) anchors you in reality. Even if each step is slow, and the face in the mirror is alien and full of shadows, each day the pets must be taken care of. For what did they know of change? It was not their fault. Mark Doty understands this well: 'A walk is a walk and must be taken; breakfast and dinner come when they are due. The routines of the living are inviolable, no hiatus called on account of misery, spiritual crisis, or awful weather.'

The year was falling towards Christmas, the feast that was always so important in our family – a festival of lights indeed. But J was not coming back; this would be the first Christmas for 35 years that we would spend apart. The situation was barely tolerable. My father had suffered a heart attack and (more or less) recovered. My daughter had been ill in hospital again and (more or less) recovered. In between all this, Malcolm Love and I had made radio programmes with the novelist Ian Rankin (in Edinburgh) and Professor Sir Robert Winston. Looking back, I don't know how I managed to string two words together, let alone ask good questions. My days felt as if I were stumbling across a field in darkness, only just managing to stay upright, hearing my own breath as the men with lamps and guns closed in. At night I would lie bolt awake and listen to the sounds outside – those sudden screeches and mysterious rustles of the countryside – and it was as if it was all happening inside my head, not out there: wildness scrabbling to be let out.

I'd had a few sessions with a local psychotherapist, in an attempt to make sense of what was happening, but when I entered her peaceful office and told the quiet woman my story, I could almost see her flinch. Oddly, I felt sorry for her, sensing she would be happier coping with a little local depression than this manic, self-analysing woman, whose savage determination to *cope* was a shield too strong for gentle therapy. In those days I knew little about such matters; since then I have wondered if J and I had been able to talk to somebody together we might have managed to save our marriage. Yet nobody suggested it – nobody he was speaking to, nobody around me – and so we continued in our private hells. By then, not long before Christmas, all the peace I had found in Grace Cathedral had ebbed away, all forgiveness forgotten. I felt enraged that he should remain so stricken with grief for a woman he had known such a short time, furious that he seemed to have fled from me, and everything we had created. The worst thought – in those bruised hours before the dawn, when the pills are not working and even the dog has lost her sense of duty and fallen asleep – was that the wrong person had gone. I could not banish the wretched thought that had I, his wife, died he would not have mourned so much.

(I now think that the comparison is as absurd as it is hypothetical. But it was how I felt at the time.)

How were we to cope with Christmas? I put up the usual tall tree at the end of our big sitting room and festooned it with the usual multicoloured fripperies, including a scrawny red garland which had adorned our trees in my Liverpool childhood, and some decorations Dan had made as a little boy. Our Christmas tree was always laden; it was impossible to find space for any more lights and ornaments. (I like what is extravagant and over the top; that was a difference between J and me.) Most cards were addressed to me, because enough people now knew what had happened, but those with 'Mr and Mrs' on the envelope seemed to make innocent mockery of tree, hanging stars, mistletoe, everything. Who would carve the turkey? What about the sweet, silly, private Christmas rituals?

Christmas had to be diluted. In 1987 I had met a Radio 4 producer called Gaynor Vaughan-Jones. We made a literary series called *American Authors* together, and became close friends. This was followed by a series, *Turning Points*, the high spot of which was an interview with Seamus Heaney about moving from the north to the south of Ireland, which was a political/cultural/spiritual upheaval. Gaynor was now married to Ernie Rea, the BBC Controller of Religious Broadcasting, who was the person to whom I had taken the original proposal for the long-running *Devout Sceptics*. They had shared an unhappy holiday with the kids and me back in the summer and been entirely supportive, as well as sad for us all. Now the children and I decided to invite them for Christmas. When they accepted I actually wept with relief, for the gap left by J was so shocking, so enormous it had to be filled.

So, in the event, Christmas 2003 saw a surprisingly convivial gathering at the farm. It was to be the last ever. With Daniel and Kitty, my parents, Gaynor and Ernie, and Robin and his best friend Lawrence, I even approached feeling happy. J's usual seasonal toast was raised by me instead, before the presents were unwrapped. My children did everything to take their father's place, literally and figuratively – whilst Ernie, just one year younger than J, was an essential father figure. We all tried so hard we actually succeeded. Gaynor's tough little Border terrier, Bentley, stared threateningly at Bonnie as if she were a white rabbit and when he began to salivate at the sight my friend realized she should keep her dog on a short leash. The cats kept out of his way. The big dogs were the same as ever – lolloping and lovely. I wondered if they missed their master, as we did.

Yet those feelings had to be kept in check. I opened J's gift to me in the privacy of my study. He opened mine somewhere else. We spoke on the phone. Nothing was as bad for me as it was for him.

Three

MOVING

A man and a dog descend their front steps
The dog says, Let's go downtown and get crazy drunk
Let's tip over all the trash cans we can find.
This is how dogs deal with the prospect of change.
Stephen Dobyns, 'How To Like It'

Imagine a world where none of us has names. How much does a name shape your identity? Before I met Bonnie she had another name – or two other names. The small dog abandoned and left tied to a tree must have been named by whoever knew her for the first six months of life. Then the kind people at the RSPCA home gave her another name, for I remember being told, 'We call her–', but can't recall what it was. When she became Bonnie she was given a new identity. With her third and last name she became truly *mine*.

I agree with the dog-loving poet Mark Doty that the saddest dogs in the shelter are the ones without any names – because nobody cares enough about them to give them up accompanied by proper information. Like Bonnie, they have simply been abandoned, bereft of names and dates. I always feel touched by photographs of long-dead dogs (for example, the ones collected by Libby Hall and published in books like *These Were Our Dogs*) because you long to know the names, as if such knowledge would defy death by attaching importance. All of the people in old photographs rescued from junk shops once cared enough to be photographed with their pets, yet few recorded the names. But one photograph (in the book I mention) shows a moustachioed soldier sitting cross-legged with a St Bernard and a Jack Russell. On the front of the picture someone has written 'Hissy and Jack'. The reverse has more detail. It reads: 'France, August 1916. Our Corp pet St Bernard named Hissy 8 months old and the Terrier named Jack. Just after we came out here 16 months – and our Staff Sgt Farrier Len Nusse.'

The soldier who took the picture must have loved those dogs. In the carnage of France he took a photograph and recorded his affection by naming them both on the front and the back. Their identity is more important to him than that of his unit's farrier, who is mentioned as an afterthought. I like to imagine what comfort these pets gave the soldiers, their tails wagging despite the menacing *crump* of distant guns. What's more, there's something dependable and British about the solid name Jack, and equally odd and unexpectedly frivolous about the naming of the St Bernard. Perhaps Hissy was a diminutive for something more dignified – but she (surely a female?) remains Hissy for ever, a light caress contained within the word.

I wonder if a name plays any part in shaping destiny. Around three centuries before the birth of Christ, the Greek writer

Xenephon published a manual on hunting in which he gives advice on dog-rearing and also on choosing their 'short names – so we may call them easily', offering a selection, like Pylax (Keeper), Chara (Gladness), Bia (Force) and Horme (Eager). All the names have positive connotations. George Orwell called his poodle Marx, but was amused to keep it a secret whether his pet was named for Karl or Groucho. Surely you would look at a dog differently if he was named after the father of socialism and not a lovable clown?

The late Leona Helmsley, the wealthy hotel magnate, who served time in prison for tax evasion, left a fortune to her Maltese dog, Trouble. But who would give a small white dog such an unfortunate name? A difficult woman whom the newspapers called 'The Queen of Mean', of course. No wonder nobody liked the poor little rich dog who nipped anyone who came within reach of his tiny teeth. The Maltese received death threats, even when his bizarre inheritance was reduced by a judge from $12 million to $2 million. On one occasion Trouble even took flight through the traffic on Fifth Avenue as if making a bid for freedom – the event recorded on the internet. The dog who was so adored by his difficult and lonely mistress ended up living in Florida with an employee paid to take care of him. The nature of that care nobody can know. Poor dog: Trouble by name, troubled by nature. When I read about him I mused that if he were mine he would be renamed Toby and have a happier life.

In contrast, Bonnie is a name full of sunshine. In the north-east of England boys are greeted with 'bonny lad' and a girl is called 'bonny lass' – such benevolence there you feel nobody thus called could be mean-spirited or ugly. The Old English *boni* links to French *bon/bonne* meaning 'good' and Webster's *Dictionary* gives definitions: (1) handsome, pretty, beautiful and attractive and (2) merry, frolicsome, cheerful and blithe. A 'bonny baby' is rounded, rosy and full of health. The old rhyme about birthdays holds that 'The child who is born on the Sabbath Day/Is bonny and blithe and good and gay'. The name is full of positives, and so although I unthinkingly called my dog after one of my favourite singers, something more significant was happening. Subliminally, I was rewriting her destiny – transforming her from the unwanted thing tied to a tree to a well-beloved creature tied to a human heart.

At the beginning of 2004 I was transforming my own destiny too. I changed my name and I bought a house. Both were acts of almost aggressive self-assertion, although I did not realize it at the time because I was not thinking things through. I was reacting. No longer would I be tied to a home or to a married name; metaphorically I took flight along Fifth Avenue, making my bid for freedom.

I was born in Liverpool in 1946 and christened Beryl Ann Mooney. Ann was my father's mother's name, and I should have adopted it, for I thoroughly detested the name Beryl, once I was old enough to care. Like other names (Hilda, Pamela, Norma, Pearl ...) it carries with it images of plain, struggling Britain in the forties and fifties, a world of low-wattage centre lights, smoky coal fires, the sound of the hand-operated sewing machine, the smell of frying and boiled cabbage – and the family clustered around the Bakelite radio to listen to *Two Way Family Favourites*. At primary school I was a thin, shy, bespectacled child, teased as 'Beryl the Peril' and 'Gooney-Mooney-Four-Eyes', and those names, those ugly personae, turned me in on myself, to take refuge in books. Beryl went to the library and read her way through all the shelves, while at home 'Our Belle' was grandfather's darling, sitting on his knees while he plaited my fair hair. She was the princess-shut-up-in-a-tower, whose identity was secret from everybody but who dreamed of being *known*, of being beautiful – *belle*.

Through the teenage years I went on being Belle at home and Beryl in school, but when the time came to leave home for university in October 1966 I decided to reinvent myself as Bel. I liked the economy of dropping two letters from my Christian name and disliked the spelling 'Belle' because of its too-flattering meaning. After all, I had only just got contact lenses, was able to see myself properly for the first time and realized that there was a way to go with the metamorphosis.

So at university I introduced myself with a variant of the pet name, and it did indeed coincide with a feeling of being handsome – *bel*. The new persona fitted. But when I married J in February 1968 I took on yet another, changing my name to his. Henceforth my passport and everything else would belong to somebody called Beryl Ann Dimbleby, although I was always known as Bel. When I became a journalist I had no hesitation in keeping my maiden name for professional purposes, since my husband's surname was far too well known. Remember that the small, insignificant wedding of two university students in 1968 was covered in newspapers under headlines like 'Dimbleby's son weds'. I was an ordinary girl, unused to this. There was no escaping it – not then, or ever.

Besides, I could not so easily lose my Liverpool-Mooney identity – which was, in the end, to prove more durable than the other. It is my essence, a source of pride which transcends academic, social or professional achievement, and I like to think there was something Liverpudlian-tough about my determination to survive. For by December 2003 I was possessed by rage at a level nobody could see. I am no saint, and nor have I ever been. Something J said on one of his visits prompted me to go online to see how easily I could change my name by deed poll. He implied that I (like my ex-sister-in-law) had been quite happy with the famous surname, a suggestion I thought unjust since I had never used it professionally. So, at a stroke (well, not quite so simply, since you have painstakingly to change all your legal documents, which can drag on for months) I became Bel Mooney in law, for the very first time. This was, in effect, a 'new' identity. I received my new passport on 13 January 2004 – all too aware of the powerful symbolism of what I had done. With this, my third name, I became truly my own person.

There was also to be a move to a new house. J and I had agreed that now, after six months without him on the farm, our beloved home had become my prison. The winds punished me, the dark was oppressive and despite the level of seasonal celebration we had achieved at Christmas, the sense of loss was pervasive. My husband knew it better than anyone; he could not return and acknowledged that I could not remain. Impasse. It was (I thought much later) as if we had been together in a little boat for 35 years, rowing strongly side by side. Sometimes the water had been choppy, sometimes the motion had made one of us seasick, yet we had kept going. Then suddenly one day we were caught up in a whirlpool and he fell overboard and I rowed in circles alone, looking for him, yet the current carried me onwards away from the danger. When his head finally broke the surface I was somewhere else, unable to row backwards to reach him. ('Always go forward and never turn back.') That is how it seemed.

My children had arrived just before that first Christmas without their father, driving down from London. They strode into the kitchen and asked what he and I had decided. By then they were resigned, on the surface at least. (Never below it, but that is another story.)

'He says I can look for a house.'

'Good – that's what you need, Mum.'

'I know.'

'So what kind of a house do you want?'

Without hesitation, it tumbled out: 'I want big windows and a walled garden and … I'd like a house with a door in the middle, like the houses I used to draw when I was a child.'

Our farm had small windows and endless landscape and a rambling shape, so I was constructing a diametrically opposite dream. They rushed off to do their Christmas shopping in Bath, and Kitty called me 30 minutes later in excitement. They had seen The House in an estate agent's window. A town house built in the Regency period, it had big windows, a walled garden and a door in the middle of the elegant frontage. What's more, she told me, in the picture of the sitting room there was a small white dog on the rug. That was surely a sign.

Next day I went to see the house with my mother and daughter, who enthused. It was spacious but compact, and the woman who owned it had installed every modern accoutrement without spoiling its period feel. All I would need to do was have bookshelves built and change one bathroom. It was all terrifying, but the presence of the owner's dog helped. A

West Highland terrier called Lily, she sat on a chaise longue in the window of the master bedroom, waiting for her mistress (a widow) to return. The dog stared fixedly at the road, ignoring (after the first barks) the estate agent and us: intruders on her territory. Her whole being was fixed on the possibility of reunion. That is what dogs want.

Humans want it too, but there is a limit to the amount of time you can stare, quivering with anticipation out of the window, or waiting in the graveyard. Looking back I sometimes feel sad that I, the enlightened human, did not match up to canine example and wait for ever – as dogs will do. For example, the famous Scottish story of 'Greyfriars Bobby' epitomizes a fidelity which touches humans who fall short. Bobby belonged to a night watchman called John Gray, and the two became a familiar sight in Edinburgh, out in all weathers. But John contracted tuberculosis, died of the disease in 1858 and was buried in Old Greyfriars burial ground. In rain and snow, Bobby refused to leave his master's grave and in the end the churchyard-keeper gave up trying to chase him off and laid sacking for the poor little dog next to his master's grave. The fame of the faithful terrier spread and each day crowds would gather at one o'clock when, hearing the gun signal, Bobby left the grave and went to the coffee house he had always visited with his master, where they still put down food for the dog. His vigil continued for 14 years, until he died in 1872, at the age of 16. There is a statue to Bobby now, and a pub named after him, and the long-dead emblem of loyalty even has his own website and sells souvenirs – proving that the story (like the similar one of Hachiko, a station dog, in Japan) goes on speaking to something deep within us.

After all, a woman's husband might leave her but her dog is there for its life. I once met a Canadian truck driver on the road in the States whose journeys were shared by the half-dingo (yes, in America) mutt he had found abandoned by the side of the road in Wyoming. He confessed that he had much more to say to the dog than to his wife – and thinking of his long months on the road I conjectured that perhaps his dog were the more faithful. The difficult truth is that some humans find it relatively easy to 'replace' people they have lost (both J and I were to do this) but the dogs hang in there. Since Susan Chilcott died I had waited for my husband to come back ('come to his senses' some said) and tell me, 'That madness is over, so let us pick up the threads of our life again.' But he did not – and I knew that unless I acted, I would go mad myself. Of course, I *could* have given J some more time to be healed and then return. But suppose that never happened? Never interested in gambling, I could not stop my highly developed instinct for self-preservation from kicking in.

I remember sitting one evening listening to Nina Simone singing Jacques Brel's beautiful song 'Ne Me Quitte Pas'. The track is long; I was listening acutely to the words and began in tears but ended feeling a powerful surge of rebellion. It bubbled up during the most abject stanza, at the end of the song, where the singer pleads (sounding beautiful in French): 'Don't leave me. I will cry no more, I will talk no more … Let me become the shadow of your shadow, the shadow of your hand, the shadow of your dog. Don't leave me.' And so on.

All those torch songs which fling themselves masochistically on the floor, waiting for the foot on the head ('He beats me too,' sings Billie Holliday), made for moody listening on tipsy nights when the cigarette smoke curled to the ceiling. But in real life? Your *own* life? No, no, no. I will *never* beg to be the shadow of any man's dog. I will pack up my own dog in her smart bag and make my own way now, thank you very much. Why should I play the victim and warble that other classic French ballad, '*J'attendrai*' – I will wait? My life was slipping by with each breath and I had no time to wait, not any more.

This is a refusal of underdog status. So many negative phrases attach themselves to dogginess. For example, a 'dog' is a plain woman. To call a man a 'dog' or a 'cur' is one of the worst insults. To be 'hangdog' is to epitomize ill-treated vulnerability, and an 'underdog' is … well, amongst other things, a woman whose husband has left her. That is, unless she leaves too. Walks in the opposite direction. 'Bends with the remover to remove,' to quote Shakespeare's sonnet 116. J had absented himself from our home first; now it was my turn to move. In the words of the philosopher Mark Rowlands, 'It is only our defiance which redeems us.' I cannot read that without imaging a clenched fist raised angrily, proudly to the sky. The truth is, there had developed, alongside the sorrow, something hard and unyielding in both of us. Grief and guilt render a man (or woman) immovable – but so does a sense of rectitude. It can be as difficult to forgive a person we have harmed as it is to forgive someone who has harmed us. Whatever the reasons, I simply could not bear to remain marooned, yet clinging to the wreckage.

These days, in my role as an advice columnist, I receive many letters from people whose marriages are at an end and do not know where to go – literally as well as figuratively. I always advise trying to take back some sort of control – even if it's changing the locks or your name. If you are the one who has been left you feel utterly demoralized. You forget to wash your hair and you take to your bed, only to remain sleepless. You go to your doctor and pour it all out until those professional eyes slide away, aware of the rows of patients waiting outside. Then you are given a prescription for amitryptilene to help you sleep, but feel like a zombie all day. You burst into tears when you hear somebody talking about love on the radio, and a scene in a film (as when Emma Thompson's character in *Love Actually* realizes her vain husband has bought a necklace for the sexy girl in the office, but knows she must put on a brave smile for her children . . .) can leave you prostrated with grief.

So, as displacement, you spend an evening watching a Jackie Chan action movie or some tedious sport coverage, as if you were somebody else. And indeed, you *have* become somebody else now – the person who was left. You never thought you would meet this person in your mirror; you can stare at her in numb disbelief for ages. You pace your home and everything in it mocks you for having failed. Because you *have* failed, and nobody (not the well-meaning friends, nor the slightly inadequate therapist you find to burden with your woes) can tell you otherwise. You thought other people's marriages broke up but now you stare into the abyss of your own and believe with all your heart that *you* should have had the power to steer both of you in a different direction. The old house is falling down around your ears, but you don't blame the earthquake: you blame yourself.

22 January: I go to see SM – pretty, dark-haired solicitor in a businesslike trouser suit, taking the remnants of my marriage in hand. It will be the gentlest type of separation since we have decided a divorce is too brutal and I don't want it. She says, 'He's not only lost his wife, he's lost his best friend.' But he hasn't lost my friendship. That must continue. There are seconds when I think I could step across the gulf between us and beg, 'Come back.' Or he could say, 'It was all a mistake – I love you – take me back.' But it doesn't happen. And now I really do want to live in the new house and imagine its clean, empty spaces with delight. The farm is chilly. Cold weather forecast. The fields grey and muddy. A fence broken. Billie and Sam look sad and bored. Tonight I went to the American Museum for drinks and took Deirdre McS aside to tell her my melancholy news and her shock affected me. Yes, it is shocking and ought not to be happening. So I returned home even more melancholy, to pick at food, and cough, then fall asleep early by the sitting room fire. I feel silent and don't want to talk to anybody much. Even Bonnie palls.

'Taking in hand' is the key phrase there, although I could not have known it at the time. I realize how privileged I was to be able to think of buying a new property, because most people cannot. The London base we had bought in 1986 – which had been a happy family home at one stage, and which provided lodgings for various friends over the years, as well as being a working office for productions made under our company – would be sold to buy me this house. So I was lucky – in some ways. Still, it is vital for people who find themselves in a similar situation to realize that taking even the smallest action to fight their own corner (a needlessly aggressive phrase, perhaps) will help. The key is not waiting for things to be done 'to' you, but to step forward and make autonomous decisions, even something as small as booking a new haircut and a facial. I know that some will think such counsel trivial; they do not understand that small decisions and undramatic actions form the bricks which, one by one, can build a new home where the self can learn its changed identity.

At the end of January my daughter left for a six-month backpacking trip with a friend; she had done what she could for both parents and now needed to escape. Her brother and I waved her goodbye, then drove back from Heathrow in silence, each knowing how much we would miss her. When she returned I would no longer be living in the family home. Dan and I wandered along Portobello Road, had lunch, talked quietly about all that had happened. I drove the 100 miles back to the empty farm and that night a blizzard raged about the house as I lit my wood stove and went through papers in my study, preparing to pack.

Messages come from the strangest quarters. Signs from the gods, I mean. A couple of weeks after Kitty left, in London to meet my agent I was very gloomy. There had been a hold-up with the mortgage and I was afraid I would lose the new house; J and I were in constant contact through melancholy emails, phone calls and meetings to discuss the division of property – at the end of which we would hold each other with wordless sorrow. Gradually we told acquaintances in a wider circle that we had separated, because it was still not generally known. Again and again I saw faces show shock – then sadness. I wondered if it is because the world holds up a long-married couple as a beacon – especially if, like J and me, they have always been honest about complex and difficult times. I could almost hear people thinking, But you've come so far, experienced so much together, survived it all – *don't give up now*. I went to a book launch and whispered the truth to a very distinguished historian, writer and art expert, many years older than J and me, with whom we'd enjoyed a warm relationship over many years. In a room crowded with people clutching glasses of champagne he actually shed tears. It was good for me to give comfort to someone else for the sad story which, I'm sure, seemed to call all marriages into question.

So there I was with an hour to kill before meeting my agent. And I wandered into the John Lewis department store on Oxford Street, feeling events bound round my heart like iron bands. With the new house in mind I wander to the basement where household and electrical goods are sold, and find The Message on a floor display. There is an iron, an ironing board and clothes drier, all in my favourite lilac and white, with a big sign suspended, proclaiming 'NEW START'. I blink and gaze around me, and it is as if everything is illuminated: glittering and surreal. There are signs everywhere: 'REFRESH', 'RESTORE', 'RENEW'. The spring colours lift me, despite myself, and I realize that nothing will ever prevent me from making a new start. No torch song in my brain, but the disco anthem, 'I will survive.'

12 February: I write sitting alone in the library. Good to be alone, even though I don't use my time well. Today I usefully terminated a lot of standing orders and direct debits. I'm overwhelmed by all the financial/organizational things I have to do on my own, for the first time. But then ridiculously pleased when I do them. J and I were so old-fashioned in the division of our life: did it have to be that way? Will I ever regain my confidence? Will I do any good work again? I feel tired and bereft of energy and – yes – love. I read poems about love, all alone in the library. Not – not alone. With Bonnie. And it was all right. And will be.

All this time I reviewed the occasional book for *The Times* and tried to develop a book proposal but other work was impossible. I drifted through the days with the three dogs and the cats, packing up those books, ornaments and pictures I would take with me, and labelling the furniture which would fit my new house. At night I curled up with Bonnie and my diary, noting that '*the complete silence of the house and valley deafens me. Yes, I can hear it like a muffled roar in my ears. If I put out my hand I know I would be able to feel it, soft as cotton wool.*' I missed J terribly. My diary spurts savage rage at Susan Chilcott ('*her selfish, greedy snatching at* our *life*') that stemmed, in part, from the need to blame. I could not bear to resent the man I had married and so I transferred all my rage to the woman he had loved for such a short time. And still loved too.

One day when J was visiting I told him that if you can *love* someone who's dead you can *hate* someone who's dead.

Bonnie and I went shopping. People in Bath always notice her. Maybe it's the size, maybe the perpetual motion, maybe the wardrobe of collars and leads that tend to match whatever the foolish woman with her is wearing. The girls in the shoe shop fussed over my little dog as I tried on heels higher than any I had worn, savage shiny black things with Perspex sides. They became mine. Three days later I bought some vintage red stilettos with lethal pointed toes, and wrote, '*I am overdrawn with no work and a new house looming and yet I buy high heels. The symbolism is obvious. I want shoes which have no place on his stupid, stupid farm ...*'

Similarly, Valentine's Day found Bonnie and me hanging out with a dealer in vintage jukeboxes, about 20 miles south of Bath. I have always loved rock 'n' roll, and Americana, and the Beat poets, and girl groups with bouffant skirts and hair who sing and move in unison while their universal question joins the harmony of the stars: 'Baby, baby, where did our love go ...?' In the basement of the house I was buying was a huge recess in the wall where an ancient kitchen range would once have been. On the first visit I had known that there, in the room that was to become office space, I would install the jukebox I'd always wanted. As a teenager in a small Wiltshire town I would hang around the cockroach-infested Milk Bar inexpertly puffing on cheap cigarettes and feeding the jukebox as I slurped milk shakes. I'd shimmy my shoulders to Little Richard and Roy Orbison (oh yes – 'Crying over you') and Jerry Lee Lewis. Such behaviour – then and now – was as remote from J's world as I was from his show-jumping or from Susan Chilcott's opera stages.

That is why I wanted a jukebox. It was another statement. The 1964 Wurlitzer with Cadillac lines, a sunburst etched on plastic and vertically loaded '45s became mine with a *click, whirr, hiss.* Although I did have to defer both delivery and payment, since I had no house and no money. Yet.

By March the press phone calls had begun in earnest. There had been some back in the summer/autumn of 2003 and the

Mail on Sunday's door-stepping visit while I was hosting a charity reception. I lied to all enquirers, saying that the soprano was much loved by everybody and a friend of 'ours'. But why, you might ask, did the end of one marriage merit such intrusion? For the same reason that we were snapped by strangers on our wedding day: there was no escape for the scion of a famous dynasty, or in turn for his family, when he became famous in his own right. J never came to terms with that. In his own eyes he was a professional writer and broadcaster, known for the seriousness of his work. He loathed the idea of 'celebrity', but in this he was out of tune with the times. In any case, Susan Chilcott was a beautiful performer in her own right, so whether he liked it or not, this was a 'story'.

I was packing up one house (the one in London sold now) and painfully extracting my own things from our proper home while being waylaid on doorsteps by junior gossip column writers who looked embarrassed ('Look, I'm just a hack, like you,' I protested) and telephoned by section editors I knew who said things like, 'The editor wants me to ask you to write about it all – this is awful, I feel like a vulture.' It was grim. Some days it was as if there were a door perpetually banging upstairs in my mind, deafening me, driving me crazy. Pathetically, I told myself that I didn't deserve this – but once you dare to raise the notion of just deserts you remember premature death, and ask yourself, 'Did *she* deserve *that*?'

For many people journalists rank very low in moral standing; certainly newspaper intrusion into private life and the lies spread by cheaper gossip magazines do damage and cause hurt. I am often amazed by the certainty with which colleagues will call a well-known person 'obnoxious' (just one example) when they have never met them. Over the years J and I were written about from time to time and I felt violent towards those who slighted him, but (perhaps because Liverpool people are bred tough in that bracing wind off the Mersey) did not care so much if people were rude about me. I was always reduced to rage at what I saw as any injustice to him, especially when he was working on the Prince of Wales project, indignant that people forgot all the serious achievements of a long career and reduced his journalism to one question about adultery.

But even at this, the worst stage, I could not hate the people who fed on gossip about us. To want to savour the most intimate detail of other people's relationships and to delight in seeing the mighty fallen are ancient human impulses; as someone who loves the classics I know that Roman poets like Martial, Catullus and Juvenal beat any modern writer in the nastiness stakes. In any case, I *like* journalists – hugely. I have worked for tabloids, broadsheets, a left-wing magazine, for colour supplements and women's magazines, and some of the most enjoyable times have been with my fellow scribblers. If I see one on my doorstep my instinct is to offer a cup of coffee – even though it is *our* flayed hearts which are the 'story'.

Nevertheless, the *Mail on Sunday* headline, across two pages, made my knees buckle, so that I had to sit down at the kitchen table. It said, 'Jonathan is in love with a ghost', and was illustrated by a press picture of the two of us arm in arm, handsome and happy, at some event or other, another a blurry snatched shot of him looking gaunt a few days before the piece appeared – and, in the middle, staring out at me, an enormous picture of Susan Chilcott, beautiful in a blue costume for one of her operatic roles. It filled me with horror, even though I knew the paper was planning an article. It was as if that face would stare at me for eternity, telling me that she had won.

On 10 March the new house became legally mine and it felt correct that I crossed the threshold with my son, who was seeing it for the first time. The two of them had spotted the place in the agents' window; Kitty had visited with me; now he was escorting me into my new home. With Kitty away, I leaned on Dan. I was consumed with a sensation of unreality which increased over the next two weeks. One day I was in London agreeing with a publisher to edit and contribute to a collection of stories on mothers and daughters, which would be published simultaneously in Britain and the USA; two days later the removal van was at the farm and the grim business began.

> *19 March: 'I wake at 7 knowing that this is the day I walk away from – not my marriage – but J's obsession with the ghost of the Soprano, because I will not live with her malevolent spectre. She possessed my oh-so-wonderful husband and has put a curse on his past and future. So. A morning of making coffee for removal men and watching my life (no longer our life) disappear into boxes, entering the van. I call Mum and Dad and as always they are there for me, going on to the house to unpack boxes. So. At 12.30 I look down and notice my left hand and scream. The large diamond in the ring my beloved J bought for our thirtieth anniversary is no longer there – torn from the setting. How to look? How could any search be possible? I was shocked and in tears. I called J to tell him and he was so sad, so sympathetic, so like the old J, before he met her.*

He said, 'I'll buy you a new ring.' I had to overcome the loss of the diamond (talk about symbolism) and of my marriage and concentrate on leaving my home to J and the ghost of SC – watching vanload after vanload depart, and rushing to the new house to see mum and dad unpacking and unpacking, being so 'up' despite their age and despite this massive contradiction of everything I have based my life upon. So overwhelmed by contradictions: my new house is lovely yet so much smaller and with traffic outside instead of the farm's peace. Fuck traffic! I like it! Oh how strange it all is. What SC has achieved is a geological shift. All is broken – and new. Tonight at 12.30 I feel full of grief and bitterness. Why isn't one allowed to feel bitter? Because that's too non-PC, or something. Yet everybody does, if they are honest. It is late. I am tipsy. I love J.

The last thing I did before leaving my home was lay a fire in the 'new' sitting room I had created for J (the old dining room) so that when he retook possession of his home, alone now, he would only have to strike a match to be warm. That action came from the same place as his spontaneous 'I'll buy you a new ring.' Although we were living apart we were to discover, during the coming years, that we would never move far from that place.

Bonnie was ever-present, the silent witness. But it was sad to be leaving Billie and Sam and the cats. My own cat was Louis, an impossibly elegant Burmilla, who was given to me by J when I reached 50, together with a medieval manuscript and a mother-and-child sculpture executed by an artist friend. (He knew my tastes so well.) Naturally I imagined Louis moving house with me and Bonnie – the smaller, less beautiful creature he regarded with indifference. But the reality of the main road on which my new house was situated made me quail. The cat had only ever known the freedom of the farm and I knew (having moved with cats before) that he would inevitably seek to return and, in all probability, meet his fate beneath the wheels of a bus. So I would leave him with the other pets, to be looked after by J's groom Fran, who had moved with her family into the cottage Robin had vacated to house-share with a friend in London. (In that sense Billie, Sam, Django, Louis and Ella were fortunate. When Bonnie became mine I was told at the Bath Dogs and Cats Home that increasing numbers of pets come under their care because of broken relationships.) But the truth is, Bonnie had triumphantly supplanted Louis in my affections; the cat lover had fallen in love with one small dog and there was no returning to the former state.

As long as my dog was with me, I would survive. One of the most beautiful possessions of the British Museum is a medieval manuscript called the Luttrell Psalter, an illuminated book of psalms created between 1325 and 1340 for Sir Geoffrey Luttrell of Lincolnshire, and world famous for its detailed scenes of medieval village life. In one of the illustrations an elaborate carriage (looking like a covered wagon) is setting off on a journey. It carries four ladies of high birth. One of them, dressed in gold with a blue veil from her coronet, is leaning from the back of the carriage towards a squire riding close behind. He is stretching over his horse's neck to hand a small white dog, wearing a pretty collar, to the lady. The curve of her body is tender as she leans forward to take the animal. The precious lapdog is about to make a journey with her, wherever it might take them, and you just know it is essential to her comfort.

That is how it felt when I moved house.

I was spending money wildly (a new TV and radio, mirrors and so on, for I had not removed such things from the farm) yet none was coming in. J and I had embarked on the complicated business of disentangling our finances. As usual I left everything to him, and payback came one day early in April when I went to the bank with just £3 in my purse, only to be refused money. With tears in my eyes, I begged the teller to increase my overdraft; clearly feeling sorry for me, she set the wheels in motion and said I would be able to get cash the next day – but the damage was done. I plunged into gloom, wanting my old safe life back.

Yet even then I had an underlying sense that this was *good* for me. While I found it lonely to register for council tax as a single occupant, after so many years as half of a pair, there was one part of me which thought it was time. For what? Coping with everyday reality, I suppose. When our baby son was stillborn in November 1975 my grief was all-encompassing, but an epiphany came on the day when my cries of 'Why me?' were transformed into the quiet question, 'Why *not* me?' So it was now.

That query expresses an awareness that you are one tiny part of suffering humanity, and that it is your destiny, as it is the destiny of so many others, to endure without understanding why. Strange as it may seem, I knew that I must learn from (temporarily) not having any money for shopping. Even though I was not born into a wealthy family, I had never known want. That day, with £3 in my purse, I experienced the panic which afflicts the vast majority of humankind who are not as protected as I had been. And why should I be protected? Even when I felt so low, so bewildered, I could stand outside what was happening and see it as a source of future strength. The day before the bank incident I had written (after a visit by J during which I played him my jukebox): '*We hugged on the path when he left and the truth is – so much of my heart and soul stays with him, wherever he goes and whatever he does. Meeting him was the making of my life and the leaving of him re-makes it – because I know how strong I am.*'

I needed the absurdity of my dog at this time: her face all squashed when she had been lying down, her ridiculous frou-frou back view, the fearsome growls when she attacked a scrap of paper. Konrad Lorenz, great animal behaviourist that he was, had this to say about choosing a dog: 'I think that the great popularity enjoyed by some comical breeds of dog is largely attributable to our longing for gaiety. A Sealyham's love of fun and his fidelity to his master can prove a real moral support to a melancholy person. Who can help laughing when such an amusing little creature, bursting with the joys of life, comes bouncing along on his far-too-short legs ...?' Any owner of a small dog will recognize that. Putting my books on the shelves in the new house and grieving for the old one, I felt dazed. It was torture to visualize J alone at the farm, just a couple of miles up the road, while I was sitting on one of a pair of old sofas (he had the other) wondering how I came to this strange place. That was the greatest absurdity, that we had come to this. So my little dog's antics were an essential antidote.

Five weeks after moving I left Bonnie behind with my parents and flew to Bangkok to meet my daughter. I hadn't seen her since 27 January, thirteen weeks earlier, and had arranged to write a travel piece about the spa resort Chiva Som, to give the backpacker a little luxury. To see Kitty waiting at the barrier and be given her welcome gifts, to wander through the night market with her and take a boat along the canals, then to be collected for the two-hour drive south to Hua Hin and a week of peaceful luxury … this was balm for the soul. At Chiva Som you have a daily massage, staring down through the table at a glass bowl, lit from underneath and filled with floating flowers. One day, in a reflexology session, the Thai therapist told me she detected a pain in my heart. Shocked, I whispered, 'My husband has gone,' and she simply bowed her head and laid a hand on my leg in sympathy.

But each day I relaxed more, and the unhappiness receded to a point where my marriage and family life on the farm seemed less real than the Golden Buddha on Monkey Mountain, which we reached by a 30-minute walk along the beach very early one morning, as the sun was rising in a mother-of-pearl sky. We lit joss sticks and I prayed that Kitty would be safe as she continued alone to Vietnam, Cambodia and Laos. That afternoon we left the resort, and the driver and I dropped her off in Bangkok on my way to the airport. I watched her small figure until it disappeared, weaving through hundreds of strangers on the Koh San Road in search of a cheap backpacker hotel. In the back of the car I snivelled, until the morose driver took pity on me and said, in his stumbling English, the only three words that matter, 'I am sorry.' Kitty and I had talked so much during the week and promised to be strong for each other. Now we were back on our different journeys, with a sense of new beginnings, as well as old loss.

At this point, returning from the holiday, I stopped keeping a daily journal (although I continued to keep notebooks). The recording of what seemed to be a mundane life (arranging furniture and books, sorting out the spare room and so on) became intolerable. The Bath International Music Festival began and when I took a friend called Stephen to a jazz concert I could sense people all round us staring, wondering if this was the new boyfriend perhaps? That's the problem with a small city. A couple I knew slightly asked me to dinner and I realized with astonishment that the spare man at the table was there for me. I felt withdrawn, although nobody could have detected it; naturally I was grateful that people should want me to find a new partner but the attempt to set me up embarrassed me. In any case, he wasn't my type.

The Bath Music Festival was one of the highlights of our year – and had been since 1981, when we had been living in Bath just six months. As Chairman, J was enthusiastic and innovative; he had forged a close friendship with the Chief Executive and Artistic Director, Tim Joss, whose wife, novelist Morag Joss, was a friend of Susan Chilcott. It was at their house that J and Susan had first met, at the fateful dinner party just 19 months earlier, and J had spent much time with them since her death. It must have been during the doleful months after Susan's death that it was decided that one of the highlights of the 2004 festival would be a special concert in her memory, from which all ticket sales would go to the hospital's on-going charitable appeal. When I saw this in the brochure I was deeply upset. It could not but feel like a slap in my face.

On 12 May Iain Burnside was on Radio 4's *Woman's Hour* to talk about Susan and publicize the concert. The presenter,

Jenni Murray, told listeners that Susan Chilcott had just been posthumously named Singer of the Year for her performance in *Jenufa,* and recalled the triumph of her 2002 debut as Lisa in Tchaikovsky's *Queen of Spades* opposite Placido Domingo. Iain Burnside extolled her talent and told of her courage, going on stage in 2002 between sessions of chemotherapy. In a soft Scottish voice, all the more impressive for its perfect control, he told how she was loved by her fellow singers, how fantastic she would have been in the next 10 years, how the cruelty of her premature death was already affecting a whole generation of singers.

Jenni Murray asked how, since Iain is gay, people viewed his guardianship of his best friend's child. His reply was memorable:

> *'When she gave me the choice that I should step up to the mark ... I think ... somewhere at the back of her mind, in the very black days before she died, there might have been some comfort in the thought that ... I am unlikely to have more children, I am rather unlikely to marry, and that perhaps he would never be in a position where he could run to another woman with open arms saying 'Mummy.' She knows that Hugh will always be the sole focus of my love and attention and in that sense the choice of a gay Dad is perhaps not so strange as some people immediately presume.*

On the night of the concert I was sitting in my new house on the green sofa with my little dog. Just a 10-minute walk away the beautiful ballroom of the Assembly Rooms was full of people (including my husband of course, making a short speech) celebrating the life and achievements of the gifted soprano whom, naturally, I blamed for the destruction of my marriage. I felt abandoned by everybody, except Bonnie. My new home was still. There was nobody to talk to about it all. The question in my mind was, is this what life comes down to, that I lose my precious diamond, and then someone, somewhere sings in celebration?

Journalist friends had rallied round and one of these, the editor of *The Times Magazine*, Gill Morgan, knew what leaving the farm had cost me and asked for a meditative essay on my idea of home. The article appeared in July, with a full-page portrait of me sitting on the pale Bath stone stairs with Bonnie – of course. She looks serene (because the photographer was dear, familiar Robin and she would have barked furiously at a stranger) but I look tense. Re-reading the article now, I realize how cathartic it was to write – to take a journey through the homes of my childhood and the homes of my marriage, attempting to make sense of the latest stage:

> '... like many women, I have measured out my life with crowded rooms, until sometimes I felt like Alice grown too large, her head against the roof. Husband, children, parents, pets, parties, food, working at home, fitting it all in ... the ceaseless struggle for perfection. Now, in these cool autonomous spaces, it's tempting to come out with the clichés of the independent, separated woman ... 'I feel liberated ... I can be myself ...' and so on. But the truth is, I was myself in all our homes; it's just that I'm not sure whether I made them or they made me.
>
> Walking down a street at dusk, the lamps lit, the curtains not yet drawn, you see rooms illuminated like stage sets for

the comedies and tragedies of other lives. In just such a way I find myself looking back through lighted windows at my own life unfolding under different roofs, and ask myself – with due humility – how I got to be so lucky …

Now I wake to the sound of buses, the distant hum of a small city. There is nobody to consult over the colour scheme in the bedroom – which happens to be lilac and purple again, after all these years. If I want to festoon the place with butterflies and fairy lights, then so be it. I pay my own bills and turn the key in the door to a new world – awestruck by the generosity of its consolations. In the words of Sylvia Plath, 'I have a self to recover, a queen' …

For about three years I had been admiring a Chinese statue, for sale in a Bath gallery (since closed) which specialized in Asian art. She sat on a plinth opposite the entrance: a bodhisatva (enlightened being, follower of Buddha) carved from what looked like sandstone, and standing about a metre high. This was Kwan Yin, the goddess of compassion. The particular iconography of this statue had drawn me into the shop time after time, because Kwan Yin (often shown with a fish, or pouring a liquid from a gourd) was portrayed seated on a lotus and balancing, on one ample knee, a small manikin – a human child. His tiny hand clutched her large one; the echo of Christian iconography was haunting. When everything began to fall apart I continued to visit every few weeks to stroke Kwan Yin's cheek, while chatting to the owner about all the other beautiful works on display.

One summer day I was walking Bonnie down to the centre of Bath and went into the Lopburi gallery as usual to greet

Kwan Yin. The statue seemed to me to be a perfect representation of universal love – all the more appealing because of the small, crude areas of restoration and the discolorations of the stone. At some point, I think, she had lost her head but now she was put together again. The metaphor was unavoidable. Clumsy and flawed yet a thing of great beauty – that's how she seemed to me. Her downcast eyes, her glimmer of a smile spoke to me of acceptance in the face of time, loss, decay, death. Kwan Yin's serenity was what I most wished to attain, and had never even approached. Suddenly I realized that if the day came when I walked in only to find her no longer there – bought by a collector – I would be overwhelmed by sadness. At that moment I realized I *needed* her – as the icon of my new life. The gallery owner agreed to take three post-dated cheques and said with a smile, 'I knew she had to be yours.'

My goddess-protector soon had her first jobs, taking care of me and my small dog in equal measure. Exactly three weeks after she was installed at the end of my garden I heard that J was in a new relationship with a woman one year younger than our son. I do not intend to write any more about it; suffice it to say that I wandered blindly down the garden to put my arms around a statue. He and I were separated and yet the news was a bombshell. I had been worrying about his welfare all the time, but there was no need now. I had not expected this to happen so soon.

Three weeks after that Kwan Yin performed a miracle – yes, I do believe it, for how else to account for the extraordinary good fortune? Permit me to be fanciful; it is more consoling than trusting to random fate or chaos. I like to think it was the benign influence of the goddess which saved the life of my small dog.

By now I was touting for work. That is all the freelance writer knows how to do, but marriage to J as well as my own success had lessened the need. Now Kwan Yin had to be paid for, and so I was back to selling ideas with additional purpose. To that end, I was due to have lunch with three editors (all women) from different sections of *The Times*. My parents always looked after Bonnie when I went to London but my father was in hospital once again, my mother would spend part of the day with him and could not cope with a dog as well. Therefore I would take her on the train, and Robin agreed to meet us at Paddington and take care of her while I headed east for my rendezvous.

At the beginning of lunch my phone sounded but I put it off without listening – still unused to carrying one and embarrassed by the intrusion. It was not until 3.30 p.m. that I checked my messages. To my horror, I heard an extremely rough London accent say, 'We got your dog …'

Now we must cut to West London, where at about 12.50 p.m. Robin (who was doing up a house with his friend Lawrence) turned his back for a few minutes to move a piece of wood across the terrace. Perhaps looking for me, perhaps fascinated by that distinctive West London scent of bus and burger with top notes of cannabis, Bonnie squeezed through a small gap beneath a gate and snuffled off alone into the mean streets. Distraught, Robin roamed around, sending Lawrence off in the opposite direction, calling her name. Then he telephoned the RSPCA, police, Blue Cross, Battersea Dogs' Home and another dogs' home in Kensal Rise. He was too afraid to call the council's cleaning department, as the police advised, because he couldn't bear to think of her being picked up dead off the road. He couldn't imagine how he could ever face me.

Back to the restaurant, at the sound of that recorded voice I naturally thought of the thieves who stole Elizabeth Barrett Browning's Flush, and their modern counterparts who hold dogs to ransom. Heart thumping I rang the number, heard the gruff voice answer and (oh joy!) it was telling me that he and his brother had found my dog on the street, telephoned the number engraved on her tag (my Bath home), picked up the mobile number from the message and tried that three times. Quickly (because his credit was running out) he told me the address where he and his mates had the dog. Rather shell-shocked, I called Robin, whose voice changed from despair to elation. He jumped into his car and collected Bonnie from a housing estate – and I was reunited with her in as much time as it takes the Underground to go from Aldgate East to Ladbroke Grove. Bonnie's own journey had been just over half a mile – which is quite a trek when your legs are only 5 inches long. The only evidence of her adventure was a reek of cigarettes on her silky fur.

That might have been the end of it. But, haunted by what might have happened, I wanted to meet Bonnie's rescuers and thank them in person. So after a couple of weeks, I rang the number, introduced myself to the man who answered ('Hi, Alan, I'm the lady whose dog you saved'), and arranged to meet him and the others, to hear their story. As estates go, Henry Dixon Court is quite pleasant, and the sun was shining when four men in their early thirties emerged from one of the blocks. There was Alan (the voice on the phone), his brother Richard (principal rescuer, it turned out) and two friends. One had 'LOVE' and 'HATE' tattoos on a fist, another bore a tattoo proudly proclaiming 'SKINS' and I was especially taken by the little cross tattoos on earlobes. These were tough-looking guys.

Richard told me he and his brother had seen her sniffing around the parked cars. He saw the traffic whizzing by, said to Alan, 'She's not a stray, she's too well kept,' and tried to catch her. He told me, 'When I got her she wriggled but I held her tight, and looked around, but there was nobody.' So they improvised a lead from some copper wire and string they found lying around, met their friends and took her back to their flat, where they tried to give her food and water, which she refused. That's when the phone calls were made. I asked Richard what they would have done if I hadn't made contact and they said there would have been no choice but to take her to Battersea Dogs & Cats Home. So Bonnie's life would have gone full circle. The thought was unbearable.

So that was it. Smiling at the unlikely vision of the tough guys mooching along with my lapdog, I said, 'She's not a very butch dog, is she?' Alan shrugged, 'Yeah, well, she's your dog, ain't she?' 'Oh yes,' I said, clutching her tightly. Then I pulled out my purse and gave them the reward they had not asked for. Off they went for several beers, looking as happy as I felt. Bonnie had survived her second experience of being alone in the wide world and I vowed it would never happen again.

I'm sure Bonnie never went looking for whoever tied her to that tree in 2002 because she knew she wasn't loved. But surely she must have been searching for me that day? She would have walked miles, hoping to find me. Whenever I drive into London and pass those streets she roamed, see the volume of traffic and all the strangers passing by, I know how close I came to losing her. The odds against a reunion were impossibly high. Four years later I included the tale of the dog loose in London and the unlikely rescue in one of my six 'Bonnie' books for children, which star a boy called Harry and his little Maltese dog with a big heart. And I allowed my characters to draw the quietly optimistic conclusion:

For a while Harry, Dad and Kim walked in silence. Harry had brought Bonnie's lead, and she just pulled ahead, sniffing at walls and gates, as she always did. Each of them was thinking of what might have happened to her – but none of them wanted to speak. Harry imagined a kidnapper's demands. Kim imagined a woman just stealing Bonnie because she was such a cute lap dog. Dad imagined the little creature getting run over – and couldn't bear it. He'd have been responsible, he thought, and would have found it hard to face Harry or his Mum ever again.

But it was all right.

At last Harry said, 'They were really good guys, Dad.'

'They certainly didn't look *it!' said Kim.*

'Just goes to show ...' said Dad, thoughtfully.

'Funny, isn't it?' said Harry. 'I mean, you see people like them walking along and you feel ... you know ... a bit scared. But they took care *of Bonnie, Dad! Aren't we lucky?'*

'That's for sure,' said his dad, letting out a whoosh of breath.

By the autumn of 2004 I was beginning to feel fortunate myself and could not help but attribute it to my superstitious purchase of Kwan Yin. Everything was falling into place, and that word 'lucky' chimed like a bell through my thoughts. Human beings will always search for an external reason for happiness, although perhaps I should have remembered that anaesthetist who had told me, at the darkest time, 'You make your luck.'

With the quiet approval of my parents and children, my life was changing. Robin returned to Bath that autumn to start his long-planned post-graduate course in website design at Bath Spa University and came to stay in one of my spare rooms until he decided whether he truly wanted to give up photography and forge a new career. The person I had first met in 1984 as a rather unprepossessing, bespectacled builder of 18 had now grown into a handsome 'walker' and best friend (apart from my women friends), and the woman he had first seen as a glamorous, achieving writer of 35, married to a famous man, was now single, which was something that could never have been predicted. Robin had changed, I had changed but little, and his absence in London (not to mention the dinner party with the designated 'spare man') had reinforced my need to have him in my life, a person who knew me well and who had always been there – notwithstanding the fact that he had led his own life, travelled widely, worked abroad, dated, started a business in France and so on. Robin had always been (as J himself was to write) 'a fixture and a fitting of our lives': supportive and loved, friend to our children. Robin told me that all he had ever wanted was to look after me, and I realized that all I wanted now was not romance – no, most definitely not that – but to be looked after. I've always believed that true friendship should be at the heart of any couple's relationship and been wary of destructive passion. Recent events had certainly reinforced my doubts about the wilder shores of love. So it was that Robin and I slipped into a new version of being, without knowing if it would work, or where it would lead, or whether I should take the step of changing the council tax registration to two.

Thanksgiving Day (25 November) 2004 saw us in Santa Fe, New Mexico on a travel assignment, the city glittering with snow and ice, chilli *ristras* hanging outside doorways and every rooftop outlined with *luminarias*, seasonal candles in weighted paper bags. The air was scented with pine and Thanksgiving turkeys. We had spent the previous night on the floor of chaotic O'Hare airport in Chicago, as vast jets of steam worked in vain to defrost all the grounded planes and people shrieked in frustration at ground staff because they wanted to get home to their families for the feast. The goddess and my dog were calling to me from home, saying they could give me a better day than this one.

I couldn't help thinking of our assignment to, or via, Chicago as ill fated. On 11 September 2001 Robin and I had been on a flight heading for O'Hare on assignment when (unbeknown to anyone) American air space was closed, the plane was diverted to Toronto and we learned of the unbelievable atrocity against civilization which happened that morning in New York. That travel assignment was about the legendary Route 66 and we had completed it, united in a love of the United States. We had done so many jobs together over the years and made a perfect writer/photographer team. He would notice a freaky person's conversation in a bar and tell me; I would spot a good picture and point it out to him. He reminded me to make notes when I got lazy; I bossed him into trying shots when he just wanted a beer. We had seen each other at our worst, picked each other up when we had drunk too much and knew each other so well that even when we fell out it didn't matter – or last for very long.

This new commission was for *The Times Magazine* January travel special and had to be turned around quickly. Gill Morgan wanted me to convey something of the spirit of Santa Fe in the winter. It was a perfect job; I'd fallen in love with the place one blazing September – its energy, spirit, history and light – and was excited to end this year of extraordinary change with a return. In winter a place is stripped back to its true soul – and the end of a marriage does that to you too.

On my first trip there had been no time to make a literary pilgrimage to the D.H. Lawrence memorial, near Taos. Now I was determined to go. The Kiowa Ranch, which Lawrence's wealthy friend Mabel Dodge Luhan gave him in 1924 (in exchange for the manuscript of *Sons and Lovers*) lies about 15 miles north of Taos, 5 miles down a dirt road. To get there we had to hire a huge Chevrolet Trailblazer. The four-wheel drive crunched through a foot of snow as I scribbled a haiku in my notebook:

Steep silence beyond Taos
Snow on the wind
Clouds oppress coyotes.

Apart from us, animal tracks were the only sign of life and heavy clouds above the dark trees were the outward symbols of my mood. It wasn't that I was dispirited – far from it. But some landscapes force you to realize your essential loneliness, the hugeness of skies, trees and mountains compelling you to confront human vulnerability and the great cycles of living and dying.

The sky lightened but the pines wept snow. I thought of J and how much he would love this place of distant mountains and stillness. Robin is good with silence; he understood that I often brooded about J and if ever I apologized he just asked quietly, 'Why wouldn't you – after so long?' Knowing about Lawrence's own marriage I thought ruefully of how, back in the sixties, both J and I would have applauded his ideas of passion and individual freedom. Lawrence and his wife, Frieda, (especially Frieda) tried to live according to such wild notions but their restlessness was destructive. They loved each other, yet theirs was a quarrelsome, tempestuous love, founded on an extraordinary mutual dependency. As Lawrence's friend Aldous Huxley wrote of them, 'The mysteries of human relationships are impenetrably obscure.'

Trudging to the little shrine I brooded on their way of life, and thought too of Jean-Paul Sartre and Simone de Beauvoir, who also experimented recklessly with human emotions. J and I studied them when we were young and now, gripped by the cold, I pictured the head of my young husband bent over Sartre's great work *Being and Nothingness* as he took notes for one of his philosophy papers. A tender line of a song ran in my head: Paul Simon singing 'Still crazy after all these years'. Or, at least, not crazy any more, but still tender.

As we reached the small building which is Lawrence's shrine, I reflected that those notions of passionate individuality to which we had subscribed will always lead to pain, to many bitter quarrels and reconciliations, to much selfish sensuality. And how, in the end, all passion spent, it came down to this – a memorial to two people under trees burdened by purifying snow.

Lawrence's short life ended in the south of France in 1930. He was 44. Frieda was at his side. She wrote to a friend, 'He has left me his love without a grudge, we had our grudges out; and from the other side, that I did not know before his death, he gives me his strength and his love for life.' So despite all their problems, she honoured the love they had shared with words I find intensely moving. Oh yes, let people have their grudges out – let them forgive each other! Later Frieda went back to live in Taos with her Italian lover, Angelo Ravagli, 12 years her junior. He had left his wife and three children in Italy, moved in with Frieda in 1933 and married her in 1950. It was he who finally (with almost comic difficulty, in 1935) brought back Lawrence's ashes and built the humble little shrine in the hills, cementing the remains of the genius into place. It has yellow walls, a blue wooden roof and a round window painted crudely with a sunflower. Lawrence's symbol of the phoenix forms the altar, which is (sadly) an ugly thing cast from concrete. But at least Ravagli tried. Perhaps he had a guilty conscience.

In the absolute silence I laid my 'wreath' there – a tiny chilli *ristra* to symbolize the heat of the Lawrentian flame. In 1956 Ravagli buried the woman whom Native Americans called Angry Winter outside the door of the shrine, and after that he returned to Spotorno, near Genoa – where his patient first wife had waited 25 years for his return. He spent the rest of his days with her, until his death in 1976. Huxley was right. As I grow older I become more and more aware of the mysteries, and how impossible it is to assess what unexpected chemistry between this man and that woman will result in a lasting love. People will say, 'They don't go together,' or 'She's not bright enough for him,' or 'He's just not up to her,' but how do they know? When well-meaning friends occasionally intimated that they could not quite understand why I still felt so devoted to one man (and entirely defensive of him) whilst living with another, I just smiled and shrugged. But inside my head I retorted, 'So you don't understand? Well, that's *your* problem, not mine.'

Turning to flick through the visitors' book with numb fingers, I noticed that some anonymous sceptic (dragged there by whom?) had recently scrawled, 'This is the height of silliness.' I read it out to Robin, and we exclaimed in disbelief at such a failure of imagination. But there will always be those who will enter St Paul's Cathedral and see only religious excess, who are immune to the sound of a violin adagio, who view a tree as a green thing in the way of a development, who regard a visit to an ancient place as an excuse to search for tourist trinkets, who reduce human relationships to lowest common denominators like sex and pride, and who will travel to a literary shrine only to remain indifferent to the art (forged in what passionate fires) it commemorates. Yes – and Kwan Yin is only a lump of stone and Bonnie only a dog. So easy it is to beat a drum for reason and drown out the music of the stars.

Robin photographed me by Frieda's resting place, where I dropped a single chilli, scarlet against the grave's snowy quilt. Then we climbed back in the wagon and drove on to Taos to see D.H. Lawrence's crude paintings at the Hotel La Fonda de Taos. In 1929 these 'forbidden' works were confiscated by the police from the Dorothy Warren Gallery in London, on grounds of obscenity, and were in danger of being destroyed until Lawrence agreed to remove them from English soil. After Frieda died, Antonio Ravagli sold the nine oils to the owner of the hotel, who was a great admirer of Lawrence. To this day nobody knows how much money changed hands, but in any case the Italian would hardly have wanted to cart the daubs of bare-breasted women back to the first Mrs R. in Spotorno. I hope he spent some of the money from the paintings on some New Mexican turquoise jewellery for her, as a peace offering.

Lawrence summed up his first impressions of Taos thus: 'In the magnificent fierce morning of New Mexico, one sprang awake, a new part of the soul woke up suddenly and the old world gave way to the new.' When we flew back home to Bonnie (always so thrilled by reunion – as we were), I was aware that something like that had happened to me too. Twelve months earlier I had felt despair. In Santa Fe and Taos, and driving the empty, frozen high road between the two, Robin and I had shared a form of spiritual awakening. We knew we loved the same things: Mexican art, tin crosses, Catholic kitsch, cowboy boots, Danny Lyon photographs of bikers, the skulls of steers nailed to posts and the stacked brown adobe of the Taos pueblo in the fading light of a winter afternoon. We laughed a lot, and that was more important than anything. Frieda Lawrence's words about her Angelo were an echo of my feelings too: 'He is so human and nice with me and *real,* no high falute, but such a genuine warmth for me – I shall be all right ... We have been fond of each other for years and that an old bird like me is still capable of passion and can inspire it too, seems a miracle.'

Settled in my new house and living more contentedly, more simply with this man and one small dog than would have seemed possible, I too felt the old world giving way to the new. I suppose it must – just as old leaves fall and mulch down to aid new growth, with no choice in the process. Another Christmas came, the first in the new home and therefore a huge step forward from the previous year. From now on the tree would be smaller, and the pile of presents too, and the old traditions would be remade to suit this new place. Of course, somebody was still missing, and I could not help wanting Daniel, not Robin, to sit in the important place at the head of the table. The greatest good fortune was to be loved by somebody who did not mind, who understood how complicated were my feelings. And that it is impossible to love two people in the same way.

Each night when I drew the cream curtains the previous owner had left behind in the sitting room, I lit candles to give thanks for hearth and home – and for the limitless resilience of the heart. The passage which closed my *Times Magazine* article inspired by the new house, earlier in the year, stands as a fitting summation of where I found myself as 2004 came to an end:

> This house is telling me the meaning. That all the joys and sorrows of the generations who lived in it are recorded since 1820 on its stone tapes. That the pleasures and pains of all the homes in my life were burnt on the CDs of their walls as well as on my spirit, and I carry it all with me, to dance to the old tunes here. I've already abandoned my plan to replace the 70s green 'dralon' covering my mother chose for the rosewood chaise longue with something more … well … *designer*. I can't be bothered. There may be smart skirting level lighting up those pale stairs, and brushed chrome plugs and switches, yet my Nan's brass hearth set and trivet stand by the marble fireplace, and will remain polished to a glimmer. Nothing demolished. Everything reclaimed. Now I can gaze back through those lighted

windows, glad of the bricks and mortar of what we all built together – grandparents, parents, Jonathan, Daniel, Kitty, all the dear friends who shared the good times.

And I know that moving is (after all) only a single letter away from loving.

Four

REBUILDING

I am I, because my little dog knows me.
Gertrude Stein, 'Identity a Poem'

J and I first saw Venice in 1972. In what was probably our favourite city we had a special affection for the Scuola de San Giorgio degli Schiavoni, and within that building we especially loved one painting.

Between 1502 and 1509 Carpaccio decorated the small guild (founded in 1451 by Slav merchants) with a sequence of jewel-like paintings narrating the lives of Saints George, Tryphone and Jerome. This one, the most enchanting picture, shows St Augustine writing to his friend St Jerome, unaware that he has recently died. Suddenly his elegant cell is flooded with light as a voice from heaven gives him the sad news. The saint sits, pen poised, transfixed by the vision. To his left, sitting in the wide, pale space of the floor, is the little bichon-type dog, ears alert, leaning slightly backwards, as if in wonder. Perhaps my long-standing passion for this picture was prescient. Surely even a non-doggy person could not resist those pricked-up ears?

I always used to think the animal was overwhelmed by awe. But now, in my enlightenment, I know that every fibre of his being – each curled white hair, those two bright, black eyes, the whole quivering *selfhood* of that animal – signifies eagerness. The dog is in the 'now'; the saint is in eternity. The animal concentrates on the man while the saint concentrates on heaven. The small dog is saying, 'Hey man, can't you leave those books alone now and take me for a *walk?*' And, 'Stuff God, master, don't you know it's *you* I love?'

That's what our dogs do: they bring us back to life, haul us into the present, make us get on with things instead of moping. They do not let us escape our humanity but save us from its worst aspects. In another Venetian museum hangs Carpaccio's *The Courtesans*. In it, two elaborately dressed and coiffed women sit on a balcony or loggia, lethargic and bored. Their faces are vacant – and yet at least the one in the front is teasing a big dog (head and paws just entering the frame) with the stick in her right hand, while her left hand holds the two front paws of the smooth-haired lapdog sitting up at her feet. Looking directly out at us, he is the one source of vivacity in the painting. You can almost hear the bells on his collar chiming to break the *ennui* as he begs his mistress for attention. I think he too is desperate for a walk – and hopes she will listen, forget satisfying the sexual needs of rich clients, slip on her pattens and stroll out into the grubby teeming streets to watch the gondolas crossing the grand canal, one of them containing a frisky, red-collared Maltese rather like mine (lovingly painted in another of Carpaccio's paintings, *The Miracle of the Relic of the Cross*, in the Accademia). I feel sure the artist loved the dogs that roamed the streets of Venice.

Yet maybe that is sentimental. Perhaps Carpaccio painted dogs simply because they assisted the composition. Perhaps the many dogs that appear in pictures by Veronese and Titian are not 'true' pets (which is to say, owned by somebody who cares, whether painter or subject) but merely exercises in painterly skills or props. How do you, as viewer (or, for that matter, reader), know what constitutes the truth? In an essay called 'Borrowed Dogs' the photographer Richard Avedon considers the carefully constructed falsehoods of portraiture. He remembers that when he was a child his parents used to borrow dogs to make the family portraits more stylish, posing the family with the dog on loan in front of smart houses that were also not their own. He says it was 'a necessary fiction that the Avedons owned dogs'. But why? It must have been because a dog conveyed a message of family stability as well as prosperity. Avedon believes that the images in their family album represented 'some kind of lie about who we were, and revealed a truth about who we wanted to be'.

Back in July 1994 when I had presented J with his fiftieth birthday present, the beautiful black Labrador puppy called Billie was not a borrowed dog, but one to be owned and loved, who would own and love right back. This animal would indeed put the seal on the kind of family we had become. There is certainly truth in the photographs which record that day: the children blindfolding J, me placing the beribboned puppy in his arms, his wide grin. I still carry, tucked in my address book, a later picture of J at the farm with Billie and Sam, on a summer evening, the valley spreading behind them. The one who is left with the family photograph albums becomes the custodian of all such truths (and some untruths too, like those smiles on days you know you were unhappy) and must fight the bleak feeling that subsequent history turns what was into an untruth. For a wedding photograph is not deprived of meaning because a marriage ends. Snaps of adorable young children should not be sullied by the frustration and disappointment caused by their evolution into difficult teenagers. Photographs inevitably make you sad, since they remind you of the time and of mortality. Yet the good can still be clung to – that this did happen.

It *was.* We existed.

At the beginning of February 2005 Robin and I went to Egypt. It was my first visit to Cairo but not his – and this was another travel commission. From our hotel we gazed through high-rise hotels and low-rise ugliness, to where the pyramids stood, their silence reaching across the cacophonous city.

'It smells so different to home,' he said, looking over our tenth-floor balcony.

'Yes, it does,' I said.

But in fact I could detect no smell – apart from traffic fumes. I agreed with him because most of us collude about the expectations of travel, the yearning for the Other which requires those aromas of spices and shisha, of different body smells, of donkey droppings, of alien and malfunctioning drains, which would have met intrepid travellers in earlier times. Safe within the international hotel we agreed on an imaginary Egyptian ambience which contradicted the polluted reality of the twenty-first century, because that is the way humans construct the truths they long for. Most of the time we live variations of a lie. Ask any married couple what happened and you will hear variations on the old 'Gigi' song 'I Remember it Well' – when he remembers being on time on the Friday and she says he was late on the Monday, he recalls her in a golden dress but she knows it was blue, and so on.

I was thinking about the visit J and I had made to Luxor just three years earlier, just after we had celebrated our daughter's twenty-first birthday with a big party. We were intensely excited by the glories of the Valley of the Kings and when we visited the Luxor Museum, we decided that a huge, battered king and queen (or god and goddess?) sitting side by side, just touching, were our alter egos. We invoked one of our favourite poems, Philip Larkin's 'An Arundel Tomb', and stood there amidst gods and grave goods, joyfully reciting the poem's last verse, word perfect, in unison:

Time has transfigured them into
Untruth. The stone fidelity
They hardly meant has come to be
Their final blazon, and to prove
Our almost-instinct almost true;
What will survive of us is love.

I wrote:

13 January 2001: ... Tonight, another delicious dinner and talking about Egyptian culture. How well J and I get on! He said today he could not imagine re-marrying – being with anybody else. Let's hope the tiny 18c god Ankh he bought me today brings me the luck of many more years of life with him.

I've put it on the gold chain with the 'Long Life' charm Kitty brought me back from Hong King when she was 12.

I only know such things because they were recorded in my diary – the chronicles of lost time.

So now I was back in Egypt, and life had changed utterly. Several times each day I would find myself wondering where J was, what he was doing, still amazed that now he had a new partner and so did I, but we went on missing each other so very much. Sometimes I felt guilty to be thinking of him; it was a strange turn-around to be secretly obsessed with the husband whilst travelling (and having a wonderful time) with the new partner. Even when we did something we liked (watching a belly dancer, for example) but I suspected he would not, I could not banish J from my thoughts. I wondered if he was followed around by a wraith shaped like me, whispering poems in his ear even when he was with his new lady.

Robin and I were looking at the Great Pyramid of Cheops, stung by a dusty wind (and soon to be stung by hucksters) when my mobile phone brought news which made us sad. Daniel telephoned to tell us that Billie had died. She of the velvet ears, the dependable paws, the thumping tail and melting expression had been ill and would salivate over her meals no more. 'Only a dog' some might say, and of little value in the great scheme of things – symbolized by those pyramids and the mysterious Sphinx, not to mention the everyday modern sorrows of East and West. But in Egypt of all places I knew differently. I could mourn Billie more truly far from home. Away from the added sentiment of familiar places, I could remember her as über-dog: beautiful and gentle in equal measure. She should be enshrined for ever on the wall of a tomb, I thought, to prove to future generations that she existed.

The Ancient Egyptians loved their pet dogs, and adorned them with fancy collars, just as we do. In the Cairo Museum we saw a Twelfth Dynasty coffin belonging to Khui, a man wealthy enough to have a decorated casket. On it he is painted with his dog Lupu (very like a Dalmatian, rather than the usual Egyptian Basenji) who trots along behind his master on a white lead. You can see the affection between them; it links dog lovers over centuries. On steles (grave markers), coffins and wall paintings their dogs are painted, and over seventy dog names are recorded, from ones referring to colour (Ebony, Blackie) to character (Reliable, Brave One) to qualities like speed (Antelope, North Wind). Apparently one Ancient Egyptian mutt was called Useless (unfortunate antecedent of Leona Hemsley's Trouble) but that could have been affectionate. So greatly were dogs valued that some were mummified to accompany their masters into the afterlife: faithful friends for eternity.

For the Egyptians, like all other dog owners throughout time, there was a distinction between the outside dog and the inside dog. They had their fighting dogs, their hunting dogs – and the dogs beneath the chair. But a Labrador like Billie makes the transition: the working dog turned into a pet. The Jack Russell is fierce in his pursuit of rats, but the Prince of Wales's Tigger had the status of Royal lapdog, even though the term is one all self-respecting Jack Russells would scorn. What interests me is the message the dog sends out about us. The savage youth with his pit bull is at one end of the scale; at the other is a symbiotic relationship which defies rational explanation.

Writing about his golden retriever Beau after the dog's death, Mark Doty recalls the golden, 'blonde shine' which is 'gone from the world forever' and yet '... something of it remains absolutely clear to me, the quality of him, the aspect of him most inscribed within me.' So for him the essence of the dog remains in the part which most correlates to its owner. In Cairo I laid Billie permanently to rest within my memory, with the realization that her quality – her absolute essence – of ever-hopeful love (no more, no less) was indeed a perfect correlation for her owner.

If dogs are held to look like their owners, what did a small white dog communicate about my own essence? It cannot be appearance, since I am assiduous in my mission to keep all white hairs disguised, and my eyes are blue. Yet I do move quickly – and so if I had to sum it up in one word I would choose 'eagerness' as the essence. It pleases me to think that I share at least one of Bonnie's best qualities and do not believe that anyone in the world (except Robin) has her true measure. Once a teasing friend said, 'Let's face it, Bel, your dog has a brain the size of a peanut.' And it was Robin who riposted, mildly, 'Well, surely a *walnut?*' Habitually we addressed her as '*silly* little dog', imbuing the adjective with honeyed affection. As a student of the English language, I know that the meaning of 'silly' has changed over the centuries, and choose to revert to the Old English meaning of 'happy' or 'blessed' when applying it to my dog. She is not foolish – no, not at all.

Yet widespread prejudice sees her as a 'handbag dog' – with all the connotations of leisure, style, money and ladies-who-lunch. I often see Maltese dogs used as props for photo shoots – as sweet and sick-making as cupcakes, but clearly viewed by marketing people as just as desirable. At one end of the scale of aspiration is the Paris Hilton syndrome, where it is as important to be photographed with your chi-chi pet as with your Prada handbag – but pity the creature if it pisses on your carelessly dropped Dior. At the other end are the people who choose a lapdog as an accessory because of all those smart associations, with no understanding of the particular neediness of the small breeds.

I met a young woman who worked in a dress shop in Bath. Her teenage sister had been clamouring for a chihuahua, was given the little dog by over-indulgent parents and then ordered a variety of 'designer' collars and leads online. Months later I found out that the girl had 'got rid of' the poor chihuahua. Why? 'It was so *naughty!*' explained the sister. The novelty of pink collars had worn off and the dog was left unsupervised in a field, where it was trodden on by a horse. The chihuahua's little leg was broken and so they had to find it another home – and all this was recounted to me as if the mishap were entirely the nuisance-animal's fault. Rescue homes worldwide give succour to thousands of dogs whose owners were just too hopeless, mean or stupid to take care of them. What other explanation can there be for the presence of Bonnie in my life? Especially at a time of economic hardship (like the one afflicting Europe and America as I write this), when dogs are abandoned in even larger numbers. I do not understand it, for I would share my last piece of meat with my dog. How else can we prove to our dogs that we are the people they think we are, other than by raising them beyond accessory status?

If artists in previous centuries used dogs as props (like the columns and aspidistras in later studio photographs) it was, after all, because the dog had *meaning*. People were attuned to symbolism in a way we are not now. When van Eyck painted the famous Arnolfini wedding portrait in 1434 he layered much symbolism within the frame – so much so that scholars are still debating whether this is a wedding or a memorial portrait (arguably commemorating the death of the wife, Giovanna) and what the single candle in the chandelier means. But at the right-hand front there is the dog, a Brussels gryphon, and surely nobody can argue what he signifies? The little dog communicates loyalty, faithfulness, trust. What else would you want a picture of a marriage to say? Contemplating this work of art in London's National Gallery I find myself thinking how much better are our dogs than we are. In general we don't do so well on the fidelity front – although how can we know the truth of the Arnolfini couple? Did they take care of that dog? Did they take care of each other?

In 2005 I was, by a strange turn of fate, to gain my first real, coal-face knowledge of the pervasiveness of aching romance, sexual passion and subsequent marital misery.

I needed more work. In archive boxes somewhere I still have records of what I earned as a young journalist: columns in the backs of diaries listing the article, the fee and whether it had been paid. Some of the amounts were pitifully small even in 1972; both J and I wrote for the *New Statesman* (then under the inspired editorship of Anthony Howard), which was not known for largesse. The years of having to keep such proudly independent (that was their importance to me) records had long gone; now I was in that position again. What's more, I believe in work as therapy. When married women give up *all* contact with the world of work (which may be voluntary or part-time) to keep house and raise a family they leave themselves so vulnerable. Your children will grow up and leave home and your husband may find himself a new love – and then what will you do? In my opinion, sorting clothes in the charity shop (when after all you can chat to fellow human beings) is better than sitting home alone. It was a jest of mine that in a terrible revolution, when the intellectuals were hunted out, I would survive – because, as a good seamstress, I could sew uniforms for the tyrants, and build a subversive *style* into each seam.

So – touting for work. For years I'd been contributing to *The Times*, under six different editors, but had never met the current assistant editor (Features) face to face, although we had spoken on the telephone. In the businesslike knowledge that you get more work if more people know you, I suggested a meeting. Sandra Parsons invited me to lunch at London's latest fashionable restaurant, The Wolseley, on Piccadilly – and, by quirk of fate, picked the date which would have been my thirty-seventh wedding anniversary. Looking back it seems 'meant' – that on that day I would shake hands with her as one person and rise from the table with a different direction, a new door opening in my career, for we were talking (as women will) about work and the problems and guilt of juggling a demanding job and a family, which I had been through and Sandra was still doing. I felt for her – and, without realizing it, gave some advice. Then I hit my own forehead and said, 'Listen to me! I sound like an agony aunt *manqué*.'

This was the first time I have ever *observed* what is called a light-bulb moment.

Her face lit up and she leaned forward. 'Have you ever thought of doing that?'

'Er – *no!*'

When a talented editor gets hold of an idea he or she will not let it go. Sandra persuaded me that I was just the person to write a problem page for *The Times*, and begged me to consider it. I was unsure – and went on feeling like that for a couple of weeks, although when I asked friends they all agreed it was something I would do well. But I was planning to write more fiction for adults and children, to continue with the radio work and get myself some regular 'proper' journalism to pay the bills. Becoming what is popularly known as an 'agony aunt' (a term I dislike, because it tends to be patronizing) could never have been part of my life plan.

But now, in an instant, it was.

Still, for a short while, I feared it might make me look ... well ... less than serious. This did not reflect (I must emphasize) my own judgement on the role, but an awareness of the snobbishness of those who sneer at all popular journalism (that slight curl of the lip, making the smirk look even uglier, and the tinkling question, 'Eeuw, you write for the *Daily Mail* ...?'), wherever it may appear. Thinking hard about that, and feeling the old rush of irritation, was enough to make me say, 'What the hell!' As the iconoclastic Victorian writer Samuel Butler wrote, 'The great pleasure of a dog is that you may make a fool of yourself with him and not only will he not scold you, but he will make a fool of himself too.' Me – I've tended to rush at things with an uncool enthusiasm to match my dog's, as long as I could swiftly gain control over whatever it was I found. So at this point in my life I was prepared to head off down the side road suddenly presented to me, just to see what was there. To try, even if I might fail.

The canine readiness to breathe the whole of odiferous life up into its nostrils, to hurl adoration at you by the front door when you've only been absent for 30 minutes, to sense it is party time when you put down your pen and murmur, 'Right then ...', to know that just around this next corner awaits something *so* exciting it must be raced towards immediately ... This is a way of living – even a state of soul – that we should learn from our dogs. There is a certain level of British society which holds that to be enthusiastic, to bounce around wagging an imaginary tail, is deeply unsmart – and (worse) probably lower class. These are the snobbish people who use that tedious, tinkling little word 'agreeable' as high praise – so that to say that the evening was 'perfectly agreeable' means you had a superb, amazing time. Dogs do not find anything 'agreeable'; they are wild enthusiasts.

Still, as curious and excited as I was at the idea of a new start, it frightened me too. Even then I wasn't to know how hard I would find the transition. For one thing, *The Times* sent the feature writer Catherine O'Brien to interview me. The sensible thinking was that I could not possibly deal with other people's problems unless the readers knew I'd had plenty of my own. Readers will trust you if they think you know what you are talking about. Virgil understood this, 19 years before the birth of Jesus. It seems to me another strange trick of destiny that in 1963, aged 17 and a keen classicist, I copied into my commonplace book a line entirely relevant to this new branch of my career – almost predicting it. It is from the *Aeneid* (book 1, line 630) spoken by Dido, Queen of Carthage. The beautiful doomed Queen tells the visiting hero who will betray her, '*non ignara mali miseris succurrere disco*' – 'not unacquainted with grief do I learn to help the unhappy'.

Yes, I thought, I may not have any formal qualification to advise people on emotional issues, but it takes more than a piece of paper to understand pain.

There would be no choice but to answer questions about the end of our marriage, which until this point I had avoided. The journalist was intelligent and *sympathique*, and Sandra Parsons had promised me sight of the copy before it was published. But that didn't make it any easier. It was as if J was in the room with me – always – shaking his head. He had always been more conscious of personal privacy than I. Columnists are accustomed to drawing on their lives; even this book is an extension of that impulse to say, 'This is how it is for me.' Yet I hated answering questions about our life, about Susan Chilcott, about how I felt. It was still too recent. Although I knew that the price of the job was a degree of revelation, the interview set up a frisson of dread.

Then, unexpectedly, I was invited to the wedding of Prince Charles and Camilla Parker-Bowles, at Windsor on 9 April. The last time I'd seen J, I had asked if he had had an invitation – then joked that he should take me. After all, we had shared the gruelling experience of his writing of the biography of the Prince of Wales and the making of the television film which caused such sensation. No couple could have been more at one, at every level. We had sat side by side and watched in open-mouthed horror when Princess Diana's brother, Charles Spencer, had made a funeral oration which, to us, lacked all taste. We shared disbelief at the rotting-flower stink of public sentimentality after Diana's shocking death, and support and affection for a Prince we thought much misunderstood and cruelly maligned. So it seemed to me fitting that we should witness his wedding together – even if fate had now set us off on separate paths.

J smiled somewhat sadly and shook his head – but in any case, I knew it would not have been protocol for him to telephone and ask to bring a guest. Things do not work that way.

Then my own invitation came. It says little for my confidence at that time that I was surprised to be treated as a person in my own right. Even though it was daunting to go alone, go alone I would. Every woman will understand that the worst problem was deciding what to wear. I trawled Bath and London seeking inspiration, when finally I saw a black silk dress, patterned with butterflies. Then I spent the day before the wedding, ill in bed, stitching feather butterflies on a straw hat. Obsessed with symbolism as I am, I knew that the early Christians saw butterflies as representing the soul, and therefore rebirth and transformation, whilst in Islamic stories the butterfly Sadaquah brings good news. For Native Americans the butterfly teaches that change may be painful but is necessary. Best of all, in ancient Chinese legend two butterflies symbolize the spirits of two lovers who find eternal married happiness together. Perfect. The Prince would like that, I thought, even though my symbolism, like the Arnolfini dog's, would be subliminal.

Robin drove me to Windsor and dropped me off. Inside the Chapel of St George I saw J, seated in the row in front of me, but about seven people to the left. It was impossible not to fix my eyes on him, not to think that we should have been there together, not to wish (with an ache) to be by his side. It must have been just as difficult for him. I gazed up at the great stone vault of the roof springing from stone pillars that look too delicate to bear it, and saw it as a metaphor for the survival of all that I believe in – from tradition, custom and ceremony to human optimism which somehow defies the gravity that always threatens to pull it down. The stone angels which run all round the interior of the chapel are resolutely facing upwards – winged like my butterflies. There is nothing to do but hope for better times, and that was the prayer I made for us both.

I found myself thinking of the sour people (especially in Cornwall) I had seen interviewed on the news the night before who mumbled that they weren't interested, that the wedding 'had nothing to do with me' … moan, groan, gripe, snipe. What a failure of imagination! You might as well say that the terrible tsunami which had begun the year with suffering on a vast scale, or the death of the Pope, or even your country's best athletes running their hearts out … all have nothing to do with you. I link those examples not carelessly but because I passionately believe we are all joined by ties of the spirit which enable us to reach out with compassion, grief, exhilaration, empathy or pride towards what goes on in the lives of others. That is why I felt, as we all made confession of our 'manifold sins and wickedness' in unison, 'Yes, this has *everything* to do with me.' And everything to do with the man on whose head I fixed my eyes once more. Conscious of imperfection, I reflected that all we can do is stumble along, like the Prince and the Duchess, hoping that after the darkness the light will shine.

And it did. At exactly the right moment in the service. The actor Timothy West had just finished reading the passage Prince Charles (very revealingly) had chosen from Wordsworth about the 'delight and liberty' in the human spirit, experienced naturally by children, but forgotten as we grow, when life gets so much more complicated. But the simple joy can be recaptured, the poet says, in maturity, through intense experiences of mind and heart. The Prince and his bride listened, then the orchestra and choir began a sublime Bach anthem, and the pale sun triumphed over those chilly April clouds and burst through the great east window. The day was telling us that all things go on, and can be made better. That, as the passage from Revelation read by Lord Carey says, ' … there shall be … neither sorrow nor crying … for the former things are passed away … Behold, I make all things new.' The smiles on the faces of Diana's sons banished the dark clouds of the past, and the pride in their father's expression boded well for the future. I always believed in his capacity for kingship – and now even more so with this wife by his side. That shared conviction was part of all our rejoicing.

On the way to Windsor I'd seen other people going to other weddings, and thought how the season kicks off now – each Saturday all the couples, of all ages, going forward in their finery to take their places in the ranks of the hopeful, toasted by their friends. And what is there to do but wish them well? Some marriages will fail, of course. Yet I realized – there in the chapel and later mingling at the reception – that being separated from J had in no way diminished my faith in the institution. Public statements of love will continue to be made because the need to affirm is a part of the human condition.

And here in the grandeur of Windsor Castle it was the same. After thanking his parents, family, staff and friends, and (very movingly) remembering his grandmother, the groom praised his bride. Adjective after adjective of love and gratitude, and finally his heartfelt thanks to her 'for having the courage to take me on'. His self-deprecating smile brought more cheers from the floor. But Camilla Parker-Bowles (now Duchess of Cornwall) is so English, so reticent. With nothing of the poser or smooth public figure about her, she shifted her feet and looked attractively embarrassed.

I felt elated for them and sad for myself. After the cruel criticism of her looks (mostly from other women, which is equally astonishing and loathsome) Camilla looked striking and elegant. And I thought how refreshing it was that here was a man in his fifties choosing a real friend one year older – not the cliché younger woman most men seem to want. As we raised our glasses my personal toast was to long-time love, to middle-aged marriages and to down-to-earth weddings – instead of stupid 'fairytales' which end in disappointment and disillusion.

When it was all over Robin collected me at the time we had arranged and drove me through the paparazzi and back to Bath. One of the truly amazing things about him was that he was (as he said) quite happy to play the driver. On our trip to Egypt I had walked through a hotel with the public relations manager, with Robin walking a few paces behind us, taking everything in, intensely interested but relieved that he was not required to play the PR game, as I had to. He joked that he was like the Duke of Edinburgh walking behind the Queen; his quiet sense of selfhood required no outward trappings of status. He and I were particularly delighted to discover a particular

Texas blues-rock number sung by Angela Strehli called 'A Stand By Your Woman Man'. Yes, that was it, and it was a source of celebration. I had told *The Times* journalist Catherine O'Brien that this practical man 'can fix anything including me'. He seemed increasingly like the intricate web of scaffolding which shores up a building and enables it to be renovated. He loved a poem I read to him one night, which uses this as a metaphor. By U.A. Fanthorpe, it is called 'Atlas' and begins:

There is a kind of love called maintenance
Which stores the WD40 and knows when to use it ...

The poem celebrates 'the sensible side of love' and is a public tribute to the life partner who 'keeps/My suspect edifice upright in air' – just as Robin was doing for me.

J is a fourth-generation journalist who epitomizes what's finest about our trade. His trajectory began in local television but switched to mainstream political radio after one year, presenting Radio 4's flagship *The World This Weekend.* He then carved out an extraordinarily successful career on television both as an international reporter and as a political interviewer, tackling heads of state while still in his twenties and winning a BAFTA award for his epoch-making 1973 report on the terrible Ethiopian famine that had been hushed up by Hailie Selassie's regime. *The Unknown Famine* became a catalyst for the destabilization of the quasi-feudal regime. J was allowed to make an unprecedented appeal on both main television channels, which stimulated the largest amount of public generosity ever seen at that time. Treated as a hero of the

Ethiopian people, he was allowed unique access to the country – which led to films that excoriated the violence and oppression of Mengistu's Marxist-Leninist regime and J being banned from the country he loved. He was a brilliant reporter – working dangerously under cover in Pinochet's Chile, coming under fire in Cyprus when the Turks invaded in 1974, exposing outrages all around the world and so on. As well as those reports, he made a name for big documentary series analysing, with equal meticulousness and style, the ongoing stand-off between Russia and America and the plight of the Bolivian tin miner, to name but two.

In a meeting-of-minds-marriage your partner's achievements are as your own. I was very proud of him, searched the newspapers for reviews and once backed the now-distinguished novelist Julian Barnes against a wall at a party to berate him, then a humble television reviewer, for being flippant about one of J's films.

J began presenting the current affairs programme *Any Questions* on BBC Radio 4 in 1987, and the year afterwards *Any Answers* was reinvented as a phone-in, which was a perfect format for him. He went on to front BBC1's first Sunday lunchtime political programme *On the Record* from 1987 until 1992, and then, in 1995, started to present a similar programme on ITV, called *Jonathan Dimbleby* – which continued the ruin of family weekends. As ITV's most experienced political presenter he anchored general elections in 1997 and 2001 – and now, in 2005, he would do the same again.

The point is, I could not tolerate the prospect of *The Times* profile of me, heralding my new column, appearing days before his mammoth election-night endurance test. It made me feel frantic and so, torn between the prospect of perhaps destabilizing (and certainly upsetting) my separated husband and my new job, I chose him. I suppose this was my own version of canine loyalty. The column was postponed.

On 5 May I sat up, as I had always done, to watch him as the results came in, giving Tony Blair's New Labour win its third consecutive victory with a reduced overall majority of 66. In 1997 J and I, like so many people, had been elated by Labour's victory; the theme song 'Things Can Only Get Better' was genuinely inspiring. We all felt that the country needed change. Even with hindsight, that was right. But now all was changed, changed utterly. After supper out with friends, Robin went to bed and I watched J by myself in my own house, lying on the sofa with Bonnie, aware of our old home empty just up the road. We're all older and more bruised, and things rarely get better, I thought. In any case, I dislike change. That's why I could not kick my habit of staying with the exhausting election coverage through the night and into the morning, dozing fitfully to wake and see him on screen.

So his life was still my life too.

A new series of *Devout Sceptics* was in production. The general election over, I knew that *The Times* was planning to use Catherine O'Brien's profile on 18 May. This was the day Malcolm Love and I were to drive to Cornwall to stay overnight before recording an interview with Tim Smit, the charismatic founder of the Eden Project, one of the region's most beautiful and significant tourist attractions. I confess I was excited at the prospect of seeing *The Times* article – public sign of a 'new' life. A piece which (written with sympathy) said, 'Here I am, this is what I have experienced and this is what I have learned.' Robin had taken a beautiful set of photographs of me (and Bonnie) to accompany the profile, which would be the cover story.

But when I rose early to retrieve the newspapers from the front door I was shocked to see a small photograph of J and me on our wedding day on the newspaper's front page (trailing the profile) and then that same image blown up, covering the whole front of *The Times 2* features and arts section. Beneath was blazoned: 'MRS DIMBLEBY MOVES ON'. My knees buckled; I clutched my dog and wept into her fur. Pictures of our wedding are readily available; as I've explained, there were press photographers outside the registry office, which was the first shock for a girl from an ordinary background. Yet to me there was something thoughtless, even cruel, about this use of the photograph without consulting me. It seemed to me to be insensitive to hire an established writer to write a brand-new column for your newspaper – a column which would consider people's deepest feelings – and cause her real pain by splashing her wedding picture on the pages, with no warning. Did nobody think I might mind?

I hated them all and wanted to give it up – and this with the first advice column, called 'Life and Other Issues', ready for the following week and now thoroughly 'advertised'. I fired off an angry email to Sandra Parsons (who had wanted to use one of Robin's photographs on the cover, as well as inside, but had been over-ruled by the paper's editor) which concluded: 'I have no words for my shock (and misery) at the cover you have chosen. It makes me feel so terrible – as if I have been done over by the very people I trusted and I am supposed to be working for/with. It defines me as "Mrs

Dimbleby" and looks back to 1968 instead of forward and is terribly, terribly sad. In the words of Plath, I simply do not see where there is to go to.'

I was still very upset when Malcolm Love came to collect me. We had been working together for a very long time and had no secrets from each other. We had talked about his loss of the faith of his childhood, my seeking of spirituality, his deeply held beliefs, and our feelings about love and marriage. We had strolled the streets of San Francisco where women came up and told him he looked like Richard Gere (which is true) and he had managed to haul me back to the hotel one time after I had drunk too much on Fisherman's Wharf – and with an interview with Isabel Allende to do the next day. Now, like a true friend, he listened to my wailing and understood when I confided that the worst thing about the picture went far beyond what I had written to Sandra.

First, I simply could not bear to think of how it must have upset J – although I did not telephone him to explain that I had not known the picture would be used. Silence seemed the safer option.

Second, I felt overwhelmed – staring at the familiar monochrome image of that 21-year-old in a mini-dress and the 23-year-old in his kipper tie looking so happy, so in love – by the feeling that I wanted to rush back through time and *protect* them. I wanted to tell them not to get it wrong, for they were meant to be together and must not dilute that meaning with the prevailing 'anything goes' mores of the zeitgeist. I wanted to beg them to take *care,* to not be stupid, to not fail each other. Too late.

Malcolm heard me out.

But over dinner in the hotel that night it was my turn to listen. My producer and friend knew a lot about love and was wise to its glories as well as realistic about its limitations. He told me that you should never say that a marriage has 'failed'. You should see it as having run its course, like a journey which has reached its destination. Perhaps, he suggested, J and I were fated to be together for 35 years and then to take different paths, as now. There is no need to damn the outcome with the word 'failure', he said. And there was no need to be so angry about the picture in *The Times*. It had happened, people are careless, nobody could have realized the effect it would have on me and it was time for me to move forward, without looking back. Hearing this echo of the advice on the laminated card given to me at the door of the Carmel Mission, I knew he was right. Now I was to become an advice columnist I must learn to take advice. Malcolm and I would go on with our series, I would be brave and start *The Times* column and see where it would lead – and J and I would go on loving each other under separate roofs.

Which is what happened.

Nothing was said about the article by J or by me, then or ever afterwards. But a few weeks after it had appeared a flat parcel arrived for me from J. It contained, with no explanation, an embossed metal 'vintage' advertisement for the 1958 Harley-Davidson Duo-Glide. He knew my tastes so well.

There is no doubt that since leaving the farm, I had become more attached to Bonnie than ever. 'Just you and me against the world,' I used to murmur, and it felt true. I doted on my Maltese as much as the Roman Governor of Malta doted on his, in the first century. The poet Martial commemorated this military man's love of his *'deliciae catella'* ('darling little dog') in a gently mocking poem called 'Issa'. Almost certainly a Maltese, the lapdog Issa is described as naughty, pure, precious and seductive, and *'sentit tristitiamque gaudiumque'* ('feels sadness and joy'). There follow four lines which every one who lets an adored lapdog sleep on the bed will recognize:

et desiderio coacta ventris
gutta pallia non fefellit ulla,
sed blando pede suscitat toroque
deponi monet and rogat levari.

('And, compelled by the impulse of her bladder, not a single drop has dirtied the covers, but with her sweet paw she nudges you from the couch, warns you that she needs to be put down and asks to be lifted up.')

A dog on the bed, no matter how small, is not a good idea. But Bonnie had been sleeping with me for two years and since she had been my companion and consolation through the months alone, I was not about to banish her because there was another partner in my deliberately feminine (because not designed with a man in mind) boudoir. The dog and I were a unit. Fortunately the instruction 'Love me, love my dog' was one Robin found easy to obey. He genuinely loved Bonnie, even though a pair of beady black eyes watching everything you do hardly encourages intimacy. The husband of that medieval lady in the Luttrell Psalter would have had no need to furnish her with a chastity belt as long as she had her small white dog on the bed.

Re-reading Virginia Woolf's quirky, charming biography of Elizabeth Barrett Browning's spaniel Flush (a book I could not see the point of as a student), I was able to see parallels with my life with Bonnie. Woolf writes that Flush's life had been lived 'too close' to humans. He had 'lain upon human knees and heard men's voices. His flesh was veined with human passions; he knew all grades of jealousy, anger and despair.' You may think that fanciful, but to the owner of a small dog it makes perfect sense; there is no other way for a lapdog to be. Interestingly, Woolf invokes that idea of symbiosis: ' … made in the same mould, could it be that each, perhaps, complemented what was dormant in the other?' Whatever the truth, I suspect that had Flush not arrived the great woman poet would have slipped slowly into the greater darkness, where there are no poems and rebellion is pointless. That Virginia Woolf (who liked dogs and gave people she loved doggy nicknames) should devote a whole book to this literary dog demonstrates that she did not believe he had a mere walk-on role.

Elizabeth Barrett, already an invalid, was plunged into depression after the death of two of her brothers in 1840. Then her friend Miss Mitford offered the cocker spaniel puppy who was to transform her life – even within her gloomy, stifling sickroom. Everything the little dog did alleviated her depression. His excitement at a carriage ride (the eternal dog with its nose in the wind) made her smile; what's more, Flush strengthened her sense of self and somehow encouraged her to rebel against her fate. Her male doctor forbade the dog on the bed, so she hid him beneath the coverlet; her tyrannical father came to check on her meals, not knowing she had slipped food to her dog to clear the plate. And when she stood up unaided for the first time in two years it was with the help of her dog: 'Think of me standing alone, with only one hand upon Flush – he standing quietly on the sofa ... to steady me.' Yes, it was Elizabeth and Flush against the world.

Until Robert Browning came along. No wonder poor Flush was jealous. At least Bonnie *knew* Robin; poor Flush had to contend with a stranger who burst into the sickroom exuding equally powerful scents of poetry and testosterone. Elizabeth Barrett's first book of poetry (containing verses to her dog) was read by Browning who, six years younger than Elizabeth, was just making his name. They began to correspond, poet to poet, and at last he came on a first visit, carrying a bunch of flowers from his mother's garden.

Flush was used to total attention from his mistress and resented the interloper. No wonder he bit the secret suitor more than once. In love with the man, Elizabeth punished her pet, and wrote to tell Robert all the details.

> *I slapped his ears and told him that he should never be loved again, and he sat on the sofa ... with his eyes fixed on me ... with an expression of quiet despair on his face. At last I said, 'If you are good, Flush, you may come & say you are sorry' ... at which he dashed across the room & trembling all over kissed one of my hands & then another & put up his paws to be shaken & looked in my face with such great beseeching eyes, that you would certainly have forgiven him, just as I did.*

I can imagine Browning sitting in his club telling a friend, 'Good God, sir, if it were not enough to love a woman a man must offer his fingers to her lapdog!' But he wrote back that he loved Flush 'for his jealous supervision'. Next time it happened, the hitherto doting mistress threatened a muzzle. But the poet bribed the dog with cake instead.

Five months after their first meeting the poets were planning to elope, but Elizabeth could not think of going to Italy without Flush. Robert reassured her. But far less reassuring was his response when Flush was dog-napped for the third time by the notorious gang called 'The Fancy'. Miss Barrett was used to her father's indifference and the mockery of her brothers, but now her true love let her down as well. Browning wrote (sounding horribly like her father) to tell her that paying a ransom encouraged the crime, and that were the dog to be killed, 'God allows matters to happen.' Monstrous! He realized his mistake and wrote to apologize, but now the once-reclusive invalid took matters in her own hands. She jumped into a cab with her faithful servant and descended into the underworld of slums to find her dog. Even today her action would be brave; in 1846 the sights, sounds and smells would have been truly daunting. I find it incredible to think of this sheltered woman having the common sense to seek out the wife of the gang's ringleader and get her on side. Flush was returned that evening. Through her love for her dog Elizabeth Barrett had discovered she needed no brother, father or even husband-to-be to help her. She was *strong* – her courage channelled through the love of her pet. That strength, as well as her love for Browning, took her into her clandestine marriage on 12 September 1846, and a week later to France, with her loyal maid Wilson carrying the dog.

Two bronze relief portraits of Elizabeth and Robert (made by J's brother, the sculptor Nicholas Dimbleby) hang on the red-brick garden wall of the house my children found for me – beautiful talismans which remind me of this story each time I see them. And I feel that the spirit of possessive, forgiving, adoring Flush lives on in my dog – who was not kidnapped by London ruffians, nor ransomed, and did not ever bite Robin, nor could be bought with cake, but is brave in protectiveness and savage with strangers and envelopes in equal measure. She gives the amused postman no quarter.

Living with Bonnie and with Robin in a house that was far more manageable than the farm, I began to feel new contentment. Virginia Woolf encapsulates this in a description of her own life after she and her husband Leonard acquired Grizzle, a mongrel fox terrier of dubious beauty. ('These shabby mongrels are always the most loving, warm-hearted creatures', she wrote to Vita Sackville-West, a dog lover herself). She valued the dog as both companion and watchdog, but he became more: a third presence who helped to create that everyday family life people take for granted. She wrote, 'The immense success of our life is, I think, that our treasure is hid … in such common things that nothing can touch it. That is, if one enjoys a bus ride to Richmond, sitting on the green smoking … combing Grizzle.'

In the same way Robin and I found immeasurable contentment in shopping and cooking together, wandering around our garden to 'visit' Kwan Yin and the Brownings, and bathing Bonnie – which is itself a sight of such rat-like pathos it would make a sculpture laugh. 'Instant entertainment,' he would say, about her waddle, the way her tongue stuck out like a stray petal, the way she snuffled at the grass like a miniature ruminant, the wholeness of the humour of the small white dog.

That was just as well, for there was little to laugh at in my new job. The role of advice columnist is old and honourable. The nineteenth century produced a number of books on how to live a happy life, but William Cobbett's *Advice to Young Men* (published in 1830 with the subtitle 'And (Incidentally) to Young Women') is perhaps the only one still read, albeit by very few people. Cobbett's classic work of socio-political reportage, *Rural Rides*, was one of J's favourite books; he had been working towards recreating the rides (as a superb horseman himself) and commenting on modern Britain but the project foundered because of the notorious inability of BBC television executives to make decisions. Now it was my turn to be inspired by the great radical; if giving advice was good enough for Cobbett (who, by the way, paid great attention to the welfare of his dog and was particular about its collars) it was certainly good enough for me.

'Happiness ought to be your great object,' says Cobbett near the start of the book, which takes the form of 'letters' written to 'a youth, a bachelor, a lover, a husband, a father and a citizen or subject'. Naturally this first advice manual is an old-fashioned read and yet at its core are some sensible values. The eccentric polymath addresses problems which affect the ability of people to live together, to make each other happy, and subjects like jealousy and fidelity. He counsels against frowns and advocates 'loving kindness' – although he believed that 'adultery in the wife is a greater offence than adultery in the husband'. Still, I cannot quarrel with him when he writes, 'Happiness, or misery, is in the mind. It is the mind that lives; and the length of life ought to be measured by the number and importance of our ideas, and not by the number of our days ... Respect goodness, find it where you may.'

At 59, having written millions of words of journalism and six novels, I thought I knew quite a lot about human nature but becoming an advice columnist taught me how much I had to learn. Nothing could have prepared me for the depths of human unhappiness in readers' letters – and for the first two months I felt overwhelmed. It did not show on the page, just at home, when the would-be wise woman (for that is surely where the concept of the agony aunt began?) would cry helpless tears over the stories of sorrow, jealousy, infidelity, boredom, ineptitude and (worst of all) warring families that came with increasing regularity into my email inbox and through the letter-box. I knew that agony aunts with more experience, like psychologists, learn to remain detached. The neophyte could not.

So, after a month, when a woman wrote to me about her devastation at finding out about her husband's affair after 25 years of marriage, I wrote:

> Pain like yours is both universal and particular, and plenty of women reading your letter will cry out in sympathy and sisterhood. Your husband has done what many men in their fifties do, and although there is no gender monopoly on infidelity (after all, his lover has been unfaithful to her husband) it's strange that many middle-aged men choose to open themselves to this turmoil. Because it is a choice. All romantic indulgences about the *coup de foudre* will not persuade me that adults can't control their feelings, unless they will it otherwise.

Re-reading that reply now, I feel less sure of that point than I did then. But the ending of that article is revealing:

> Your children will lead their own lives and you and your husband may or may not survive this ... Whatever happens, you will be left with your sense of self. I ask you to look in the mirror and contort your face in a silent scream of rage many times. Then let your features relax and study that face. Is it really broken and bitter? No. See it as the new self-portrait which is still a work in progress and which will bear your own name.

The readers knew about my own experience because they had read the profile weeks earlier. Many wrote to tell me that they could write to me precisely because they knew that I had not been born with a silver spoon in my mouth and had endured many of the painful experiences that were bothering them. As the weeks passed I cried less, read more – and knew that this was the job I had been waiting for all my life. I also knew that had my marriage not broken up it could never have come about. The paradox – that I could miss J so much and yet feel happy and even be grateful to him – was overwhelming.

13 July 2005 [written in pencil]
The ancient Persians said, 'If fate throws a knife at you, you can catch it by the blade or the handle.'

I write that on a day when I have my column in The Times, *a comment piece in the* Mail, *and I sit in the new white study Robin has built for me, sun pouring into the conservatory, Bonnie curled up on the old cane sofa and I'm asking myself if it is possible for things to be better. Wanting to be nowhere else but here. Heat and stillness folding together; the garden dense and green; distant hills like the background to a painting by Leonardo.*

I am holding the handle I have caught.

[in ink] To write in pencil is to be afraid, like a child first learning who will reach for the eraser to cancel mistakes.

Robin calls me from the Alps but I am embedded in solitude, greedy for the silence of the garden. Now 9.30 pm, pearly dusk, pink sky in the west, a chalked half moon, distant lulling of wood pigeons. You could live like this: efficient in the eyes of the world, existing through the telephone, the internet, your work – and yet all the while dropping below the horizon like the sitting sun, ready to make the long journey to the underworld.

These days I no longer think of The Soprano with compassion, and that in itself is cause for resentment, for she has taken away something from my core. It was a terrible death, I know; yet she toppled into the void and dragged the man who was mine with her.

Yet he of all people, how could he prove so vulnerable? Maybe this will be one of the many tasks I will set myself in the future: to understand.

The sculptor Henry Moore wrote, 'The secret of life is to have a task, something you devote your entire life to, something you bring everything to, every minute of the day for your whole life. And the most important thing is – it must be something you cannot possibly do.'

The white lobelia glimmering like thousands of fallen stars.

15 July

9.20am and a vapour trail lit up, like a snail track in the sky. A cloud shaped like a bird. Robin absent. Why am I content? I feel I will never truly need *to be with a man again. Not after so many years. I read all the emails and letters from* Times *readers and am over-awed by the unhappiness that they carry to me, evidence of the eternal human capacity to make a mess of things. But still, sitting here with Bonnie snuggled up to my side, watching the silver moon assert itself in a deep turquoise sky, knowing somebody who loves me is drinking beer in the French Alps, I catch my breath at my blessings. I work, I sleep … It's as if never before was life as simple and harmonious as this. Yet the act of writing those words feels like a betrayal of the past. Still … did I really get so stressed all the time? Did I usually feel very far away from the autonomous peace I feel now? Yes, it is true.*

That summer brought a new shock. J was to sell the farm. I understood his reasons but had trusted he would live there for a while yet, as intended. But he had a new life to make and understandably no longer wanted to rattle around amidst the memories. Each time he drove into Bath he had to pass my new house; each time I drove out of the city towards the motorway I had to pass the track to our old home. He must have realized that the pulling at fresh stitches, re-opening the wound, would go on until one of us moved from the city. Now the next stage had been reached, and it was right – but we all dreaded it. More boxes. More lists. A final partition of things. Another ending.

It was just as well I was about to park Bonnie with my parents and escape to the USA – again. This was another job, but it was to provide a new, subversive perspective.

The week came when I had to write three advice columns because the page had to appear while I was away. Robin and I were commissioned to produce a piece for *The Times Magazine* on the growing phenomenon of women motorcyclists; I'd sold the idea because I was curious to see Sturgis, the small town in South Dakota which hosts the world's largest motorcycle rally every August. It meant that Robin could spend a week photographing semi-naked women straddling big bikes, which struck him as a fine assignment. Then, after six days at the rally, we would head off, travelling from Deadwood to the Badlands to produce a travel article for the *Mail on Sunday*. Friends groaned at the good luck of work like that. And as always, I experienced that sense of release when the plane took off for Minneapolis. From the Twin Cities we took an internal flight over the empty plains to Rapid City.

Sometimes, at the end of a long relationship, it's essential to try to do something – anything – to reinvent yourself and to realize that (no matter how the marriage ended) this may well be a liberation rather than a loss. Which is to say, it can be both at once, but the emphasis is placed (even if by the greatest effort of will and a degree of falsehood) on the new you, the new life, the new soul. It is one key to survival. Robin and I had worked together on many travel articles, and were used to gatherings of bikers too. J and I had always 'allowed' different sides of each other to develop over the years. His tennis and sailing interested me but little, my attempt to learn to ride horses was a failure and to the end I never fully understood why he wanted to farm. He did not share my penchant for jazz and blues (especially in the 'dark cafés' of Joni Mitchell's lyric), or jukeboxes, but he regarded my middle-aged fascination with biker culture with enough amused benevolence to buy me a Harley-Davidson which, in the end, frightened me too much to ride.

The point is, the whole week in Sturgis enabled me to enact a fantasy life a million miles away from the one I had described in *The Times Magazine* the year before. All the ingredients were there:

We were supplied with a Harley-Davidson Electra-Glide by the Milwaukee-based company.

We rented a trailer.

I was travelling light, with none of the things which normally give my life structure, like (for example) books or smart clothes.

For one week I could become the kind of woman who, wearing jeans and a singlet, swigs a cold beer sitting on the trailer steps, then puts on a cowboy hat or bandana (no helmets in South Dakota) and rides off with her man to join the deafening, throbbing rumble of 500,000 other iron horses on the streets of the small town. I could become the kind of woman who had never been Mrs Anybody, or sewed nametapes on school uniforms. Never owned a library in a fine house, surrounded by land. Never had to wear that woman-of-many-committees face at a charity event. Never known the lash of the work ethic or the dinner-party imperative. Anonymous, I could cut loose. Not give a damn. It was tempting to get a tattoo of a bird, with the word 'Freedom' on a ribbon in its beak. My T-shirts announced 'Badass Girls Need Badass Toys' and 'Good Girl Gone Bad'. What I needed was a small mongrel on a string who would guard the trailer (barking furiously at the world just as I often wanted to bark, but always restrained myself) until we roared back to unload the six-packs and the food and party on through the sweaty night, with biker universe grumbling in the distance, like a summer storm.

Another life.

Sitting in the trailer one hot afternoon, brooding about the (still 'our' in my mind) farm up for sale and strangers wandering round, looking up at those carved stone corbels to ask the unknowing estate agent what they meant, and peering at our furniture wondering what sort of people created a home so unusual, so beautiful ('Oh, and how could they *leave* such a place?' they'd ask), I felt miserable. Like the ghosts which haunt your childhood – slipping into your wardrobe and beneath the bed – you have to face the truth that your worries and your loves will follow you to South Dakota or the South Pole and even outstrip a motorcycle at speed. No choice. You carry it all with you, and always will. Still, many miles away and feeling free as I did, I was able to realize how wise J was to say, with sad pragmatism, 'Houses go on and on – they're just owned by different people.'

And Sturgis was full of different people. I walked up to women leaning against their parked bikes and found out all about them, cheered and inspired by people like 68-year-old Anita Feldman, a retired airline executive, who had ridden her H-D Fat Boy from St Louis – 1,000 miles in two days. Lolling over her yellow bike in a skinny blue camisole, with the face and body of a 50-year-old, she told me about her Drag Racing 'personal best' (for the uninitiated that means reaching a maximum speed over a quarter mile from a standing start) of 110 miles an hour – 'tho' I'm still just learnin', so I'm gonna beat that'. I met 80-year-old Gloria Struck from New Jersey, who joined the women's motorcycle club The Motor Maids in 1946 (the year I was born) and bought herself a new H-D Heritage Softail for her seventy-ninth birthday. On the back of her blue T-shirt was an image of herself on a motorcycle when she was young, with the caption 'A Living Legend'. She told me, 'Life is wonderful at 80. I've made a list of the things I want to do before I die and I'm working through them. I think next is a ride through China.'

There were so many more – women of all ages, all types, married, single, divorced, gay, glamorous, greasy, scary, mothers, grandmothers – all righteously sexy motorcycle mamas. I felt empowered by them, even though I had given up my own riding dream and settled for being the best pillion rider. (And by the way, my guidelines for being the best pillion are a reasonable guide to life in general:

1. Be prepared by reading the road.
2. Move with the bike, with what happens.
3. Never complain.)

Even in the throbbing hubbub of Sturgis I knew that back home in my white study this whole experience would inform everything I wrote. That I would be telling my readers that no matter what shit circumstances throw at you, no matter who hurts you, it's up to you to learn to grasp the handlebars of your own life, face the road ahead and crank up the speed before you die. I heard, *You can, you can, you can*, in the stuttering idle of every mean machine, telling me to catch life by the throat.

One day we rode out to the Full Throttle Saloon, 'America's No. 1 Biker Bar', just outside town, where cars are not allowed. Back home only our biker friends Al and Sue would have understood this wild place; everybody else I know would have deemed it another circle of hell – and that fact added to my feeling of a new identity. I felt a strange impulse to introduce myself as a biker lady called 'Bonnie Mooney', morphing into my dog. But I never did. The bar was in fact an enormous corral full of heat and dust and the endless roar of Harleys and thousands of bikers drinking beer and generally hanging out and having a good time. Old chairs and sofas to loll on. Stalls selling things like the purple zebra-striped cowboy hat I had to buy. Smell of burning rubber and fried food. Blue smoke drifting on hot air. Big men watching pretty women wearing underwear and leather chaps. A glamorous 40-year-old real estate agent called Jessica, wearing a black bra, mini skirt and white ankle socks rolling into the corral on her 8-foot long chopper, loving the stares. Everybody with attitude, and yet the sum total of attitude becomes camaraderie. We were a pack: an insanity of bikers.

On the stage a heavy band was led by a rock chick called Jasmine Cain: beautiful, talented and tough with bare midriff, jeans and long, flying hair. She played the mostly male crowd with that splayed-leg, come-on-and-try-me stance as she hit her guitar and they roared – dogs howling for the moon. And her lyrics cut through the scream of bikes and guitars and people, words that made me want to raise a fist in exultation. The song was called 'Not Gonna Turn Back' and Jasmine was singing just for me:

I never will give up
I've sacrificed too much
I'll stand and I'll face it I might get burned
but I'm not gonna turn back now
Push me down
And I'll get back up . . .

With a Budweiser cold against my hand, thinking of all that had happened, I was saying to myself, Yes! I would rather be here, listening to Jasmine in all this infernally cool chaos than in any of the great opera houses of the world. Yes! I want to ride down Bath's premier shopping street on a massive chopper, wearing cowboy boots and black leather.

This retrospective rebellion was changing me from the feminist who would disapprove of all the blatant sexism to somebody who didn't care. Nearby, a plump young girl with bare breasts was astride a slowly bucking pony-skin-covered bronco machine, trying to keep her seat while a bunch of men watched avidly, hot puppies with their tongues hanging out. Next to me, a woman in her thirties turned and shrugged, saying, 'I think of it as an anthropological study. I mean … *guys!* Show them tits and they're hooked. Can you imagine *us* standing around for hours in case we got a sight of cock?' We were convulsed with laughter.

A blonde girl called Kelly was serving beer at one of the rudimentary open-air bars, wearing white panties under leather chaps with a white T-shirt. When she bent to pick four cans of Miller-Lite from the tub of iced water she allowed the water to pour all down her chest, to reveal large, perfect breasts. The guy she was serving gave her a tip; I could almost see his tail wag. Next in line to be served was a woman. The two girls exchanged grins as Kelly murmured, 'It's easy!' She reminded me of a playful Bichon, all white curls and curves, who knows how beautiful she is and how readily men can be manipulated.

At last, somewhat relieved, we left the trailer, the Harley and the noise, to become different people yet again: tourists in a rental car admiring the sights and wildlife of South Dakota.

Wild burro, mustangs and Buffalo under Ponderosa pines. Silence of Wind Cave National Park, and a host of prairie dogs – who reminded us of Bonnie. The little creatures stood by their burrows, front paws dangling, giving out their strange cheeping squeak of warning as they rear up. (Sometimes Bonnie dances on her hind legs, paws in the air, attacking my playfully raised fists. Attagirl! I think, take it on! Attack that air!) Towards the end of the two weeks we were longing to return home. Robin pointed out that an additional plus of having a dog you love waiting is that you always want to go home. The dog creates the home. The dog represents that part of you which never really went away.

The last thing I did in Rapid City was buy Bonnie a Harley-Davidson collar, lead, T-shirt and peaked cap. Which was about as far away from the biker-cool of black leather and Sturgis, and equally as unacceptable to any English notions of style and dignity, as it was possible to be. But why should I care? A part of recovery is learning not to care what people think, to recover the true self. And if my true self was shaped by poetry, by motorcycles, by a lapdog, by rock 'n' roll, by chamber music, by family, by freedom and by countless complicated feelings including loving two very different men – so what?

J and I saw each other from time to time, of course. We had lunches in London, and sometimes in Bath, but not very often. Not as often as we thought we would. It was always unsettling to see each other because of the impossibility of ever saying what we felt. Yet we both knew – and so felt relieved to talk about broadcasting and writing as we had done for so many years. Then we would hug goodbye and stride off in our different directions. That's how it is.

All the things I was doing – from developing the style of *The Times* column (to the degree that soon strangers would stop me in the street to talk about it), to sitting in Bonham's auction house in Bond Street, wearing (I who had never given a damn about designer labels) a Missoni jacket and hat, and bidding for pictures – were still acts I observed from a distance as if carried out by an assured stranger. Sometimes I wondered where the persona I was accustomed to – the bespectacled, nervous child in Liverpool, the 21-year-old who did not know that the middle classes she was marrying into call the midday meal 'lunch' not 'dinner' and the evening meal 'dinner' not 'tea', the young wife, the mother of somebody's children – had gone.

Sometimes I wondered if this is a usual effect of separation. Yet I knew otherwise from my letters. Again and again I read about people stuck within their lives as a fly stuck on flypaper twirls helplessly over a void. Men and women wrote asking how to move forward, if indeed there is any place to go. Sometimes the letters caused me the same discomfort as lemon juice rubbed into a paper cut, or the sharp pain from a tooth you cannot help but touch. At the beginning of November, for example, a woman in her late fifties wrote a long letter, the nub of which was this: ' … How can one remain serene in the face of dead and dying family, offspring leaving the nest, the end of a long marriage (my husband left a few months ago) and the feeing that this is it? Everything I lived and worked for and made me happy seems to be disappearing in front of my eyes.' She felt empty, with no faith to console her. Her letter could have come from any one of thousands of people.

This reply shows how closely I was drawing on my own experience. I was talking to myself:

> Like many people, you are overwhelmed by universal sadness. The trigger for these feelings was the departure of your husband, and most people reading would conclude that you have every right to feel sorry for yourself. Anybody would. Contemplating that void which was so recently filled by the whole rich, bright, multi-faceted construct that is married life, bewilderment is understandable. Some days it must seem that you are battered by a mocking snowstorm of symbolic birthday, anniversary and Christmas cards into which you stumble, cold and alone. And isn't the innocuous photograph album transformed overnight into an instrument of torture?
>
> Most exhausting of all is the retracing of steps in memory, over and over, wondering if there was anything one could have done to pre-empt what happened. And at 4am, we are wakened by the distant laughter of the universe, that we – poor creatures – are doomed to attach so much desperate importance to monogamous personal relationships when they are so unstable.
>
> Sometimes I think we are homesick for our own lives – for the fragrant land of imagining we mapped out when we were young, assuming the route would be clear, that we would claim the welcoming terrain as our own, and live happ— Oh, you know. Then in middle age we discover the limits of cartography – that those 'blue, remembered hills' are as far away as ever, though still close in dreams, still tantalizing us with what might have been. Of course, the

trouble is that we usually think 'should' instead of 'might'. Whereas the genius of the poet A.E. Housman is to acknowledge that it is 'the land of lost content' itself which is our true inheritance.

I'm saying that because I want you first to release yourself from any sense of inadequacy or failure, and realize that your feelings are normal – so much so that there will be many reading this who will completely identify with you, whether they have a spouse or not. Loss is as central to life as growth; they are two sides of the coin. Graham Greene once referred to 'the madness, the melancholia, the panic fear which is inherent in the human situation'. His own faith did not save him from depression, and after all, the great theologian Teilhard de Chardin identified the things that beset us as fear, dread, sickness, old age and death. Religious belief does not necessarily protect you from sorrow; on the contrary it can intensify the feeling of being abandoned. I have to say that most of the questing agnostics I have interviewed over the years for Radio 4's *Devout Sceptics* are not 'stuck' but have worked hard to construct consolations (art, landscape, philosophy, children, a sense of being part of a whole, and so on) to light their way forward into the darkness. I see that imaginative reaching out towards the unattainable as a thrilling, creative act, and the defiant belief in the possible a world view as profound as any religion.

I want you to see your letter, this universal experience which you are sharing with the rest of us, as itself part of the solution. You are not asking, you are giving. It always fascinates me that people choose to go on living, even when they are suffering from depression. Where does that will come from? I suppose it's a simultaneous rejection of the darkness and an innate belief in the self. That is what your letter, sad though it is, already shows. You have already made progress, and your ability to be alone is a key part of this. But what seems to be bothering you most is the sense of being 'ill equipped' to deal with all the problems which beset you – all of which are made so much worse by a terrible sense of emptiness (and anger?) at the destruction of your marriage. You wonder how to repair the loss, fill the void. So if I were to assure you that such a task is actually impossible, would that make you feel less incompetent? You must not use up energy blaming yourself for a perceived inability to do something no one on earth can do.

I will not utter platitudes which seek to diminish the loss currently central to your life. Recently bereaved people feel (for differing lengths of time) that the world has become meaningless. It goes without saying that the end of a marriage is akin to a bereavement, since the structure and meaning of life were so bound up with that other person that a period of mourning is inevitable. Perhaps you might have lost one or two friends because of it (that happens) which adds to your feeling of abandonment. In addition you have endured death within your family, and know this is just the beginning. The knowledge that one's children are growing and moving away is hard enough for many women who are still married; for you (as for the widow) the prospect of the empty nest is made bleaker by the absence of the arm on which you might have learnt to share the experience.

There is absolutely nothing we can do about the changes which happen to us, except to strive to make them happen

> for us. You're on that path, and can have no inkling of where it will lead. I hazard a guess that your children will always view home as where you are, that when (with luck) there are grand-children you will be still be central to the whole family, that the baring of your soul to the mirror in solitude will make you grow – and that one day somebody new may well see how strong and utterly worthy of love you are. But you will have constructed a new life before then, for yourself, by yourself – knowing that without the perception of universal sadness, we would have no means to transform that burden into grace.

As always, on 26 November I lit a candle for our son Tom, who would have been 30. We attach to such milestone birthdays more importance than is reasonable, especially in mourning. What do the numbers matter: seven, 15 or 23 years? Each year you think about how old your child would have been and of the stages he or she would have reached: toddling, nursery, primary school, first love. When a child is stillborn the yearly imagining is all you have, since in 1975 there was no practice (as there is now) of helping parents to deal with the loss by allowing them to see and hold their baby. Our second son was taken away to be disposed of, in the way they did then. The Catholic Church used to consign these babies to limbo since they were born unbaptized (this is no longer the case) and a strange limbo-like stasis does indeed imprison the mother who did not actually view her dead child, as if it might all have been a dream. Many years later I wrote to the hospital to ask what had happened to him and somebody from obstetrics eventually replied to tell me that stillborn babies were cremated in the hospital and their ashes 'scattered on the rose bushes'. I did not remember any rose bushes at St Thomas's. My mind quailed at the image of the furnace consuming detritus.

Still, the thirtieth anniversary did seem meaningful. It made me pause amidst the renewed activity (more travel pieces, giving talks on writing, a big interview with Salman Rushdie, book reviews, the column, the workaholism which usually kept contemplation at bay) to think about memory. I am the only person who *knew* the child I carried for eight months, and when I die that tiny memory of somebody who never drew breath will be gone for ever. I remembered how full of sorrow J was, and how supportive to me, how *good* – throughout an experience which is so hard for any couple that many marriages do not survive the shock, disappointment and grief. Nevertheless the actual date is not at the forefront of his mind as it is mine. I am the keeper of the flame, the candle is its symbol, and it occurs to me (strangely) that the loss was but a preparation for the much bigger conflagration which would set the house on the hillside alight.

I thought it ironic that I should be so full of sadness at the loss of the farm about which I was first so resentful. Night after night I found myself dreaming about the home J and I had created with so many hopes, but about which I complained so often. I grieved for the beautiful things we placed within it, in the sincere belief that we would be there for ever: rare antique tiles, a Victorian flowered lavatory, stained glass. At the same time I could hear J's voice in my mind telling me that, after all, these are *only* things, and no more. I felt anguish at the thought of the hedges he had planted which were growing tall and thick – even though I knew he was right to remind me that they would go on growing, to provide sanctuary for countless small creatures, whether we were there or not. Maybe all this had happened before in another life, and J and I were ghosts already haunting a house full of strangers.

But the trouble is I had placed my faith in the whole edifice, without acknowledging the cracks that had been in it all along. My natural tendency is to dissemble and call it honesty, to evade and pretend to be straight, to manipulate and then look surprised when what I wished for came about. But now I had lost all control. Thirty years earlier I believed that I had been punished for all my sins by the death of my baby. Now, deep down, I felt that our marriage would not have been destroyed, and our home sold, had it not somehow been my responsibility. There were times (let it be said) when I had hurt my husband just as much as he had recently hurt me.

The furniture and objects he did not want and I had no room for were stacked in the barn I had made into his games room – to be carted off to the sale room. Our children were summoned to remove some of their possessions. Knowing the rooms I knew so well (stone by stone, plank by plank) were being emptied made me weep afresh. Understanding why J was moving, I still railed against him in my heart for not wanting to preserve the precious relics. On the surface my life was good, but underneath the impending sale of the farm had a deep effect, which I kept hidden, because a brave face was my stock in trade. I was afflicted by a lack of trust in everybody and everything. One thing surprised me – I simply could not bear to listen to the soprano voice, whoever was singing. I would shiver and snap the radio off.

My notebook from this time is full of sorrow, with an obsession with home and with loss running through. My certainties had gone and it was lonely without them. Why would you place any trust in human love, I thought? Friends disappoint and work too will one day fade, your professional world not wanting you any more. How did I know Robin would stay with me? How did I know my children wouldn't abandon me when I am old? When you reach another ending in such a short space of time (the marriage, then the home) you glimpse, as if a curtain has parted on an empty stage, all the other endings which stretch ahead.

Still, this much I trusted, without consulting tea leaves or my own line of fate. The one thing you can always be sure of is that your dog will recognize you, no matter which mask you wear.

Your dog will know your voice, even when all you can utter is a cry.

Your dog will love you no matter what you have become.

No matter where you are, your dog will welcome you home.

Five

GROWING

It is a strange thing, love. Nothing but love has made the dog lose his wild freedom, to become the servant of man.
D.H. Lawrence, 'Rex'

Robin, who is fascinated by the art of animation, particularly likes Betty Boop – but especially now, because of her small white dog, Pudgy. They remind him, he says, of his 'girls'. Betty and her pet sit atop our fridge in the guise of a salt and pepper set, by the kitchen sink holding washing-up tools, and also in my study as a funny resin ornament I bought in Brussels. Here Betty is wearing exactly the sort of glittery purple dress I might choose. Naturally Robin is correct to identify me with Ms Boop – a woman whose appearance (high heels, big earrings, tight clothes) belies dark, existential depths ('Ohhh, Pudgeee, what shall we *dooo*?').

My dog is, of course, a ringer for Pudgy, if you discount the black markings which, in any case, the animators sometimes forgot. I love Betty's squeaky crooning over her little 'Pudgy-

Wudgy' in a language I understand, while Bonnie entirely sympathizes with Pudgy's aversion to baths and his jealousy of any interloper, even Betty's fox fur. What's more, when the little dog first appears in 1934 as 'Betty Boop's Little Pal' he is scooped up as a stray by the dog catcher and hauled off with other lost hounds. Naturally they make a break for it and he finds his way back to Betty, to lick her face in ecstatic reunion as the black screen circles in on them, signifying the end. And so I recognize my dog and me, prefigured seven decades before we met. Pudgy is lost, then found – and spends the rest of his cartoon life getting into scrapes of course, but watching out for Betty, attacking anything that might threaten her, and (of course) having fun.

Yet there is an intriguing puzzle at the heart of Betty Boop – another of those questions about identity. For Betty started life *as* a dog. Within that moon face beneath black wavy hair is a memory of the canine soul. In 1930 the Fleischer Studios (the only serious rival to Disney at the time) produced a 'talkartoon' called *Dizzy Dishes*. It contains a night-club cabaret scene packed with animals in which an unnamed female dog sings. It is only a walk-on role. The animator Grim Natwick who created her (and animated most of *Snow White* for Disney) explained that he just designed a little dog and put feminine legs on her, and long ears using a French poodle as the basic idea for the character. A year later this canine creation appears in another cartoon, as the abandoned wife of Bimbo the gun-totin' dog, a bandit who holds up a train full of oddball animals. Unfortunately for him, his wronged spouse turns out to be one of the passengers. Mad as hell, she whips out a photograph of his 17 kids and whups him into submission. I like that.

This virago is recognizable as Betty, but she still has dangling ears and a tiny button nose. Her jowls may have lessened slightly since *Dizzy Dishes* but she is still the humanoid dog, with a deep voice too. But the following year the Studios produced *Stopping the Show* as the first cartoon with the Betty Boop name on it, as well as the theme tune 'Sweet Betty', which was to introduce ever-single Boop animation. In *Stopping the Show* Betty has metamorphosed (who knows why?) into the iconic, oddly innocent sexpot familiar from a million dollars' worth of merchandise. The ears have become dangling earrings, she is a human cabaret artist performing impersonations to a huge audience of cheering animals – and a star is born, trilling 'Boo boop be doo'.

I am somewhat obsessed with the idea of transformation – and believe that each one of us is capable of reinvention. That's why I love the Betty story, because to *start* life as a dog (even an animated one) is surely to be a unique repository of metaphorical knowledge. Sometimes we look at our dogs and wonder what is going on in their heads, apart from devotion and desperation, of course. But, you see, Betty understands it all. Just as the legendary Greek seer Tiresias had the experience of living both as a male and as a female, thus giving him unique insight, I like to think that Betty's blend of sweetness and cunning derives from her half-doggy, half-human soul. The world of her early cartoons is populated mostly by jiving dudes in animal form – giraffes, rhinos, monkeys, cats and so on – but Betty is leader of the pack. Her habitual demeanour is surprise, she is always ready for an adventure, quickly forgets wrongs and works to put things right, is naughty and playful and appealing, and always entertains.

Yes, this is the essence of the dog in her.

Robin and I had begun to broadcast our obsession with Bonnie to the world by putting her on our Christmas card. The first one had her outside our garlanded front door, paws up against it, trying to get in (I was hiding inside, of course) but looking over her shoulder at the photographer – who was Robin, naturally. Beside her was a pair of scarlet high heels, as if kicked off by the lady of the house. The words inside said, 'Open up this Christmas – and in the coming year may you never lock the good things out.' It was a professional production, beautifully printed, but still, we half expected our friends and colleagues to mock our madness. Instead they loved the card – and one or two people even suggested we could go into business designing doggy cards. That was not a part of our life plan; nevertheless a different Bonnie card each year, complete with a meaningful message, was to become our trademark, looked forward to by friends. The cards are an outward symbol of how I have changed. The fun we have creating the concept and taking the photograph is obvious, and only a patient dog who loves her human companions would be such a long-suffering model. Yet I was the one who used to opine that the only cards sensible people should send are religious themes in aid of charity. With Robin and Bonnie to help, I could lighten up.

My first job for 2006 was an extended review for *The Times*, analysing memoir as 'the new novel'. There was a pile of books to wade through. Other people's lives. The reading snagged at the edge of my mind, as if I knew that one day I would embark on such an exercise of retrieval in the full knowledge that the truth is tenuous. How can you stop yourself cheating at Patience, and who will know if you do?

I might mistrust my own memories were it not for the diaries, which I cling to now as evidence of how the smallest things can bring light to days of unhappiness: a phone call from my daughter, getting to know her new soldier boyfriend, talking to my son, a shopping trip, a walk with my dog in cold sunshine. Diary entries which patiently state mundane things such as 'went to the supermarket' are as revealing of a life (especially, perhaps, a woman's life) than the angst-ridden musings of teen journals: 'Will I ever find love? What is the point of being alive?' And so on. In the memoirs I was reviewing, the pages of dialogue 'remembered' from childhood bothered me. How could the 'he said …' and 'she said …' have any validity after the passage of years? The writers might as well have been writing novels, or screenplays. The exponents of the 'new life writing' hold that this does not matter, but I remain unconvinced. It seems to me that it is the duty of the memoirist to leave out when necessary, but not to fictionalize.

Writing a diary is a chore, yet, having once abandoned the daily task, I took it up again because it grounded me in events. Otherwise, I sometimes felt, I might float off like an escaped balloon. So 2006 is set down in detail. Robin and I had wonderful holidays in Oman, St Petersburg, South Africa, yet what is far more significant is the record of daily life, delight, despair, divorce. And ageing, of course.

When your life changes radically you can't expect your personal growth to keep pace with events. Most of the time you feel left behind, wailing in the wake, wondering why this or that happened and (worse) why you continue to lack understanding. It astonished me, sometimes, that with the great good fortune of a pleasant house, a caring partner and a job I had grown into like a second skin, I still felt in mourning for the old house, the old marriage, the whole way of being we knew. As I passed the entrance to the farm (with the painted sign I'd commissioned for J, showing Herefords and Lleyns in silhouette), my hands would tingle, itching to flick the indicator and turn in, bumping over the cattle grids towards the 'home' that was now empty and awaiting its new inhabitants. Janus, Roman god of the first month, looks back and forward at once, back to the old year and forward to the new. So it was with me.

The idea that one can be still, yet still moving, is encapsulated in the 1912 Futurist painting which I love, *Dynamism of a Dog on a Leash* by Giacomo Balla. It depicts a dachshund on a silver chain walking beside his mistress. All you see of her are the feet (in heavy shoes and dark stockings beneath a long, dark coat) pounding briskly along. The dog trots to keep up, the chain leash swings with their motion – and each 'frame' of the action is captured in a blur, just as animation was later (paradoxically) to freeze time and create movement. The lady and her sausage dog are like Betty and Pudgy: motion in monochrome. Balla, like all the Futurists, wanted to reflect the spirit of the age by painting the movement of machines, the quantum essence of light, speed, motion. But this painting – of a woman and her small dog with somewhere to get to – represents even more: the forward movement of life itself, which we cannot escape. Small dogs (by virtue of their deficiency in leg length) *move*: they represent all energy, all life – and when I look at the Balla painting, the question I ask is, 'Who is leading whom?' Surely the dachshund has the edge on the lady? He is taking her into the future they will share, for ever linked by their silver chain. Although she may yearn for whatever she left behind, she is driven forward, impelled by the thrust of the universe, on her capable feet.

What choice is there in life? Sometimes unwanted change – and the deep unhappiness it causes – turns out to be the essential journey between two halves of your own soul. You have to make that journey (albeit running on the spot) in order to become more wholly yourself.

At first J and I had assured each other that divorce was not necessary, but things had shifted. Each of us had a new partner (although at the time still with no intention of remarrying) and therefore knew we needed to take a further step away from the past. In February, Robin and I went to Oman for five nights of peace and luxury, and when we returned to cold England the first divorce papers were waiting with the rest of my mail. I know that for some people this is a glorious relief, an essential step towards freedom from a detested marriage and a nightmare spouse. That was not the case with us. I wrote in my diary: '*How strange to think of J and me ending thus. But perhaps it never ends. No – of course not! Unless of course you hate each other, but even then it goes on ... all that you have been, for better, for worse.*'

A week later I walked by the River Thames to Tate Modern to meet him for lunch. It would have been our thirty-eighth wedding anniversary and I wondered if you go on having an anniversary when you are separated. And if so, for how long? Rain swept over the river, wrinkling the surface of the water like a worried brow, and the wind cut through my coat. Inside what is probably London's most popular gallery, a temple to

Modernism, the echoing spaces felt chilly too. I arrived deliberately early to have time to look around, but remembered too late that the last time I visited the few works of genius seemed lost amidst too much meretricious dross. Then I came across an installation by Susan Hiller, called *From The Freud Museum*, and all was redeemed. On each side of a dark room stood a long glass display case, containing about forty-eight boxes in two tiers. Each cardboard box contains a collection of objects, described by the artist as 'rubbish, discards, fragments and reproductions which seem to carry an aura of memory and hint at meaning'. It is not only a nod to Freud's collected objects (still on display in his north London home) but a representation of the many compartments of the human mind.

As you stare at the boxed collections you wonder why they were selected by the artist, knowing all the while that this is as random as archaeology: the shards, the fragments are there because they are there. You can see what you wish, make connections, remember what you wish. I imagine the boxes automatically shutting like eyelids at night, when the lights are switched off and the galleries given to darkness and emptiness. But even when a lid is closed, what lies within is permanently there, safe from dust. This installation fascinated me because I love both collecting and compartments, and used to create box constructions myself, to give to friends. I made one for J for our twenty-fifth wedding anniversary: a shallow lidded box which opened on to 25 little compartments behind glass, each containing miniature *objets* to evoke the year, and with an explanatory booklet hidden at the back. In the darkness of the Susan Hiller room I remembered it. The sudden recall was like a door thrown open on a pool you could drown in.

We met in the crowded restaurant. The windows framed foreboding, the weather getting worse. It is beyond strange to meet someone you have loved for so long, in a noisy public place, as you might meet a colleague. On the other hand, lovers meet that way too, the room disappearing as their eyes meet and they don't dare to touch because the brush of a finger would be too much to bear. It was strange that there was still something of that. We talked about work and our lives and our children and his Sunday programme on ITV and then I told him about the Susan Hiller boxes. I suggested that when we have loved somebody and endured great pain we can decide to put that person away into a box within us and then close it firmly. So we absorb the people we have loved, the things we have experienced, but we have to be safe from them. We have to bless the existence of lids. I even dared to mention Susan Chilcott's name.

I told him what he already knew, that it was 38 years since we had married. He replied that we had had 35 really good years – and I felt a strange exultation, because only we could ever know the depth of truth in that. Despite everything.

Lunch over, at the foot of the escalator we embraced and he walked away. I turned back, into the great Turbine Hall, to see the Rachel Whiteread installation *Embankment*. It was a mistake, because these boxes all but destroyed the good done by Susan Hiller and by the lunch, and plunged me into gloom. Whiteread's translucent polyethylene casts of cardboard boxes – 14,000 of them – stacked like mountains of giant sugar cubes, are about absence, about negatives, about time congealed. I felt something guarded and hostile about the whole piece; its coldness held me at bay. Whiteread maintains that her work is about memory, yet I saw nothing so human in the collection of shining white blanks. I visualized the time when I was leaving the farm and my cartons were stacked in the dining room, all containing precious things, like Susan Hiller's boxes. But this enormous installation seemed to me like nothingness incarnate and almost called into question everything I had ever loved. There seemed no way forward from this. How can you tuck something away when there is no container, simply emptiness made solid?

There was nothing to do but jump into a taxi, calling out, 'National Gallery!'

There I indulged a secret pastime – which is to walk through rooms of pictures in search of dogs, large and small. And I was rewarded. For in a fifteenth-century work called *The Mass of St Hubert* and in Catena's *A Warrior Adoring the Infant Christ and the Virgin* my eyes were delighted by Maltese dogs the image of Bonnie. As always, they made me smile.

Since my solution to all problems is always to keep moving on my silver chain, I had a new project to take my mind off anniversaries and memory. Although I had maintained that I would write no more children's books, there was now a contract for a new series, inspired (of course) by Bonnie. The first one was due in one month and I had not yet begun, but deadlines present no problems for a writer growing old in the trade. As I finished the 8,000-word story of a boy whose fantasy dog is big and rough, but who is forced to learn how to love the tiny Maltese his mother rescues from the dogs' home, I realized that (without thinking it through) I was writing out my life.

The series for which I became known as a children's author, and which took me to countless schools, libraries and festivals, starred a feisty little girl called Kitty who lived in a normal family with two parents and her older brother Daniel. Some of the stories were based on real things that had happened in our family. In time I gave them another baby, called Tom, as if constructing in fiction the life denied to us by our real Tom's stillbirth. In a sense, this merry nuclear family with their squabbles and jokes was old-fashioned; the prevalence of broken families brought a need in children's publishing for a more gritty realism, taking account of dysfunction and divorce.

I could not have predicted that such things would come to form my experience too. In the (implied) back story of the new series the mother has been left by her husband (whose new girlfriend we meet in a later book) and is struggling with the painfully altered life in a new home, with her son Harry. He is beset by conflicting emotions, worrying about his mother, missing their old life with Dad but gradually coming to terms with the new. The cute, small dog brings affection, entertainment and adventure. As each of the six books (written between 2006 and 2009) unfolds it becomes clear that Bonnie is the good angel: the catalyst who leads people to know each other and makes everything better. Most important, she is the means by which the humans relearn love. I knew that few seven-year-olds would interpret the books so overtly; they just need a good story about characters they like. But no matter: I like books which 'teach', no matter how subtly, and I knew that parents reading aloud to younger children would entirely 'get' the positive message of the stories my dog inspired.

* * *

One day I took Bonnie to visit my close friend Gaynor in the north of England. Robin was in France at the ski chalet he owned with two business partners. I hated him being away, and had grown used to him being there at my side, driving me places and generally being indispensable. I've always loved the song from *My Fair Lady* which celebrates (even if wistfully) the realization that becoming accustomed to somebody's face can indeed 'make the day begin'. Robin was certainly 'second nature to me now'. My much-vaunted independence was diminishing, and I was glad. At a service area I stopped to stretch my legs and let Bonnie pee on the grass verge. Suddenly the lead jerked from my hands and she hared away out of sight. I panicked, and ran in the direction she must have taken, horribly aware of all the cars and strangers who presented instant danger to a small white dog.

A couple walking towards me called out, 'Have you lost a dog?'

'Yes,' I panted.

'It's over there,' they said.

I turned to see a big motorcyclist undoing his helmet, clearly bemused to see a white fluffy thing jumping around excitedly at his feet, her lead trailing on the ground. I raced over, just as he revealed his face. Confused, Bonnie froze and shrank back, panting.

'She thought you were my partner,' I puffed, 'because he's got a bike.'

He grinned, perhaps thinking this was a novel way for a middle-aged lady to pick up strange men. But Bonnie's tail was down. She was disappointed not to see the man she loved. So I led her back to my car, and told her she really must learn to distinguish between the whine of a Japanese motorcycle and the sexy rumble of a Harley-Davidson.

People say we can learn a great deal about anxiety in humans from studying dogs. Of course we are very different species, and dogs do not feel emotions like ours, do they? Well, actually they do. They feel depressed and anxious and are usually miserable to be left alone; their lives are marked by disappointment and intense joy, as ours are. They experience jealousy, and grief too. All dog owners tell tales of how their pets anticipate the holiday before the suitcases come out of storage, as if they understood the word 'hotel' and saw the vision of a sun-lounger through your skull. Then there is the terrible anxiety about whether or not they will be taken with you, or to the kennels, or the minder ... To hear the word 'stay' when the human companion is heading for the door is the worst disappointment. It strikes at the canine soul.

Bonnie always knows when I am going out; she reads it from my clothes, but how I cannot tell. The gym kit tells her I will be absent, but so does the smart dress. Perhaps her ability to read my wardrobe is one aspect of her femininity. Clothes apart, a sure sign of my intention is the application of make-up. Then her brow furrows and a terrible intensity possess her tiny frame and sets it quivering with anticipation. All I have to do is look at her sadly and shake my head for her to turn hers away sharply in reproach before allowing her whole body to droop. I always try to reassure her with 'I'm coming back' – just in case she remembers being tied to that tree. Dogs, like babies, suffer from the condition known as separation anxiety and it seems that psychological trauma in puppyhood is largely to blame. Often they are dogs who have been acquired, like mine, from a pound or dogs' home.

According to Dr Nicholas Dodman, professor of veterinary behavioural pharmacology, in his book *The Dog Who Loved Too Much*, anxious dogs usually have the canine equivalent of a dysfunctional human background. Many of them have been left too much alone, as well as, in some cases, suffering outright abuse. Dodman asserts that the relatively modern use of psychoactive drugs to alter animal behaviour 'seems to imply that animals have a psyche (which they do) and that they're prone to mental disturbances similar to the ones that affect people (which they are)'. He draws parallels between problem behaviour shown in dogs and equivalent behaviour exhibited by human beings, and points out that dogs' problems can be studied 'as relevant models of human psychiatric disease'.

Once I would have shaken my head in disbelief at such theories, snorting, 'Hey, come on, it's just a *dog*!' Now I read the experts, and marvel how their collective research experience is backed up by my own. It reminds me of what happened when I gave birth to Daniel in 1974. I knew nothing about babies beforehand and had shown no interest in them. Suddenly the world was full of them: other people's squirming, cooing, dribbling infants which fascinated and enchanted me almost as much as my own. Similarly I will now cross the road to ask about somebody's dog (huge or small) that has caught my eye, whilst encountering Maltese owners, whether in Florida or France, turns me into a babbling fool. If a single small white dog can thus enlarge one woman, is it not reasonable to acknowledge that there may just be a sum total of wisdom and feeling in the canine world, which has a greater potential for good in human terms? That learning from dogs can make us *better*?

The truth is that the more I was exposed to the woes of readers through my *Times* column and the more psychotherapy I studied in order better to equip myself for the task, the more I realized how hopelessly ill equipped most individuals are to deal with relationships. To put it simply, when (in that first summer) my six-month-old Maltese chewed my new children's book and I swatted her with it, making her tremble so piteously, the speed of her forgiveness was superior to any human response. Who, therefore, should I learn from – my dog or people who enmesh themselves in bitterness and recrimination until their souls starve to death? Whenever Bonnie saw J she covered him with joyful licks. Why should I not, metaphorically, do the same?

I often think that nobody should be allowed to have a baby until they have shown themselves fit to care for a pup and that a recognition of the importance of animal welfare should be a part of the moral education of all school children. For by learning more about how animal minds work and what they need, we gain insight into our own humanity. In his brilliant book *The Dog's Mind* the vet Bruce Fogle draws a parallel between the 'primal' need for touch (for example) in young animals and in humans. He describes how baby macaques who were deliberately isolated from their mothers at birth grew up to suffer from 'overwhelming and serious behaviour disturbances', banging their heads and sometimes mutilating themselves. It comes as no surprise to read that 'touch is the earliest and possibly the most important of all the canine senses' so that 'dogs that are deprived of touch will grow to become subordinate, fearful and withdrawn.' Anyone reading that who has had the distressing experience of visiting a children's home will recognize the description.

What's more, Fogle describes the mutual benefit possible when human and dog share this essential craving for physical reassurance. Touching is a two-way street: soothe your dog and it will soothe you. Learn to be soft, kind, giving, and your dog will help the world to send those qualities back to you in spades. All those who use dogs in therapy with old people, sick people and disturbed youngsters know that the truth goes even one step further than Fogle's observation: petting a dog which you do *not* know, but which is trained to respond therapeutically, can often be as rewarding as any session on the couch with a human shrink. Dogs can do this for us. Bred as hunters, guards and companions (to name but three roles), they are above all *helpers*. I suspect we are only just beginning to find out the extent of their capacities, but the important thing is: they respond to praise, example and affection, and the more we give it the more *we* will receive.

I can't separate this awareness from my (increasing) knowledge of how people can behave when a marriage ends. Sometimes it's hard to avoid seeing the humans who write to me as ill-treated dogs (and obviously no insult is intended from the terminology), backing into their lairs to lick their wounds and snarl at anyone who approaches. Some lick themselves so obsessively it becomes self-mutilation. Some display the greedy cunning of the sneaky Border collie who waits until the humans have gone and then jumps up on to the table, scattering the cats to steal their food – as Sam used to do at the farm. Some cower, beaten and whining. Others are angry because of what has been done to them, and never regain trust. Worst of all, some charge each other like savage dogs of war – and at the end of the battle their own children lie mangled and bleeding on the battlefield.

But some will always recall (and dogs have good memories) the best of times, the sublime moments when the air was full of the sweetest smells, the treats tasted delicious and every moment was full of possibility. They remember the mutual touch which gave such pleasure, and the loyalty which was (for a while) its reward. Some fortunate human hounds are locked into that primal 'training', and although they may feel disappointment when suddenly the present reality changes, still they choose to forget the tree they were left tied to – and instinctively summon up all the rest.

Yes, I am so glad to have learned from my dog.

The tail-sweeping, ear-drooping disappointment of the 'No' is something we humans have to get used to as well. Back in 2003, in the middle of the worst of times, when J had gone but few people knew, I had to fulfil an obligation to present the sixth-form prizes at a smart, academic girls' school and – very unhappy and nursing a (not unconnected) hangover – decided to talk to them about the forbidden subject of disappointment, instead of success. 'Girls, you will fail one day!' I said. I told them they should be prepared for it, because failure can help you grow – as in Samuel Beckett's staccato wisdom: 'No matter. Try again. Fail again. Fail better.' So get used to the real world, girls!

The unscripted talk was a hit; I could see the girls were relieved – even if their over-ambitious parents would have preferred a pep talk about university. Then three years after that day I had to come to terms with more disappointments of my own. First I faced the disheartening truth that adult fiction and I would probably part company. My sixth novel, *The Invasion of Sand* (set in Australia and the result of cumulative years of work), had only found a modest publisher and received just one major review (which was excellent). J had always been passionate about this book and could not understand why others did not feel the same; his belief in me had not changed, but now that seemed to me as sad as all my work on a novel into which I had poured my heart. It was tough.

Then Malcolm Love called me to say that the new Controller of BBC Radio 4 had decided not to recommission the interview series *Devout Sceptics*, which we had been making since 1995 and which had won an award for religious broadcasting. Even before it began, I had been a regular contributor to the station since the eighties: interview series, reportage, literary programmes, talks. People would stop me in the street to say they loved listening. Now it was over – and Malcolm and I would work together no more. These are the things you have to face as you get older in a competitive trade: the previous station boss takes you out to lunch and gives your series the prime 9.00 a.m. slot; the new man is not interested. It's tough too. But that's how it is in journalism and you have to face it.

More painful was watching J present his last eponymous Sunday programme on ITV on 7 May. Commissioned by the BBC to make a big documentary series on Russia, with a book deal too, he had to relinquish his political interviewer's chair. Naturally I watched. His guest was Charles Falconer QC, Lord

Chancellor, then Secretary of State for Constitutional Affairs, and close friend of Prime Minister Tony Blair. J was as good as ever, his unique blend of terrier tenacity and perfect manners as much in evidence as it ever had been. Still at the top of your game, I thought. But at the end Charles Falconer surprised him by turning the tables and doing a pre-arranged spoof interview with the presenter, after which the programme showed a montage of his 11-year tenure. Such high spots, such scoops … I felt the familiar surge of pride at his talent. But a second later I realized that was no longer 'mine' to feel. There would be a post-programme party and it was overwhelming to think that I would not be sharing it with him – I who had shared his whole career. He was with another partner now. In comparison with these still-new realities, ephemera like books and radio programmes dwindled to nothing.

Later that afternoon he telephoned to say he felt it all too. Of course.

The lesson of all these experiences is that jobs will come and go, creative work will have varying degrees of success, children will grow up and leave home, marriages may end, precious pets will inevitably die one day just as farm animals have to die … and that is how it is. Just as dogs have to get used to perpetual disappointment (the walks that don't happen, being left …), so do we. There's no escape – other than moving forward yourself with all the changes. Keeping pace. In the words of Rilke, you have to:

Want the change. Be inspired by the flame
Where everything shines as it disappears …

I will not deny the difficulty, but pain does lessen once you have learned to accept. What's more, there is an irony there – that to learn perpetual motion may bring you to a condition of Zen stillness. Like Betty Boop and Balla's dachshund you have to animate yourself in order to survive and, in surviving, you may learn how to 'be'.

There was nothing else to do, after J's last programme, but join Robin in the garden for three hours of punishing labour around Kwan Yin's temple. I slashed at grasses while Bonnie looked on in puzzlement, before retreating to search for the creatures who live beneath the lawn. The terrier in her always lives in hope that she will root them out – and the fruitless, grubby activity never ceases to make me laugh. Florence Nightingale was quite right when she noted the healing properties of dogs: 'A small dog is often an excellent companion for the sick, for long chronic cases, especially ...' Perhaps my ongoing obsession (for that's what it was) with my ex-husband made me a chronic case too.

Just four days later in Dorset I experienced one of those life-changing moments, which led me to realize yet again that you can go on remaking your life, and sometimes need a shock to force yourself to try something new. This was hardly one of those intense spiritual realizations. Instead it was rooted in an awareness of age and the realization that to indulge vanity can be the boldest affirmation, after which I decided that it was time I made myself 'better' in a very particular way.

Robin and I had taken Bonnie to Lulworth Cove for just one night and visited the famous beauty spot Durdle Door, which happened to be voted the best view in south-west England by the readers of a publication that would never be on my reading list, *Country Walking Magazine*. The giant rock archway juts out into the sea far below the cliffs; you descend from the ugly car park to the pebble beach on steep steps cut into the cliff. Bonnie hopped down like a small mountain goat, stopping to look back every few steps to make sure we were following. It was a very hot day. I sat with her on cushiony pebbles listening to the withdrawing roar of the sea, aware that it was shaping that Jurassic coast into strange caves even as I listened: the Portland stone eroded, the rocks crushed, the whole process happening in eons and eons of heartbeats. Although I cannot swim and dislike boats I love to look at water. Perfect contentment would have left me there all day, running smooth stones through my fingers and listening to the waves, with my little dog lying at my side.

Full of energy, Robin had gone to roam about and take photographs. After a while I looked about for him and spotted him on the clifftop, waving. He made a sign of pointing to his watch; we had planned to visit three ancient churches in the area before lunch in Weymouth. It was time to go. Reluctantly I hauled myself to my feet and walked across to where the steps began. I looked up. Bonnie scrambled ahead. The ascent looked impossibly exhausting and after about twelve steps I was puffing and had to stop. Hating all exercise, I had always turned laziness into attitude, and would rarely go for a country walk, even though we had lived amongst beautiful fields since 1980. Suddenly, at Durdle Door, I realized I had become a woman approaching her sixtieth birthday, in a relationship with a man 17 years younger – who was even then standing at the top of a cliff watching her huff and puff as she struggled to join him, carrying (at the end) her tired dog. I kept my head lowered, thinking, I look so old, I feel so old, I look so bloody, horribly, breathily, wretchedly, wrinklingly *old*, at every step. That was the turning point. Robin smiled affectionately at my state when I reached him, chest heaving, face hot and screwed up with effort. I said nothing but hated feeling and looking as I did. As we closed the car doors my thought was, You are a woman any man in his right mind would leave.

We drove to Osmington and walked to the church with Bonnie. Inside we found a 700-year-old font as well as a monument bearing a description of man's life in childlike letters: 'Man is a glass: Life is as water that's weakly walled about: Sinne brings Death; Death breaks the glass: So runs the water out: Finis.'

'Cheerful!' Robin said.

I said nothing. The message got to me.

After that, we went on to a little village called Chaldon Herring, on the edge of Winfrith Heath, called Egdon by Thomas Hardy. On a ridge above the village are the Bronze Age mounds called the Five Marys where, in excavations carried out before 1866, they found a deep chalk-cut grave in one of the tumuli, containing an adult male and female skeleton, buried sitting together, each with stag antlers on their shoulders. What was that about? I knew that stags' antlers have ancient associations with sexuality and fertility and that hundreds were found at the site of Stonehenge. But who were those people who had been buried up on the windy ridge? Was it a committed couple who were sacrificed? Or had they sinned against the tribe? Reading about them in the guidebook made me shiver, as though the spirits of the long-dead were all around, revenants dreaming of coming back to be christened in the church's two ancient fonts.

Our next destination was Winfrith Newburgh, where we intended to admire the gargoyles and stone corbels (we love such things) as well as the two Norman doors. But we found the church all prepared for an imminent funeral, while at the same time local ladies were getting ready for the weekend flower festival. I was intrigued by the twin spectacles of death and mourning, growth and celebration in one tiny church among trees. As we left the village I spotted people wearing black walking towards the church and it was then that the lessons of the whole morning burst like the 'Hallelujah' chorus in my head. I pinched my own arm, saw the signs of age like the rings on a tree or the branches of an antler and thought, *I am alive.*

Four days after that, for the first time in my life, I signed up with a personal trainer for two sessions a week in her ladies-only gym. No longer would I be that proudly indolent lady with flabby arms used only for pouring a glass of wine and turning the pages of a book. I would remake myself. And so it has been from that day until now. When the boxing gloves are donned or the 4-kilogram free weights lifted I know I am still a work in progress, becoming a person I never thought I would meet within my own mirror. My trainer, Debbie Robinson, smiles at how much I have changed – and I know that J would be amazed at this new person I've become. If I were back in the old life I would stride in our beautiful fields with him every single day, answering the perpetual doggy plea for walks. Too late. But that is the point about knowledge, change, regret. They whisper incessantly the message I learned at Carmel

Mission – that you can't go back. It will never come again as it was.

That indeed is what I wrote to J on the day in August when our divorce became absolutely final. It was (as I emailed him):

> *... a very strange feeling because I thought we would be married until one of us died and then probably afterwards too ...*
>
> *But you can't run back through time. You can't change the bad things – but the wondrous side to that coin is, you can't un-write the good things either. And we – unlike so many sad, bitter couples – have not done that, and so we reach this point on our life journey taking different roads but waving to each other across the intervening grass verge. It's a proud testimony, isn't it? So we should always celebrate it. As Dolly Parton sings, 'I will always love you' – and with sweet memories.*

He wrote back immediately, in exactly the same vein.

I was alone in the house, thinking about the past and (as usual) being consoled by my dog. ('*Thank goodness for Bonnie*' is in the diary). Then an impulse made me do an unusual thing. I printed out the long emails we had exchanged and sent them to our son, with a covering letter. You know how it is: we have our children, watch them grow and wave them off into the world, but forget to engage with them as adults in all but the most easy, practical ways. The individual, faltering heartbeat is drowned by family chatter. We forget that you need to go on *showing* them and allowing them to understand you, adult to adult. It was that need to share important truths with one of my children which made me write:

Saturday night
12 August 2006

Dearest Dan
I'm going to scrawl this note and post the letter before I think about it. Enclosed is the email corresp. Dad and I exchanged today. I want you to see it, and keep it somewhere as a testimony to all that your parents had … and have. Because I know it's rare and I write this in tears, so I want you to KNOW.

I don't want you to be cynical about relationships. Read what Dad and I say to each other thirty-nine years after we first fell head over heels in love, and marvel at the miracle. You shouldn't say, 'Because they made mistakes and finally split up, it proves love can't last.' You should say, 'Because they love each other so much in parting, it proves that real, deep love can triumph over all. Even over death.'

Because that's what I believe. Nothing has changed it. And I so want you and Kitty to be proud of your parents – not for any worldly reasons but because we are two flawed human beings who had ideals, betrayed them and each other, yet somehow – as a result of the final, fatal betrayal – achieved some extraordinary private glory. A sort of ideal.

As for the road between Dad and me – the leaves may blow across it but it's as if I could walk that way in a dream and find the path back to our first home together and know that place as if for the first time.

But it's all OK, darling, because we will make it so. We aren't like other people; we never bought into petty possessiveness and corrosive jealousy and (although we got things wrong) we still don't. Your parents both love you and Kitty more than anything and anybody. And now, given that confidence, I want you to forgive us our transgressions and fly freely into your own *destiny.*

With all love
Mum
PS: You can show this to Kitty. I can't write it twice xxxx

So – it was done.

It made me very sad.

One of the most interesting memoirs I read (three-quarters through the writing of this book) was *The Philosopher and the Wolf* by the philosopher and academic Mark Rowlands. The subtitle is 'Lessons from the Wild on Love, Death and Happiness'. Rowlands analyses, in complex detail, his relationship with his 'pet' wolf Brenin, describes how he trained the destructive cub and reflects on how the lessons he learnt from his majestic animal companion served ultimately to transform his personal life – and to go on transforming it even after Brenin's death at the age of 11. If I had feared sometimes that readers might think me somewhat eccentric (or sentimental) to ascribe to small dogs an emotional significance and a moral purpose so much greater than their size, Rowlands has reassured me. He writes of his life with his lupine 'brother': 'Much of what I know about life and its meaning I learned from him. What it is to be human: I learned this from a wolf.'

One of the lessons Rowlands learnt from Brenin is defiance. The wolf bestowed on him the profound awareness that 'it is only our defiance that redeems us.' The epiphany came when he was still a cub, attacked by a pit bull terrier which pinned him to the ground. Instead of squealing in terror, the smaller animal let out a deep growl and the pit bull let him go. That defiance is, I realize, as much a part of my own being as my control freakery, vanity and love of books and art. When things go wrong my inner wolf growls, 'I'll *show* you!', not with malice, just resolve. The small girl from Liverpool still sticks her tongue out at the world, almost with no choice – just as my small dog's tongue lolls out like a scrap of pink felt, because the bottom front teeth have gone. (She is getting older whether I like it or not.) Rowlands takes his cue from the memory of a wolf cub; I take mine from the absurdly small dog who yaps her heart out in defiance of the man in black at the door, disguised as a postman but carrying a scythe.

Getting older too, whether I like it or not … I was approaching my sixtieth birthday, and my response to the strange sensation of divorcing someone I had never ceased to love – indeed to all that had happened in the past three years – was to celebrate. I planned two parties, one in London, one in Bath. The extravagance would say, 'I'm still here, still ready to party, no matter what happens. So there!' When I was 50 I had written two essays about ageing in *The Times* – and here I was again, asked to write about being 60. For the cover of *The Times 2* section Robin photographed me and Bonnie under a scudding sky, on top of Little Solsbury Hill at the edge of Bath. I wore my biker jacket, jeans and purple gloves; she looked like a small cloud briefly tethered to earth.

That evening we set up a second photo shoot at home, given a contrasting style by purple velvet and full make-up. I cooked pasta while Robin edited the pictures. Then, to my surprise, he invited me to go with him out into the garden. It was dark, dank, chilly. My dog and I peered dubiously out of the back door, only to see that he had already switched on the lights which illuminate Kwan Yin in her gazebo-temple at the end of our long garden.

'Come on.'

'Where are we going?'

'To Kwan Yin's house.'

'Why?'

'Just come!'

High heels in damp grass. The dog detests all wetness but will not be left behind. The Chinese goddess glows apricot, with no other lights around. I have no idea what we are doing, but fall silent for once, probably because I love our destination so much. (I have a habit of drifting out to Kwan Yin, stroking her stone face and telling her things.) I am guessing that Robin wants me to look back at the height of the house, where we have been busily preparing for my big birthday party four days away, because his inhabitance of it is so relatively recent and still gives him pleasure.

Instead, once we are in the gazebo beside the statue, he takes a box from his pocket and tells me that this is not a birthday present, and he knows that I have said I don't want to get married again and that (such a long preamble, this) it doesn't matter at all and he won't mind if we never actually get married, but still … 'Will you marry me?' He sounds so nervous. I am totally surprised; the control freak did not see this coming. Bonnie sits and looks up at us and Kwan Yin's smile is serene. I love my two witnesses, and I love the ring – an intensely dark blue opal (they call them black opals) flanked by two diamonds. I recognized it immediately as one I had admired a couple of weeks earlier, walking through Bath with Kitty and gazing in the windows of jewellers as we always do. So my daughter was a part of Robin's great plan. Now he stands looking at me and everything is quiet and I am so moved by this unexpected thing: this gift of steadfastness which (it seems in that moment) only my dog and my statue can match.

'Yes, I will,' I say, not knowing what I have done to deserve this.

'Phew,' he says, with that lop-sided grin.

We go inside to dance to the jukebox and I wonder if it is possible to feel happier. Yet human beings so have a tendency to stand outside the moment, don't we? As soon as it is there, greeted with joy, we consign it to memory and start to worry. For I knew that I had been happy once before, that Robin was 17 years my junior (with all the complications that implies) and that – in my deepest heart – I really didn't want to be called Mrs Anybody again. We were contented just as we were; therefore I saw no need for more change, in the form of an actual marriage. Let's just stay committed, I said, and he agreed. Still, at my birthday party on Saturday 7 October, to my great surprise, the hitherto rather reticent man jumped on the chaise longue in our sitting room and announced to the guests that he had asked me to marry him and I had accepted. Everybody applauded.

The next day was my actual birthday. When lunch was over, and even my children had left for London, and Robin and I had moved all the furniture back, J came to visit me. Robin opened the door, shook his hand and then disappeared to the basement office to give us privacy. J brought a perfect gift: a limited-edition volume of poetry published in 1970, containing work by some of my favourite poets. Bonnie greeted him with a flurry of ecstatic licks and twirls as if he had never gone away – or as if I had never gone away – and everything was the same. That is the beauty of dogs. They carry their old allegiances and affections right at the front of their minds, ready to prompt the always optimistic tail. (Once, I encountered J at Paddington Station – he off the train from Totnes, me from Bath – and he had Sam with him, that needy muzzle greyer now, his hearing failing. Sam remembered me, of course, and the old collie thrust his face into my hand as he had done when he was a puppy and I brought him home for J's Christmas present.)

There is, surely, a choice as to how you choose to view a dog's excitement at meeting one who is no longer part of the pack. It is easy to sigh and say how sad that the faithful animals retain their loves when their humans have hurt each other and the pack is rent asunder. But look at it from the opposite perspective and learn from the small dog – and the old one too. Why not defy human weakness and sentimentality, and rejoice with the dogs at all fleeting reunions? Why not wag our tails and take the past along with us, like an old scent a dog will pick up and recognize for ever?

There was much of the spirit of our shared past in the article which appeared in *The Times* the next day – celebrating becoming 60. In it I made a link between Paul Simon's 'Still crazy after all these years' and Bob Dylan singing 'Forever Young' on Planet Waves, suggesting that if you can achieve the former then the latter will follow. The article goes on:

If the miracle were possible, why wish to be forever young? Crazy indeed to be deluded – spending more and more money on face cream and clothes, to hide 'the skull beneath the skin'. So let me get the vanity stuff out of the way, because it's not what this is about. In the sixties I had Quant hair, in the seventies long hair; in the eighties it was Big, in the nineties scrunched – and now I have plughole hair. Not good. I've had botox twice, and 'filler' injected into my smile lines and cheeks – all to write about, I must add. I've never paid for the stuff, but I'm quite prepared to, because I like the difference it makes, and hate the way certain newspapers delight in 'exposing' women who have 'confessed' to a bit of help, as if they'd been caught out touching up teenage boys behind the bike shed. The extremes of cosmetic surgery are sad, but if women (and men) want to 'prepare a face to meet the faces that they meet' (to quote T.S. Eliot) – where's the harm? It's a statement about life, not mere terror about aging and death. It winks at the guy with the scythe, chuckling, 'Not yet, baby!'

Somebody asked recently, 'What's the secret of staying youthful?' and I mumbled something about always be ready to reinvent yourself. But that implies putting on masks, trying to switch your selfhood as you might redecorate a room. Of course, it's meaningless. What is important is to ADD all the time, opening yourself to new experiences, never allowing yourself to congeal, always topping up the sum total of who you are, surprising yourself. Instead of saying 'One door closes, another opens,' you fling open ALL the doors. The truth is, never before have I felt such a powerful passion for life. I relish the biker-hen look one day and boho chic the next – because it's all authentic: the multi-faced self ...

The universal story is of aging; what I can bring to it is my own narrative. We baby-boomers are surely the luckiest generation. Born in 1946, we imbibed post-war relief and optimism with our mothers' milk and experienced a safe and structured childhood during the undervalued fifties. I was brought up in a Liverpool Corporation flat by young parents who demonstrated by example that if you worked incredibly hard you might one day be (almost) as good as 'them' (meaning, the ones with class, money, power). You stuck with what you started, did your homework, never whined over knees grazed in a hopscotch tumble, and accepted rules and hierarchies just as our medieval forebears accepted the Great Chain of Being. We had serious public libraries (which fed me), ultra-clean hospitals ruled by fierce matrons, and rigorous schools like my crowded state primary, Northway, which saw a top class of 50 all pass the 11 plus. As a clever child, I had to listen to younger, very poor 'D' stream children read aloud. Smelling neglect and feeling instinctively that it wasn't fair, I realized I was lucky. My home wasn't wealthy, nor always harmonious, yet love sat on the table with the bottle of tomato ketchup. Each day now I give thanks for that upbringing, as much as for all I possess.

Idealism born of a sense of gratitude – did that fuel us baby-boomer protesters? Liberated by the late sixties and early seventies we preached tolerance and challenged the old structures in as many ways as we could. For me CND and Movement for Colonial Freedom at 17, then feminism, then anger at Vietnam, racism, then Labour Party membership – all seemed much more significant than the so-called 'Summer of Love', in a world that was changing more rapidly than our parents could have predicted. When I became a journalist it was because I believed that writing could improve the world – you would tell it like it is, write passionately about the disadvantages which weigh people down, and then somebody with power would say, 'Hey, we'd better change that.' It's easy to be cynical now and say, 'No such luck,' and since 1946 history does show that human beings can take the long, slow road to improvement; 'things can only get better' indeed. There's no space to list the acts of parliament and liberalization of attitudes, but no amount of disillusionment or despair should blind us to progress …

I confess I went through a period of quiescence and complacency, enjoying the ivory tower; but as Dylan sings, '… I was so much older then,/ I'm younger than that now.' For I've returned to feeling that things can – and must – be fought for. If you don't cherish, deep in your soul, the conviction that things ought to be made better, you die slowly inside. It can happen to people in their twenties; we all meet them sometimes – so much older than they should be. It may seem crazy to cling to idealism when proofs to the contrary come in every day, but don't forget that crazy can mean 'mad' too – and the things that make me mad as hell drive all fluffiness away. Bad parenting; indifference to the environment; all fanaticism, racism, tribalism; greed – in whatever corner of the globe it raises its ugly, bloated head; the assumption that people cannot be stretched; cruelty and cynicism; selfishness and defeatism … need I go on? 'Cry shame' said Martha Gellhorn – and never before has Yeats's famous line seemed more true: 'The best lack all conviction while the worst/Are full of passionate intensity.'

When I was fifty I wrote a piece for this newspaper which said 'I didn't plan it this way. I wasn't supposed to get old.' Well, the good news is – I didn't! Things didn't work out the way I thought they would, but I celebrate the fact that you can come through a divorce with mutual love and respect, and work out pain, sorrow and regret, murmuring 'That's the way it was fated to be – dammit – but now let's move on.' And I know that somewhere in a trailer park in Arizona, or a block of flats in Marseilles, or a village outside Kampala, or a cottage in the Highlands, a woman is weeping because she has lost what she thought would last – that whatever the differences in our lives, we are the same. I celebrate the will to challenge corruption and war-mongering, and Susan Sarandon's rebellious victory sign at the Oscars, and Bob Geldof's endless, mouthy championing of the poor in Africa. I celebrate 'love thy neighbour' as the only way to live, and admire those who preach it.

You see, somebody has to speak out, and up. Always. That faith keeps wrinkles on your mind at bay. You're rejuvenated by the absolute certainty (even after six decades of life and so much experience) that the good ones are always beavering away, never giving up – real heroes, people brave in body and soul, humans full of love and compassion, whose deeds outweigh the evil. It makes me throw back my head with joy – because I am young again.

Re-reading those extracts now I realize how much the spirit of my life with J shines in every sentence. Although we will not descend into querulous age as a couple we were young and passionate together, and that is all that matters. He – idealistic philosophy student and angry young journalist (inflamed by all injustice) – played such an important part in moulding the better side of me and nothing can alter that.

I was busier than ever: interviewed Gordon Brown twice for a 4,000-word *Times* profile, did events at literary festivals, reviewed books, was a guest presenter on Radio 4's *Something Understood*, answered people's problems, learned to feel slightly less depressed about them, took part in discussions for *Woman's Hour*, went to South Africa with Robin to write a travel piece, prepared and delivered a keynote address for PEN for the Day of the Imprisoned Writer inspired by our visit to Robben Island, wrote a piece on angels for *The Times* and various comment pieces for the *Daily Mail*, signed letters as President of an appeal for a new neonatal intensive care unit in Bath … and on, and on. Through the years of marriage I used to shake my head to friends at J's workaholism, and now it was as if I had learned it at his knee.

'*Friday December 8: It's exhausting, but how can I make 2007 different? Too busy for everything has become an unwelcome mantra. I had a pain in my chest when I went to the gym. Stress? I feel old and stiff and too tired to play with Bonnie.*'

As Christmas drew nearer and I made all the usual lists and preparations something happened which inevitably disturbed me. J wrote to tell me what I had already heard from our daughter: that he and his partner were expecting a child. His letter was short but beautiful – and loving. Which made the news it contained even harder to bear. I picked up my dog and stared out of the window at the wintry garden and took several deep breaths. Robin was away; there was only the dog to tell. It was the day of our local parish Christmas craft fair which I had planned to support, determined to spend money in aid of the church, even though at such events there is often little I really want to buy. But now I wanted to hide in my house with my dog and not see a soul. Yet my church-going (admittedly only about one a month) had become strangely important to the questing agnostic who had made so many *Devout Sceptics* programmes. Stepping out of our front door and looking to the right I see the Victorian church tower; during the strange months after moving to my new house alone I had found refuge in St Stephen's and its thriving congregation. It made me feel that I belonged somewhere again. So why should J's news stop me doing what I had intended to do, which was not to let the organizers of the craft fair down? Surely I was made of sterner stuff ...

Making yourself go out, you are forced to don a smiling mask, and when people ask, 'How are you?' you inevitably answer, 'Fine!' That lie can move, by degrees towards a truth. There is research which shows that if you make yourself smile a lot you will actually cheer yourself in the end. So I walked around greeting my neighbours and buying second-hand books I did not want. Then came the shock. In one corner of the basement community centre an elderly lady was selling her own old-fashioned, lacy hand-knits for babies, most of them in rather ugly colours – artificial pink, saccharine blue, screaming citrus. Nobody was buying the clothes and I felt sorry for her. I stood staring down at the tiny jackets and bootees and suddenly the room swam, and I didn't know what to do. The size of the garments, the memory of being pregnant with Dan, the thought of Tom, baby Kitty's ill health, my longing for a grandchild, the sense of how unfair it all is ... all overwhelmed me on this the day of J's important piece of news. It was like a panic attack. I could not move.

Do so many men (I wondered) leave their wives for younger women because of their powerful, instinctive need to go on having babies? In one sense, who can blame them? With Robin away in France there was nobody to talk to about these things, nobody to wail with ... that *we* could not be so blessed. But the truth is, gaining control as I stood there, surrounded by Christmas decorations, home-made cakes, cards and jam and the murmur of good people, I felt neither real sorrow nor anger, but just a flat, bedded-down *angst.*

What can be done?

Then I found the thing to do. I picked out a cardigan, unusual for being white and plain, and bought it for them. How pleased the old lady was to get a sale. And how pleased I was to go home to Bonnie, wrap the small garment immediately before I could change my mind, address the parcel – and by those actions begin the process of acceptance.

Six

UNDERSTANDING

A little Dog that wags his tail
And knows no other joy
Emily Dickinson, 'A Little Dog that Wags his Tail'

Cruising along the M4 at night, the moon low in the east like the end of a lit cigar, Ray LaMontagne's breathy agony filling the car, I wonder idly if all the words from all the centuries' sorrowful poems and songs of love, placed end to end, would reach to that indifferent, orange moon. Robin and I had just seen *Treats* at the Theatre Royal Bath, with Billie Piper starring in Christopher Hampton's bitter comedy about the eternal triangle, in which the good man is ditched for the bastard (as so often they are – or the good woman left for the siren) and you know it must end in tears.

More tears.

'Life is long, my love is gone away from me,' moans Ray – and for sure he will be listened to by a million lost souls who know what that is like. It is easy to immerse yourself in such a mood. On the other hand (as I often tell readers, since advice columnists must offer some encouragement, even when the individual case does sound pretty hopeless) love can possess an extraordinary, surprising resilience too – not so much a melancholy moon as a rubber ball, bright orange and still bouncing.

As an old-fashioned children's reading book might say:

Here is the ball.
Watch the small dog run after it.
Watch the lady pick up the ball and jump.

Displacement works in many ways. Sometimes self-indulgent melancholy can be driven away by indignation. So it happened that, at the beginning of 2007, I was refusing to brood on J's impending marriage, mainly because those who sniped at the fact that he was marrying a very much younger woman enraged me so much I found myself entirely on his side. The incontinence of comment (on the web and in newspaper columns) is one of our age's most bizarre pollutants: everybody has an opinion, and the meaner the better. Who are they, these people who get out of bed only to log on to this website or that, or read newspapers online, in order to spew their ungenerous comments about anybody they might have read about, or heard on the radio or seen on television? Desultory venom and vitriol hold sway. Is it living a life, to use up your precious time thus? Even chat rooms set up to offer mutual help (for mothers at home, for example) too often degenerate into gossipy snippets about this celebrity or that, crowding out thoughtful responses to each other. Sometimes (especially reading BBC online comment) I'm reminded of packs of starving, snapping curs. Of course, I do understand that curs usually get nasty because they haven't been taught any other way.

It was the same when J's new daughter was born that summer, and again 18 months later, when he and his wife were expecting their second child. There seems to be a widely held assumption that there is something perverse and/or pitiable in (a) an older man fathering a child (b) a younger woman wanting to be with an older man and then conceiving a child, and (c) a child being born to such a mismatched couple, when Dad will look like a grandfather and all too soon pop off to meet his Maker – at which point he will be eternally damned for the sin of loving. Or so the critics would have it, rubbing their hands in glee and chortling all the way to the guillotine.

The confusing, painful, dazzling truth – that life is infinitely various and coloured in many shades of grey – passes such commentators by. I realize that Chaucer too made merry with the idea of 'January–May' marriages, but they happened then, as now, the world over, and were/are often successful. If any young woman is forced or cajoled into a reluctant marriage with *any* man of any age (and they so often are, in other cultures) that should spark indignation. On the other hand, observation tells us that young fathers all too often neglect and abuse their children, then move on to repeat the pattern, whereas a man in his fifties or sixties with a second chance at fatherhood usually makes the most tender, intelligent and attentive of parents. I like to imagine a world where all our birth certificates were lost and so we presented ourselves each to each unfettered by chronology – when some people in their twenties would come across as more mature than some born-again teenagers of fifty.

In any case, what can I – happy in a relationship with a younger man – say, but that the issue of age is a distraction from the complicated truth about love? Which is that you never know how or when it will strike. That's what Ray LaMontagne is singing about on all his albums. That is why Edith Wharton asked, '... how many of us could face each other in the calm consciousness of moral rectitude if our innermost desires were not hidden under a convenient garb of lawful observance?'

This was the point in my life when I realized how important it is to avoid ossification. Just a year earlier, with my sixtieth birthday beckoning, I had announced to my children that I was not interested in mobile phones (except to call an occasional taxi), would never text because it was something else to have to think of, and could not see the point of iPods. Anyway, how did such things *work?* Why would I *learn* all this stuff, I asked – not understanding that such attitudes are as ageing as out-of-date clothes. They are the dreaded wrinkles on your mind.

On the other hand, an important process had begun with the unlikely exercise regime, and my constant message to readers was (and is) that you *can* change yourself. There is no need to be stuck in the selfhood that used to own you.

So, halfway through 2007 I was crossing Regent Street in London, stranded on a traffic island in the middle of the two lanes, having just purchased my elegant white iPod (which of course I knew how to work, since by then I wrote listening to iTunes) from the Apple Store, when my mobile phone (now full of texts sent and received) played its jazz riff. It was a journalist from the *Daily Mirror*, asking me for a comment on the fact that my ex-husband's baby daughter had just been born. The buses roared, the taxis did their U-turns; no time to stop and think, just to speak truly: 'There's only one thing to say when a healthy baby is born to two loving parents and that's … Wonderful.' I expect they wanted a terse rejection (what volumes are spoken by 'no comment'!) but to my surprise my quote was printed. That serves to confirm my innate optimism (one of the qualities I share with my small dog) that every now and then, a small voice bringing simple, good news will be allowed to be heard over the din.

Did I ever ask Robin if he was jealous that J and his wife could have a baby? No. But was I certain that he would have loved a child and would have made the most perfect of fathers and did that make me sad? Yes. Would I, in fantasyland, dream of having a child with him? Oh, a thousand times yes. Would we follow the example of desperate people who seek options like surrogacy or overseas adoption, at enormous financial, emotional and even moral cost? No.

Because, after all, we have Bonnie.

The American psychiatrist Aaron Katcher says that pet owners look upon their pet dogs as 'four-legged Peter Pans caught between nature and culture'. Their nature tells them that they are dogs, and they expect their human companions to act like dogs – play, hunt together, sleep in the same den and so on. Yet we expect our dogs to take the place we have allotted them within our human culture – to be biddable, decorative, loyal and so on. We need small dogs, especially, to be our dependents. John Steinbeck expresses his distaste for this human need in *Travels with Charley*, the quirky, charming book about a road trip with his dog:

> *I yield to no one in my distaste for the self-styled dog-lover, the kind who heaps up his frustrations and makes a dog carry them around. Such a dog-lover talks baby-talk to mature and thoughtful animals, and attributes his own sloppy characteristics to them until the dog becomes in his mind an alter ego. Such people, it seems to me, in what they imagine to be kindness, are capable of inflicting long and lasting tortures on an animal, denying it any of its natural desires and fulfilments until a dog of weak character breaks down and becomes the fat, asthmatic, befurred bundle of neuroses. When a stranger address Charley in baby-talk, Charley avoids him. For Charley is not a human: he's a dog and he likes it that way.*

Reading that makes me guilty, because I talk baby language to my dog and swear she likes it. What else would I think? The smaller the dog the more we are likely to treat it like a surrogate child. This is not to infantilize, in the sense of treating them in such a way that it denies their dignity – because the very concept of such maturity is not relevant to a small dog. When Bonnie was six months and had just come to live with me, a friend picked her up and, feeling her featherweight fragility, exclaimed, 'Oh, she's a permanent puppy!' You cannot (easily) pick up a Labrador to cuddle, but the small dog always remains the right size, whilst our innate instinct is to make the same sounds to any small animal as we do to babies. That the small animal is in fact *old* has no bearing on the way it looks.

Neoteny is the existence of juvenile features in an adult animal, the word coined in the late nineteenth century from *neo* (new) and the Greek *teinein* (to stretch). So newness of youth is stretched out into adulthood, and it is thought that any lapdog breeds were bred specifically to retain puppy-like traits, like short legs and relatively large heads. They may also have traits which resemble human babies, like high foreheads, short muzzles and relatively large eyes. Some small breeds resemble the puppies of larger breeds, for example, a papillon, like some spitz-type breeds, possesses the facial characteristics of an infant wolf. There can be no doubt that *some* of these puppy-like traits are the result of selective breeding, and although such breeding is controversial my point is only that such characteristics contribute towards the particular relationship between the adult human and the small dog. To put it simply, the dog is permanently *cute*. Therefore you want to baby it.

Me and many others. In January 1920 the writer Katherine Mansfield wrote to her husband, literary critic John Middleton Murry, from Menton in the south of France, where she was convalescing from the tuberculosis that was to kill her. Mansfield's stories were the first in England to show the influence of Chekhov, whom she greatly admired. Her letter to Murry shows a keen observation of a lapdog in action which surpasses that of the author of the famous short story I quote in my first chapter:

> *Connie came yesterday to see me, carrying a baby Pekinese. Have you ever seen a really* baby *one about the size of a fur glove – covered with pale gold down with paws like miniature seal flappers – very large impudent eyes & ears like fried potatoes?*
>
> *Good God! What creatures they are … We must have one. They are not in the least pampered or fussy or spoilt. They are like fairy animals. This one sat on my lap, cleaned both my*

> *hands really very carefully ... His partner in life when he is at home is a pale blue satin bedroom slipper. Please let us have one ...*

One stillbirth and two further miscarriages (or abortions) and a tempestuous private life did not equip Katherine Mansfield for motherhood. She desperately wanted Murry's child but couldn't achieve it and constantly grieved over the reality. She and Murry consoled themselves with fantasy children – which he went on to have with other wives after her death. He was woefully ill fitted for fatherhood; neither was he a husband any woman would want, not even (at times) Katherine. Into that innocent paragraph about someone else's baby dog I read so much unfulfilled longing it is hardly bearable.

Sometimes we pity those who turn their dogs into child substitutes, sometimes we mock them instead. That genius of the short story O. Henry wrote a hilarious first-dog narrative (*Memoirs of a Yellow Dog*) which gets inside the head of a 'babied' pooch: 'From that moment I was a pet – a mamma's own wootsey squidlums. Say, gentle reader, did you ever have a 100-pound woman breathing a flavour of Camembert cheese ... pick you up and wallop her nose all over you, remarking all the time ... "Oh, oo's um oodlum, doodlum, woodlum, toodlum, bitsy-witsey skoodlums?"'

Because, in the pre-Bonnie era, I had shown no interest in matters canine, I was initially embarrassed that my dog inspired such nonsense-talk in me. I believed that lapdog mania, with all its attendant accessories, was a modern phenomenon. But my recent researches have brought me relief, as well as justification. The urge to pet small dogs is centuries old, and there is nothing new about turning a dog into a child substitute. In 1896, for example, *The Strand Magazine* (which first published Arthur Conan Doyle's Sherlock Holmes stories) ran a long article (uncredited, as was the norm) about an establishment called the Dogs' Toilet Club in New Bond Street, London. This canine beauty and fashion parlour was patronized by wealthy ladies who might buy a travelling leather kennel at 10 guineas or the latest dog's driving coat – the Lonsdale – made to measure, in fawn cloth, lined with dark red silk, finished off with two gold bells and a fur collar.

This makes Bonnie's wardrobe seem restrained.

The reporter documented that sometimes 'an aristocratic mistress' would say that she wished to see her precious pet bathed and throw herself on the dirty floor near the bath ('unmindful of her eighty guinea dress') and 'keep up a running fire of oral consolation – Now, it won't last long, Birdie. Ah, 'oo's all dripping wet, little darling, but 'oo'll soon be d'y. Don't pull Birdie so, naughty man!'

The article ends with a gently ironic paragraph, economical in its social satire yet as damning as any of the bludgeons used by some contemporary journalists: 'In conclusion, it may be said that pet dogs are treated by their mistresses almost precisely as though they were human members of the family; the only discrepancy in the analogy being that it is horribly bad form for a lady to drive in the park with her baby by her side, while the presence of a pompous pug or toy terrier is irreproachably correct.'

In July 1859 such a pug came into the life of my favourite novelist, George Eliot (born Mary Ann Evans, in 1819, and later calling herself Marian Lewes). The dog made the entirely serious woman laugh. She was so overcome with delight at the delivery of her new pet that she suffered a failure of grammar and wrote 'Pug is come!' to her publisher, who gave her the pet. And couldn't she who created so many living, breathing fictional characters (Silas Marner, Adam Bede and the rest) come up with something more imaginative as a name than 'Pug'?

George Eliot's novels are full of dogs. She uses them as subtle pointers to the character of human protagonists. For example, near the beginning of *Middlemarch*, over-serious Dorothea Brooke is being courted by the handsome Sir James Chettam – a catch in any woman's eyes. One day he appears 'with something white in his arms ... which was a tiny white Maltese puppy, one of nature's most naïve toys.' But Dorothea sniffs, 'It is painful for me to see these creatures that are bred merely as pets,' and goes on, 'I believe all the petting that is given them does not make them happy.' It gets worse: 'They're too helpless; their lives are too frail. A weasel or a mouse that gets is own living is more interesting. I like to think that the animals about us have souls something like our own, and either carry on our own little affairs or can be companions to us like Monk [a St Bernard]. Those creatures are parasitic.'

What can I say but foolish, deluded Dorothea! George Eliot uses the dog to highlight her lack of judgement, and condemns the young woman who dismisses the Maltese (with its infinite subtlety and generous soul) to a terrible marriage with the arid, pretentious, loveless old stick Casaubon, whom she thinks is a man of insight and intelligence. She who can't comprehend the companionship of small dogs is doomed to life with a man who mistakes a wife for a secretary. Whereas her sweet sister,

Celia, lover of tiny terriers, gets the handsome, rich, affable man as well as the rejected Maltese.

Dogs populate the pages of Victorian fiction – which is perhaps not surprising given the Queen's well-known love of dogs. Yet George Eliot has a uniquely strong sense of the relationship between animal and human, 'the glance of mutual understanding'. Her letters reveal how her relationship with her own pug ('transcendent in ugliness') developed. At first his presence promised an almost moral companionship of equals. He would 'fill up the void left by false and narrow-hearted friends. I see already that he is without envy, hatred or malice – that he will betray no secrets, and feel neither plain at my success nor pleasure in my chagrin.'

Then, just under a year after the pug arrived, comes the apotheosis of the dog baby. With her partner, the writer and polymath George Henry Lewes, she travelled Italy, leaving Pug in the care of a Mrs Bell. They always missed their dog 'terribly' – just as all dog lovers do. On 8 June 1860, GE wrote to Mrs Bell: 'You have never sent us a word of news about Pug! I hope no tragedy awaits us on our return. We have seen a pair of puppies – brother and sister – here at Venice that make us long to carry them home as companions for *our very slow child*' (my italics).

So when I call the two of us Daddy and Mummy to Bonnie, I remember the author of *The Mill on the Floss*, and smile. She proves to me that it is *allowed* – this silliness, this harmless projection of longing onto a dog, this infantile crooning.

And what of all the others – long-dead women, united with me in dog-loving sisterhood? The life of long-suffering, sweet-natured Jane Carlyle, wife of the irascible historian Thomas

Carlyle, was transformed by Nero, half Maltese, half mutt ('the chief comfort of my life'), whose loss after eleven years ('loyal until his last hour') devastated her so deeply she wrote, '... my little dog is buried at the top of our garden, and I grieve for him as if he had been my little human child.' Similarly, Peggy Guggenheim, the art collector, whose life was erratic, whose relationships were fraught with pain as well as appalling irresponsibility and who was a truly terrible mother, found consolation and uncomplicated love in a succession of Llasa apsos. In a corner of the garden of what is now the Guggenheim Museum in Venice there is a stone which marks the resting place of her 'beloved babies' – all 14 of them, all named. Next to it is another plaque which bears the words 'Here rests Peggy Guggenheim 1898–1975.'

Edith Wharton's dogs played the same role. In her French houses she sketched her sleeping Pekes, and doted on the gaggle of small dogs, led by her favourite Linky, who would survive them all. The dogs spent the mornings with her in bed and the fiercely intelligent, cosmopolitan author of *The House of Mirth* and *The Age of Innocence* dispatched photographs of her dogs to friends with inscriptions like 'Please come and see me soon – Linky.' But her friends grew irritated by the childless Wharton's excessive (in their view) doting on her little dogs. One wrote, 'Much as she loved conversation, we all complained bitterly that her frequent endearments to the dogs and expostulations on their behaviour ruined all consecutive talk.'

Most new parents will recognize that tendency. When you first have children you sit over dinner, obsessing over first words and adorable little habits, and agreeing that your baby possesses all charm, all intelligence. J and I were like that, of course; once, accidentally on purpose, we woke Daniel up because, besotted by his babblings, we needed to hear the musicality of his baby voice. (J took a photograph to mark the moment: it is 1975, Daniel is about fourteen months, held sleepy in my arms in his striped Babygro, and I'm in an old, lace Biba dress, hair permed to a fashionable curly mane.) It is a short step from this delicious, private collusion in gene worship to boring your friends too, just as Wharton bored hers with her little dogs.

J and I loved family life – even though the state of parenthood brought more anguish to us than it does to most, because our daughter spent the whole of her childhood through into university years afflicted by a condition known as Hirschprung's disease, which is (to simplify) a congenital malfunction of the bowel. This was, for J and me, intensely bonding; when those times came when I was too exhausted to ask a doctor a simple question, let alone an intelligent one, and cried that I couldn't cope, he stepped in, strong enough for us both. This was required of him, over all those years. Like most young couples we had not thought much about having children, but assumed that there would be no problems. Yet the physical mechanics of motherhood did not come easily to me. To set out the history baldly is a convenient shorthand for much stress, disappointment and grief: five pregnancies and three births allowed us to bring up two children. From time to time I would whisper miserably that I was 'no good' at having children, disappointed (like so many women) by destiny. Fortunately, as they grew, I could counter that old mood of self-blame with the unassailable fact that the emotions of motherhood came very easily, and I was indeed 'good' at loving the pair who were the centre of my being.

Assuming we would live on our farm for ever, J and I imagined that one day Daniel and Kitty would arrive for weekends accompanied by spouses and grandchildren. Life would evolve and quieten, or so we believed – although with our tendency to cram our days with work and outside obligations, the prospect was unlikely. All through Daniel's and Kitty's childhood and teenage years into their twenties, I was accustomed to their friends choosing to hang out in our home when they might not like to socialize with their own parents.

But that was the merry side. When Kitty left home I was, briefly, stricken by deep gloom and sought help from the doctor, who prescribed a type of antidepressant known as a selective serotonin reuptake inhibitor, which I took for a while, then threw away. (In the same way I had flushed the antidepressants away after Tom was stillborn, believing that I had to walk through the darkness to emerge on the other side.) Sitting in the silence of the farm where Kitty would never have her permanent home again, I realized that I was still a mother, naturally and perpetually maternal. The mothering days would never be over, but would just take a different form.

Therefore when Bonnie came along in 2002 it is no surprise that she was answering a primitive need. Her perpetually baby-like characteristics were exactly what I (like so many other women *d'un certain age*) needed. Kitty was 22 and Daniel six years older; nature had made me ready to become a grandmother, but since that remained a distant prospect, I was primed and ready to love a little dog. The dependence of my very own dog reminded me of how my children were; I was *needed* once more. But this adorable creature would never grow up to stamp a foot and say 'No' at the age of two, or start smoking at 14, or suffer anguish over a girl, or weep over exams or boys, or defy the curfew and come home reeking of alcohol, or slam a door screaming, 'You don't understand anything!' or return miserable from university, ready to drop out – keeping you sleepless because you feel so helpless, knowing it's impossible to make everything all right. Instead, the small dog would curl in her basket at my feet, and follow me around with utter devotion, and greet me ecstatically after an absence of perhaps less than an hour – as if every slice of ham and cheese and roast chicken, as well as all other glories of the universe, were contained within my embrace.

Like George Eliot and George Henry Lewes, Robin and I are incessantly amused by Bonnie. Like Peggy Guggenheim I feel sometimes that she is far easier to deal with than people; like Edith Wharton I like to talk about her and show her photograph to those who show the slightest flicker of interest. And when I call her Baby-dawg and Babba and Baby-girlfriend and Mummy's Precious and Little Treasure and all the other sweet nothings that tumble from my lips as easily as when I used to blow raspberries on my first baby's stomach, I am not embarrassed, as John Steinbeck would wish me to be, for this is nothing more or less than acting in accordance with my essential nature.

What's more, in the daily exchange of love and mutual benefit between me and my dog, a covenant is enacted which transcends the obvious notion of child substitute. An ancient Mediterranean saying has the olive tree (essential to a whole culture) telling its 'owner': 'Care for me and I will nurture you.'

It's my passionate belief that we should thus listen to all the living things, plant, marine and animal alike, which share our planet. We do not 'own' them, any more than I 'own' my dog. If we learn the art of taking care, or respecting, of love, we will be repaid.

And that is why, when I stop to think (which happens infrequently, since I am not given to brooding) that life is unfair because I cannot have a baby whilst the unequal laws of gender mean that my first husband can go on having children with somebody else, I console myself with the ever-present reality of our little dog. Not 'mine', but ours. As we are hers.

Robin refuses to take Bonnie out for walks wearing pastel collars and leads, especially (horror) the pink set I bought in Brussels, but always selects the black, knowing that her long hair will obscure the diamante trims. A man has to try to keep up appearances. One day he was walking through Bath with the dog. They passed two women, who stopped to point.

'That's cute,' said one.

'The man or the dog?' asked the other.

A confident man has no problem being seen with a lapdog, as he doesn't believe it calls his manhood into question. Why should it?

That's why I think it sexist to assume that loving small dogs is intrinsically foolish and feminine – because many men dote on their pets just as Robin does. The list could be very long, but a few examples will do. The seventeenth-century statesman and poet Sir John Harington was so besotted with his clever spaniel Bungey that (uniquely) he put his portrait on the title page of his book. The diarist Samuel Pepys was inordinately fond of his 'little bitch' Fancy, the poet Robert Herrick wrote affectionately about his spaniel too, the historian Edward Gibbon adored his Pomeranian, the artist William Hogarth is pictured with his pug and the great French novelist Emile Zola grieved for Fanfan, 'a griffon of the smallest kind'. The emotions he expressed in memory of his little dog echo the theme of this book:

> *An animal, nothing but a little animal, and to suffer thus at its loss! To be haunted by its recollection to such an extent that I wished to write of my sorrow, certain of leaving the impression of my heart on the page! … But then it seemed to me that I had so much to say … upon this love of animals – so obscure and so powerful, at which I see people around me smile, and which pains me to the extent of troubling my life.*
>
> *And why was I attached so profoundly to this little mad dog? Why have I fraternized with it as one fraternizes with a human being? Why have I cried as one cries for a lost friend? Is it not that the unquenchable tenderness which I feel for everything that lives and feels is a brotherhood of suffering! A charity which inclines one towards the most humble and disinherited?*

With the help of his small dogs Mickey Rourke, the Hollywood actor and boxer, has endured the darker side of fame: a fall from grace followed by personal redemption. He came to rely on his most cherished pet, a chihuahua–terrier cross called Loki, flying her (at enormous cost) to be with him on film sets, because he simply couldn't do without her. In 2009 Loki died at 18 (120 in human years, according to some calculations, about 85 in others) just after accompanying

Rourke to the Golden Globes. In his acceptance speech for his role as 'The Wrestler' Rourke paid a touching tribute to his chihuahuas, living and dead, proclaiming to the world the saving power of dogs: 'It's been a long way back for me … I'd like to thank all my dogs, the ones that are here and the ones not here any more, because sometimes, when a man's alone – that's all you got – your dog. And they've meant the world to me.'

When interviewed by Barbara Walters on television he credited another dog, Loki's father, with distracting him from dark thoughts of suicide. It seems that Rourke had taken an overdose but then he saw a pair of brown eyes fixed on him: 'I looked at my dog Beau Jack, and he made a sound, like a little almost-human sound. I don't have kids. The dogs became everything to me. And the dog was looking at me, going "Who's going to take care of me?"'

There we see the old transaction working: in making clear his dependence on his master, Beau Jack was saving his life. Yet nothing could protect Mickey Rourke from the loss of his favourite: Loki died just before the Oscars in 2009 and no piece of diamond jewellery received as much attention on the red carpet as the pendant bearing Loki's picture which the macho man proudly wore. In an interview he remembered his dog: 'She's the love of my life. She made it until six days ago. She left me at a time when, after 18 years, she knew I'd be all right.'

If anyone should deem that anthropomorphically saccharine, I can only cite the philosopher Mary Midgley, who argues that animals can be 'fellow sufferers and useful indicators of shared trouble'. Who knows enough to deny that one small dog might well have clung to life to a great age until she was certain her master was back in business, a player rather than a failure? That such unconditional love is an essential part of the treasured dog's medicine cabinet?

Not long ago, on a trip to a literary festival in Scotland to publicize my 'Bonnie' books, Robin and I were in the Lake District, visiting Dove Cottage, the home of William Wordsworth. We were delighted to be greeted near the entrance by a near-life-size oil painting of Pepper, a Norfolk terrier given to Wordsworth by the dog-loving Sir Walter Scott. That the poet hung it so prominently says much about his feeling for the animal companion of so many lengthy walks. More than one poem displays an acute empathy with dogs and an understanding of their interaction with humans and with other dogs, while 'Tribute to the Memory of a Dog' leaves us in no doubt that Wordsworth identified, in the lamented animal, the redemptive, moral force he perceived also in mountain and stream:

For love, that comes to all; the holy sense,
Best gift of God, in thee was most intense.

That same day we located a pub in Keswick we had been informed was dog friendly. One of the irritating things about travelling with your dog in England (unlike in France) is that the supposed nation of dog lovers bans the faithful friends almost everywhere, usually because of absurd rules of 'health and safety', but sometimes simply because the owner of the hotel or bar dislikes dogs, even tiny ones who nestle happily in a handbag. Once, on a visit to Oundle, I went into a chi-chi shop with my dog (as pretty and pristine as anything in the establishment) tucked under my arm, but was swiftly dispatched by the two ladies behind the counter. 'You can tie it up outside,' they said helpfully, clearly unaware of the phenomenon of dog-napping. I left speedily – and have kicked myself ever since for not retorting, '*Big* mistake! Ladies with little dogs spend *big* money.'

Anyway, the pub we found bore the appropriate name, the Dog and Gun, and was clearly a favourite of tough, outdoors-loving men – the kind who go ratting with terriers and would certainly regard the British Parliament's ban on hunting with hounds as a pernicious infringement of liberty. Robin and I sat in a corner with our drinks and sandwiches and Bonnie on my knee, her back straight with tension, as she watched two rather intimidating Norfolks rear and wrestle in the space in front of the bar – round and round, over and over, teeth drawn back in friendly play. A couple with an English bull terrier sat near us. The man was tall and burly with close-cropped hair and a tattoo on one arm: not a man to argue with, any more than his bruiser of a pet. Suddenly his blonde partner rose and walked across the room, out of sight. The dog watched intently, those tiny, sunken eyes fixed on the direction she had taken, the tension along the spine and down those powerful forelegs mirroring Bonnie's miniature stance. Moments passed. At last the dog quivered and his head jerked up. She was returning, packets of crisps in hand. And the big man reached down to stroke the butch creature, saying softly, 'There's yer Mam.'

In the early spring of 2007 I had to make a career choice, or rather, shift. For years I had contributed occasional freelance comment articles to the *Daily Mail*, and I knew well the way that newspaper worked. I had been told that the editor, Paul

Dacre (recognized, even by his critics, as the most influential, feared and admired editor in London), liked my advice column in *The Times* and wished me to switch allegiance, writing exactly the same column for the *Mail* and guaranteeing me autonomy. We met over lunch in February and established an immediate rapport, which surprised me. Yet the decision was very hard and I took over two months to make up my mind. I credited Sandra Parsons (then still in charge of features at *The Times* and now a friend) with the invention of my new, fulfilling persona as an advice columnist and was reluctant to show my appreciation by accepting the blandishments of a rival newspaper. I also liked writing essays and book reviews for *The Times*, whilst also being able to contribute to the *Mail*, sometimes appearing in both newspapers on the same day.

The then *Times* editor, Robert Thomson, took me to lunch and offered inducements, which could not, however, match up to those coming from Associated Newspapers. I even asked my dog what I should do – guilty that the fidelity we so admire in her kind is not matched by humanity. When you write regularly for a newspaper you come to care about the readers, and writing an advice column makes them all too real. To love a job yet be seduced into flitting after only two years? On the other hand, the Saturday edition of the *Daily Mail* (where I would be berthed) is a fine, fat and busy newspaper with a readership of over six million and I had always loved the paper's bruising swagger as well as its courage. It has its finger on the pulse of a middle England – which I understood.

My love affair with newspapers began in childhood. My parents read the *Liverpool Echo* and the *Daily Express*; my grandparents took the *Daily Mirror*, then in its mass-circulation, crusading heyday. Each Saturday night my brother and I would stay with Nan and Grandad, who would have saved the week's *Mirrors* for me. I don't know if anybody thought it unusual that a girl of eleven or twelve should be so absorbed by a pile of newsprint, but I would sit and work my way through the papers, sometimes cutting out a picture of Prince Charles and Princess Anne in their velvet-collared coats, because my grandmother and I loved such things, royalty and smart coats alike. (The bespectacled little girl furtively fascinated by the semi-naked strip-cartoon character Jane would have been astonished to learn that one day she would (a) sit down to dinner with the Prince of Wales and (b) write a column in the *Daily Mirror*.)

When I reached that stage (bizarrely called 'Britain's Brightest New Writer' on the masthead at the age of 32) I was somewhat disillusioned when the legendary advice columnist Marjorie Proops, doyenne of the *Mirror* (and the person who had recruited me), counselled me not to care so passionately about what I wrote because 'It just wraps tomorrow's chips.' Brought up on delicious, greasy, salty fish 'n' chips in newspaper, I recognized the truth of that, but rejected its spirit. Newspapers, I thought (and still think), matter, and we should be still proud of the wide-ranging quality of the British press, for all its faults.

Throughout 40 years, having written for every single national newspaper except the *Sun* and the *Daily Star*, and had columns in three papers and three magazines, I found my natural berth at *The Times*, but always admired the *Mail* for its professionalism and verve. The mixture of campaigning clout, acerbic comment, judiciously placed sentiment, wide-ranging coverage of women's issues and an entertaining habit of printing photographs you don't see anywhere else (if a tiger is born without stripes somewhere in the world they will run his picture) drew me to the *Mail.* Left-wing friends excoriate the paper (but often buy it secretly) and I myself feel uneasy about its tendency to encourage bitchiness and its occasional reversal to outdated sexism. But no one can argue that it is a newspaper which matters. In terms of 'reach' the *Daily Mail* is unequalled, and for somebody like me – who, after all, epitomizes social mobility – that is very appealing.

These media affairs are of interest only to those in our trade; the more general point is that being courted so assiduously and generously by two newspaper editors was heady for a woman of 60 and reminded me that the recent, testing changes in my life had brought me to this place. The paradox is expressed most memorably by Rainer Maria Rilke in one of his 'Sonnets to Orpheus':

Every happiness is the child of a separation
It did not think it could survive.

The irony was extraordinary. Had my marriage not been shattered by fate, I would still have been at the farm, coping with our life in the same way, trying to wind down, getting older, wondering what to write next. And (to be honest) always living somewhat in my husband's shadow, no matter what I achieved. Instead, I felt intoxicated by new opportunities. Sometimes I asked myself if I would turn the clock back, and the inner voice whispered a half-ashamed negative. The silver chain was (almost) broken.

Still, in my vacillation over the job decision, I retreated into old habit – and asked J's advice. To my surprise he thought I should move to the *Mail.* His grandfather had worked on the paper as Parliamentary Correspondent, but stormed out in May 1931 after a furious row with the editor over the proprietor Lord Rothermere's flirtation with fascism. Now J – who shared his grandfather's liberal values and his dislike of some of the attitudes widely associated with a right-of-centre paper – was telling me I'd be mad not to accept the *Mail*'s offer.

On the other hand, Robin, who tends to value contentment over worldly concerns, thought that the best course would be to stay with *The Times*, where I was happy. 'Stuff the money,' he said at first. In the middle of all this debate I tripped on a pavement, hit a wall, knocked myself out and injured my eye. With enforced time to think (although I never missed writing a single *Times* column) and looking in the mirror to see a gargoyle looking back, shocked once again by how quickly things happen and how in one second I could have lost the sight of one eye, I took the message of fate. Let it happen. You have to reach out, and go on reaching out, taking risks, allowing yourself to become excited rather than staying safe – until the moment when those reaching arms fall lifeless to your side.

I would change newspapers.

This was not the only shift of allegiance I was to make in 2007. Paul Dacre said to me when we finally reached our agreement that my new column would begin in June: 'So – you're getting married again and you have a marriage to a new paper … This is a good year for you.'

It would be dishonest not to confess that my capitulation to the idea of actual remarriage (rather than wearing a ring as a symbol of emotional commitment) was encouraged by J's own remarriage in March. This was not a matter of tit for tat – rather an acceptance that his life had moved on irrevocably, and therefore mine should too. I realized that my determination not to marry was much to do with clinging to the entirety of what we had had – the dream of home as well as the individual man. His new marriage would help me to let it go – but just as some people cling to bereavement, I did not really *want* that parting. The Nobel laureate Seamus Heaney expresses this idea with characteristic insight in his interviews with Dennis O'Driscoll: 'A wedding always has its moments of strangeness, sudden lancings or fissures in the fun, when parent or child have these intense intimations that the first circle is broken. It is in the literal sense an *unheimlich*, an unhoming.'

Another translation of that German word is 'uncanniness' and I recognize that etymological connection between the idea of being unhomed (or unsettled) and being spooked. In my imagination J and I were ghosts revisiting all the places we had known and trying to find our way home through the darkness. I dreamt of him constantly, which was very unsettling, yet I had started to accept it as a part of my new life too; the on-going journey within another dimension with somebody I had never ceased to love. It seemed miraculous to me that the unhomed love was not, in the end, homeless. It would live on as long as we did. So my strange dreams were written down in yet another notebook I had begun in 2004, jotting down passages from books, scraps of poetry and brief thoughts to help me make sense of things. Looking at it now (lying permanently on my desk) I realize how much of what I put down has to do with those ideas of home as well as of loss – the two inextricably bound, as when Philip Larkin writes: 'Home is so sad. It stays as it was left.' The mood of my notebook varies from elegiac, in Tennyson, from 'The Princess':

For when we came where lies the child
We lost in other years,
There above the little grave,
O there above the little grave,
We kiss'd again with tears.

to furious Marina Tsvetaeva, in 'An Attempt at Jealousy':

... Tell me: are you happy?
Not? In a shallow pit? How is
Your life, my love? Is it as
Hard as mine with another man?

Robin and I were fine living as we were, and he would never have pushed the situation, but it was my daughter who suggested that marriage would make him very happy. So our decision to go ahead was relaxed, even light-hearted. For a while we thought of going to Las Vegas and rumbling along to the Elvis chapel on a big motorcycle, with only Daniel and Kitty as witnesses. But then, one night when he was away on a job and Bonnie was looking anxiously for his return, I realized that I did not want a joke wedding in a tacky place. Robin was my rock, the support which he had demonstrated over so many years crystallized into something more beautiful, more permanent. We decided to have a church wedding. Back in 1989 I had published a travel book called *Bel Mooney's Somerset* and had persuaded the publishers to pay Robin (then a young film and photography student as well as Kitty's babysitter) a very modest amount to take the black and white photographs. Through the project he became fascinated by piscinae and rood screens and Norman arches. Now it seemed to us sublime and fitting that we would choose to be married beneath one.

The decision made, we parked Bonnie with my ever-willing parents and went to Bali for another travel piece for *The Times*. We stayed at Ubud, at Jimburan and Candidasa. Much-travelled acquaintances had predicted how much I would love Bali, but their estimations fell short.

I was transfixed by the ubiquity of worship. Even the scruffiest motorbike on the streets of Kuta is made sacred by decorative hangings on handlebars. Similarly a car dashboard becomes a shrine, and an open drawer in a clothes shop is transformed into an altar – complete with an offering of food and flowers on a palm leaf plate and a joss stick, reverently lit by the beautiful salesgirl. You walk along a beach, careful not to tread on the palm-leaf plates, exquisitely arranged with food, flowers and incense, which are laid down with reverence, sanctifying tourist haunts. Nowhere else have I been where the smartest, international hotels have shrines in their gardens tended many times a day by staff lighting incense and murmuring ritual prayers. There is no self-consciousness about this, even if guests gawp. Everyday ceremonies keep the darkness at bay. I was prepared to be sceptical about claims made by Bali-high friends that it is a special, spiritual place. But that greenest of islands gave me more than a good holiday. It confirmed my belief in the essential wholeness of things.

On our second day we visited the great temple at Ubud, and noticed the ubiquitous black-and-white-checked textile wrapped around priests and shrines alike, and made into temple umbrellas. It reminded me of tablecloths in fifties Britain, and I wondered why it was everywhere when the vibrant colours of silk would have been more beautiful. I discovered that the cloths – called *poleng* – are designed for protection, warding off evil spirits. The white squares represent good, the gods and health. The black ones stand for evil, the underworld and disease. Yet in the traditional *poleng* (rather than cheap modern printed versions) the two are woven together, and the intersection of warp and weft, of black and white, forms the grey squares. This is the visible confirmation that you cannot have one without the other – the grey squares are, if you like, mitigation. The grey is emblematic of the pitiful and brave nuances of the human condition. In the dull neutral lies a simultaneous acceptance of darker realities and hope for redemption.

I was once given a box of grey pastels for monochrome artwork, and I had marvelled at the range of shades – about twenty – between the black and the white at either end. In Bali, on a day when disappointing rain fell, I looked up at the multi-hued clouds and remembered those pastels, then imagined the *poleng* wrapped around all of us, offering protection against the dangerous, fanatical certainty which sees life in black or white with no shades of grey in between. In Bali's capital, Kuta, the monument to the young victims of the Islamist terrorist outrage of October 2002 is a permanent reminder of what happens when men believe they are right and condemn the rest of humanity to death as 'infidel'. That is the blackness. But the flowers and shrine and messages all around represent the opposite: the white light of faith, hope and love, which cannot be extinguished. Bowing my head at the monument, and seeing the symbolic *poleng* cloth all over Bali, made me determined to fly the flag of blessed nuance all my life, even within the portals of the mighty *Daily Mail*.

Robin and I talked endlessly about our wedding, and drew up a guest list – which was very hard since we wanted only about thirty people. It grew to just over forty, but still, some had to be left out. We decided that only people from Bath should come, although that had to change. Yet – wedding plans? Lists? Worries about hurting some feelings by not inviting? A part of me still couldn't help wondering why I was *doing* this, but the other part (the larger part) simply relaxed into the quiet, philosophical feeling that what will be will surely be. At the same time, that is too passive, for you do indeed create your own destiny – rushing to meet it with the same speed as my little dog responds to the sound of the doorbell.

Each lazy day, at some point (or two points, or maybe three) we would find ourselves talking about Bonnie, just like doting parents. Her silly little habits, the inconvenience of her sleeping on the bed, her endless reassurance that we are wonderful people – and so on. This was a part of life now, the knowledge that the three of us formed a 'pack' that was mutually dependent. One day we were exploring the faded grandeur of the palace, Puri Agung Karangasem, in the small town of Amlapura. In truth, there's not much to see there, but we both exclaimed in glee when we spotted, as part of the design on a carved and painted balcony balustrade, a strange, small, white animal. Floppy ears, long hair, furry paws, funny little face, plumed tail … it was clearly a Maltese dog. A sign. At that moment I knew I was looking at my bridesmaid. Robin was delighted with the idea.

But not so other family members. 'You can't have your dog as your bridesmaid, Mother,' my daughter protested, and was careful to get her brother on her side as well. He suggested that surely I didn't want attention to be deflected from me? 'I don't care – I want them to look at my dog,' I replied. She said people would think it silly if I walked down the aisle with Bonnie.

'Well, if everybody in the church is grinning on my wedding day that's fine by me, ' I retorted.

'But it's a solemn occasion,' she said.

'No, it's a joyful occasion,' I replied, 'and as long the vicar approves that's fine!'

In any case, I have books of historical photographs which show dogs nestling at the feet of brides in Victorian and Edwardian times. They obviously knew what Amy Tan had told me, so long ago: 'The dogs are essential.'

On 8 September 2007, my second wedding day, an article appeared in the *Daily Mail* in place of my usual advice column. It was surely a testimony to one marriage that this (polemical as well as personal) could be written just before the second:

> In February 1968, at the age of 21, I married in a registry office, wearing a purple mini dress. We had barely thought about what we were doing; the smallest, plainest wedding was less important than being madly, impulsively in love.
>
> Today, at 60, I am getting married for the second time – in another purple dress. I have thought very deeply about it, and the beautiful church ceremony will be an important

declaration of deep friendship and commitment. As it is for all those brave and lucky souls who choose to utter publicly the most important words they will ever say.

One or two friends have asked me, with affectionate curiosity, 'Why marry again?' After all, when my first marriage ended after 35 years, I believed I would never sign up for it again. I reverted to my maiden/professional name by deed poll, worked hard to develop a good relationship with my still-dear ex-husband, loving each other under different roofs – but saw no need to become 'Mrs' anybody else. In fact, I shall not take my new husband's name today, but that's an irrelevance.

My answer to the question, 'Why marry?' is that I believe – profoundly – in the importance of marriage as an institution. Or (perhaps a less stolid way of expressing it) as life-choice in which the well-being of society and personal happiness are uniquely united. This is the point at which the person blends into the political. It's easy for me to explain why *I* choose to tie the knot for the second time. I can say, simply, 'I want to belong to the one who says that all he wants is to look after me. And I want to look after him right back.' But more important is why marriage matters to us *all* – perhaps more than ever before ...

It won't surprise anyone when I say that of all the categories which make up my postbag of questions on human relationships, the largest is marriage. Any day I can pluck a handful: cries for help from young women who long for their boyfriends to display commitment, from older women who chafe at the sexless sterility of their marriages, from wives tossed aside by husbands who started affairs or just got bored and went off in search of lost youth. Whatever problems women have, men have them too – although honesty compels me to point out that the bias of my letters is borne out by statistics, middle-aged men more likely to skip off than older women …

Some marriages end with a bang, others with the most pitiful of whimpers. Yet the other side of the story needs to be heard too. There are plenty of marriages which last, nurturing children in harmony and carrying the couple into a contented and loving old age. I could not do my job if I was cynical about wedlock – or rather, if I ever lost faith in the human ability to get it right, to sustain long-term love, 'till death us do part'. I believe it is natural for human beings to want to nest in pairs, to grow together, to share, to say 'we' instead of 'me.' I repeat, why would you *not* marry?

Caught between the sorrows of my postbag and the seemingly contradictory statistics which proclaim that the divorce rate is at its lowest for decades but also that fewer people are choosing to marry – I still say it's too soon to pronounce the funeral rites on the institution. How could something which does so much good die out? The subject is complex, involving an analysis of the role of women, of changing expectations, of fiscal policy, and so on. But to simplify, let me isolate two reasons to marry. One no longer affects my personal choice, the other does.

First, traditionally, you marry to procreate. But now that there is no shame attached to having children outside marriage this is only a 'reason' to marry if it is seen as best for those children, and therefore for the long-term values and stability of the society they inherit. Personally, I have no doubt that this is the case – an assertion confirmed by so many surveys. Children whose parents marry and stay married are more likely to have stable marriages themselves and to wait until marriage before becoming parents.

One study has shown that children brought up by two birth parents until the age of sixteen have higher levels of happiness and fewer psychological problems. Children bear the brunt of a no-commitment culture. Rates of mental disorder among children in lone parent families are double those amongst children living with both parents; they are more likely to live in poverty and harm or kill themselves. The shift is partly due to marriage breakdown, of course, but mostly to the big increase in mothers who have never married. Single people are turning their backs on the institution yet regarding singledom as no barrier to accessorising their lives (carelessly or deliberately) with kids ...

Why not praise stable marriage as the ideal? Ideals are what give a culture cohesion; they must be enshrined equally within political and individual actions. Call me sentimental, but I believe that the old wedding photograph in its silver frame on the shelf possesses a symbolic value beyond anything contained within statistics.

What it stands for brings me to the second reason to marry, which has little or nothing to do with children. The exchanging of vows in a civil or religious ceremony tells the couple that they 'belong', proclaims to those who witness it that love and faith and commitment have lost none of their power – which positive message ripples out into the wider community. It's a universal affirmation ...

A few weeks ago, in Bath, we were looking for a shirt for Robin and kept encountering the same, unprepossessing grey-haired couple in the same shops. They could have been retired teachers. Making a fuss of our little dog, the lady confided at last that they were looking for 'wedding clothes.' 'Ah, so are we!' I smiled – and what we shared in that moment was a secret delight that even when you are older, when maybe you have experienced much pain, it is still possible to be renewed. And to tell the world …

In the months since we decided to marry we have both been struck by how *happy* people are to hear. To a guy cold-calling me to sell solar panels I said, 'It's really not the time, 'cos I'm about to get married.' His 'Oh, sorry … of course … and many congratulations' was surely politeness, yet sounded so genuine. Why shouldn't I think he meant it? After all, people long for good news – and the word that this couple (or that) care enough for each other to articulate that love in front of others causes even strangers to share in the celebration.

Today, when I am listening to the vicar say 'It is given that as man and woman grow together in love and trust, they shall be united with one another in heart, body and mind,' and 'Marriage is a sign of unity and loyalty which all should uphold and honour' I shall be agreeing with all my heart. When we repeat, 'to have and to hold from this day forward, for better, for worse, for richer, for poorer, in sickness and in health …' my heart will overflow. And into the Christian service I have written a famous Apache blessing (often used at modern weddings), containing words which express why I, and so many people the world over, choose to make a shared declaration of love and faith and belonging:

Now there is no loneliness for you,
For there is no more loneliness.
Now you are two bodies,
But there is only one life before you.

On the morning of our wedding I lay in bed, somewhat dazed, reading my own words in the paper, looking at the large picture of Robin and me which accompanied it, as if (for a moment) I didn't know who we were. It all felt strange. Family and friends rampaged about the house, looking for cufflinks, the iron, shouting to use the shower and so on. During the morning J texted me from Russia, where he was filming his television series. Certain that he would do so, I had rushed around the house frantically amidst the chaos, to find my mobile phone, simply to be ready for his message. He wished us luck. My text back told him I would always carry him in my heart. Because even on this golden, happy day that remained the truth.

After the houseful of loved ones had dressed, there was no hot water remaining for me, and so the mature bride endured a cold bath, compelled to play the mother's old, self-sacrificial role even on her second wedding day. The house grew quiet as they all left for church. Bonnie was on my bed, watching me get ready, quivering with nervous anticipation, in case she was going to be left behind. 'Just you and me, girlfriend,' I told her, as I put on my purple and turquoise silk dress, then decked her out in her matching purple harness, collar and lead, fixing a purple feather to her harness with slightly shaking fingers.

'You look lovely,' I said, grateful for the comic relief of that feather waving over her back, just like her tail.

'Take me, oh, take me,' was all she had to say in reply.

At last, just before noon, Daniel returned from ferrying my parents and drove Bonnie and me to Charlcombe Church, the oldest ecclesiastical building in Bath still in use. Hidden up a lane in trees, about a mile from our house, it has literary associations which naturally delighted me. In 1799 Jane Austen wrote, 'We took a charming walk to Charlcombe, sweetly situated in a green valley.' Sixty-five years earlier, one of the great fathers of British fiction, Henry Fielding, married his beloved Charlotte Crawford in the church, and in *Tom Jones* he conveys something of the way I felt on my second wedding day. I even included the longer extract as a frontispiece to our Order of Service:

> *All were happy, but those the most who had been most unhappy before. Their former sufferings and fears gave such a relish to their felicity ... Yet great joy, especially after a sudden change and revolution of circumstance, is apt to be silent and dwells rather in the heart than on the tongue ...*

Bonnie was excited and pulled on her lead. The purple feather slipped to one side. Outside the church we paused for a moment while the Reverend Jonathan Lloyd said a brief prayer, just for me. He strode ahead – and then I entered Charlcombe Church with my small dog leading me forward to the next stage of my life.

> *8 September: I walk in, smiling, not seeing any individual faces, just a blur of beaming all around me. R waiting at the front, looking happy, not at all nervous. Just a few steps down the tiny aisle. I hand Bonnie's lead to Gaynor, who gives her to Mum next to her. And then it unfolds, this beautiful, holy*

'performance' of which we are a part – like actors who are also believers – in an ancient, sacred drama. I am aware of such a great joy in that ancient place: a sharing, a confirmation. And, so quickly, it is over, and the 'Ode to Joy' booms out and we float upon it, joined by Bonnie as we walk up the aisle out into bright sun and warmth and snapping cameras and petals thrown and so many smiles and kisses …

In his address, our friend Ernie Rea (a man of the cloth as well as former Controller of BBC Religion, and Radio 4 presenter) said words that meant much to us both:

… today marks a new beginning. It is you two who matter from this moment on. Now is the time to put the past behind; not of course, forgetting all that has happened; continuing to cherish all the good things life has handed you until now. But letting go too; focusing on the joy that you two share together and all the good times that lie ahead … At the heart of what Jesus taught is the message that there is always another chance. Grace and forgiveness always have the final word over rancour and bitterness … I firmly believe that love is at the heart of the universe. That is why I believe that there is rejoicing in a little part of heaven as you two come together as man and wife.

No wonder I chose to read the U.A. Fanthorpe poem 'Atlas' to everybody, as a public tribute to the man who 'insulates my faulty wiring'. Robin's own choice was Raymond Carver's 'Late Fragment' – six lines in which the poet, at the end of his life, answers the question about the only thing he ever desired: 'To call myself beloved, to feel myself/Beloved on the earth.'

All weddings are, in essence, the same – which is something easy to forget when you have to deal constantly with unhappy letters from the ones who lost the way, lost their love. Surely, no matter how different we are, we make our vows (civil or religious) in the hope that this will last? Even when you know too well the pitfalls of marriage, you must only choose to remarry if you can restore trust (in a partner, but in yourself as well) to its essential place in the centre of the household gods' (the Roman *penates*) shrine. And when, despite those pitfalls, you have also experienced the profound rewards of a long love, it is not so difficult to set hope up there, alongside trust. Through the rest of that day – champagne, long, delicious lunch in an elegant hotel, and affecting and accomplished speeches by Robin and Kitty, followed by a mad evening of wine and Indian takeaway for the small group back at our house – I felt, above all, grateful to have come through to quiet camaraderie.

On our honeymoon, in Sri Lanka and the Maldives, Robin and I talked incessantly about our dog – as always. We reminded each other of the entertaining things she does, and the smallest gesture – like sticking out the tip of a tongue for a second – was a secret, silly signal that would evoke our pet. And as always, we were perfectly happy for the holiday to end, so we could return to our dog and our life.

Two months later we strolled into the National Gallery to be confronted by a poster which made us laugh: 'Look – it's us!' The poster advertised an exhibition of German Renaissance stained glass, called *Art of Light*, and the object shown made us rush to the exhibition to see the original. It glowed on the wall – a special message which we interpreted in significantly different ways. *Tobias and Sarah on their Wedding*

Night (measuring just 56 x 66 cm) is an exquisite panel which shows a couple asleep in their fine bedchamber. The luxurious bed has rich red hangings and a vivid blue and green patterned coverlet. The floor is tiled yellow and black, and – sweet domestic touch – a pair of slippers lies by the bed. In the foreground is a table, expertly shaded to show its bulk but also the fine grain of the wood. On it stands the snuffed candle in a yellow ceramic or brass candlestick, which lit the married pair to bed.

And there they sleep chastely, because (according to the Old Testament story) Sarah's previous seven bridegrooms were strangled by a demon on their wedding night, but the Archangel Raphael briefed Tobias to avoid this terrible fate by not consummating his marriage until three nights had passed. Their pale heads in nightcaps are propped up against soft white pillows, and – certainly assisting the vow of chastity – a small white dog nestles in its own glass oval, on the bed at their feet. His eyes are firmly closed too, his ears flop down, his tail ties him into a small ball – and the stained-glass master has shown his skill in the minute depiction of curly hair.

It was like looking at ourselves through the wrong end of a telescope: a couple, frozen in endearing intimacy, at the beginning of their life together, with their little white dog asleep at their feet. One family. One small pack. In a second, centuries of devoted owners and their dogs were strung side by side like glass beads on a thread of time.

I said, 'Just shows – people have always been as soppy as us.'

Robin said, 'Oh, you should *never* allow a small dog on your bed.'

Seven

SEEKING

Side by side, their faces blurred,
The earl and countess lie in stone,
Their proper habits vaguely shown
As jointed armour, stiffened pleat,
And that faint hint of the absurd –
The little dogs under their feet.
Philip Larkin, 'An Arundel Tomb'

The snow has fallen. The trees on the top of Lansdown, where J and I used to live, are heavy with frosting, and the hard earth glitters. One bitter Friday night we drive over the hill to drop Bonnie with my parents for company, then crunch our way through the streets of Bath to meet friends in the pub next to the theatre, for drinks, a play, then dinner. The Garrick's Head is packed and very noisy; people call out greetings – with that merry sense of mutual congratulation which agrees that on a night like this we're all rather bold and stylish to be out. Then our friend Lucy beckons me over, shouting an introduction to man I've never seen before.

'I know you,' he says. 'You're the one with the little white dog!'

'That's right!' I smile.

He does not seek to know my name; nor do I offer it. Like Chekhov's heroine (though much happier than she) I am suddenly identified through the absent Bonnie, and that suits me. This is my new persona: the lady with the lapdog. When my children were at school I had the common habit of introducing myself not by name but through my relationship with them: 'Hello, I'm Daniel's/Kitty's mum.' Now it entertains me hugely that my various changes of name and shifts of persona and career developments boil down to this uncomplicated truth: I hang out with a Maltese.

After a very long marriage, after the pain of breaking and refusal to let go, after the confused efforts to form new life and the bittersweet acceptance of success and failure alike, you often ask yourself who you really are. The answer is, of course, you are *all* the people you became throughout all the experiences. Just as the philosophers tell us that we never step in the same river twice, so I maintain that you never view exactly the same face in the mirror. Acknowledging that challenging truth can transform even the unwelcome process of ageing into an adventure. Wondering who you are and whom you may become during the next twenty-four hours, let alone the next few years, turns each day into that staple of fairytale and myth – a quest.

I was reading Penelope Fitzgerald's last novel *The Blue Flower* when a sentence jumped out at me: 'If a story begins with finding, it must end with searching.' The meaning is not elaborated; Fitzgerald knew the value of the silence between words – since what is left unrevealed must surely make you curious. I firmly believe that the ongoing inner questions – the constant queries of 'Why?' and 'What might it have been like?' and 'What if?' and 'How does it all end?' – form the imaginative workout which builds strength for our human quest.

The child within us will always cry, 'Why did that happen to *me*?' when misfortune strikes. It is only when you reach the moment of epiphany and turn that round, to ask, 'Why not?' (as simple as an acorn containing an oak) that the door of the self can swing open, releasing you into questions more fundamental than your own *angst*. It happened to me when our second son was stillborn. It happened more than once during long years of hospital visits with our daughter – when I sat on National Health Service paediatric wards with mothers whose precious children were dying but who (some of them) still managed to don lipstick, the better to defy the vicious Reaper.

It happened when I tasted the ashes of our marriage in my mouth and wondered (like so many other separated people, especially in middle age) what to do. And nowadays, when I study readers' problem letters I often feel it too – but cannot tell them. Not in so many words. No counsellor can advise a person immured in misery that this particular grief may be the making of them, may lead them through a gate into a field they never knew. The bereaved are afflicted by well-meaning souls who say, 'You can have another baby' or 'You'll get over it', but the desperately unhappy are similarly punished by breezy advice. The statement 'When all this is over you'll look back and see what it taught you' may have an important truth at its core, but is rarely helpful.

No, you have to experience the meaning yourself.

That is the quest.

It must begin with the realization that no one is immune, and therefore anything can happen to you. The test is not what you will make of it, but what it will make of you.

This particular story began with finding. A small white dog, aged six months, was left tied to a tree in a park, found by somebody, then taken to the RSPCA Cats' and Dogs' Home, to be rescued by me. Who could have known that she was destined to make the transition from toy dog to muse? Because of that miraculous transformation I find myself (now, as she sleeps in her blue bed at my feet) imagining her death. This is because the universe rolls on and sooner or later we must all come back to the beginning. My journey began with finding and ends in this chapter with seeking, and yet that can never be the end, because I must lose again, and again. This is the price of that very humanity which all the words in my library, all the birds in my garden, each stamen and petal on the flowers on my desk and all the loves I have known urge me to celebrate. What you seek can take you right back to the start, and with ending, begin once again.

The search is for nothing more, or less, than a state of grace.

It was loss that transformed Bonnie into my muse. Love and loss which changed her role and set us both on our journey – my little dog and I, sniffing our way forward, step by small step, not knowing quite where we would arrive but being stout-hearted together. I love her expressive wordlessness. Even the people you most love will sometimes disappoint through not having the right words for the moment you need them, and besides, their truth may not match your own. But the dog watches you with a mute understanding which hovers on the edge of wisdom. There are no blandishments, no words brisk or comforting, no rationales, no promises, no arguments to complicate or halt our pattering steps – as human friends would give. There is only (and how easily the cliché springs forth, like a Doberman in a dewy dawn) that old dogged devotion. My dog and I stand, shoulder to ankle, every sense alert. Seeing what we shall find.

Outside a bank in Milsom Street, Bath, a man was clearly waiting for someone, his enormous red setter sitting peacefully at his feet. Bonnie and I drew level with them. In contrast to the big dog she was restless, pulling on her lead, (in truth) badly trained. When she saw the elegant gun dog she adopted her pose of maximum aggression: chest out, back legs splayed, head jutting forward with that very 'Don't mess with me' attitude which I tend to adopt myself in situations which rattle me. Then an ear-splitting rattle of hysterical yapping fell down on the other dog's astonished head, like hail. He shrank back. His owner laughed. The setter rose nervously and put the lamp-post between himself and the tiny pest. I could imagine him thinking, What on earth is *this?* Looks like a rabbit or a cat – but that smell? … *sniff* … Lordy, lordy, it's a mad *relation.* Take it *away.*

Passers-by, noticing the confrontation between the unlikely little aggressor and the enormous softie, stopped to point and smile.

'That's a tough little one,' said the red setter's owner.

'Too right,' I said, with pride.

I read a haiku somewhere and memorized it, to give me strength when my own life requires Bonnie's splayed-leg squaring up, and her burst of angry yaps:

Big Dog towering
Little Dog versus Big Dog
Little Dog stands tall.

An experienced clinical psychologist I turned to during the difficult process of writing this book told me, with absolute seriousness, that she was convinced Bonnie had come into my life for a 'reason'. To those imprisoned by reason itself, such a statement will be meaningless, even absurd. But to those who believe that 'The heart has reasons that reason cannot know' it will make perfect sense. Robin gave me those words engraved on a heart pendant. They were written by Blaise Pascal, the seventeenth-century French mathematician and philosopher, who (despite his grounding in science) recognized alternative universes longed for by the human soul. I believe that in one of those universes the small dog has a significance far greater than the sum of its parts, or the frequency of its cuddles, or its comforting charms. In one of those other worlds, full of mystery, the small dog is the guide, leading us on a search for grace – just as Emily Dickinson believed that a dog is the fitting companion for the soul's final journey, 'Attended by a single Hound ...'

She described her beloved Newfoundland Carlo (as far from a small dog as it is possible to be) as her 'Shaggy Ally' – an endearment which will resonate with anyone who sees a dog as a confederate and other self. She filtered the world through him, put his interests above her own, and when he died at the grand age of 16 her grief went beyond all expression, other than a brief, anguished note sent to her friend and literary mentor, Thomas Higginson, editor of the *Atlantic Monthly:*

Carlo died –
E. Dickinson
Would you instruct me now?

It was to Higginson that she had confided her belief that her dog – like the hills they roamed together – was 'better than Beings', i.e. people. In the year following Carlo's death Emily wrote next to nothing, and she never replaced the dog who represented her connection to all creation, as well as her protector and guide. Many years before his death, looking ahead she had told a friend, '... do you know that I believe that the first to come and greet me when I go to heaven will be this dear, faithful, old friend, Carlo?'

It seems to me that one of the functions of the dogs we love is to lead us towards an awareness of the inevitability of loss. From time to time we have to take Bonnie to the vet, to have her teeth seen to, her glands attended to, or for booster injections. She is always terrified, her tail sweeps the floor and she quakes, while we hate the whole experience just as much, wishing she would understand that it's for her own good.

One time a vet we didn't know asked bluntly, 'How old is she now?'

'Seven,' I said.

The response was casually blunt: 'OK, so she's about halfway through her life – with luck.'

Robin grimaced. Suddenly you are forced to contemplate your precious pet's mortality – those dog years that race to catch up with your own age, and then overtake. The thought fills you with a powerful, anticipatory sorrow which is yet another aspect of the dog's saving grace: knowing he/she must die (and most likely, before you), you are put into training.

I was interested to read the results of a survey with the veterinarian Bruce Fogle conducted into his British co-professionals' attitude to per death. It seems that one out of five practising veterinarians admitted a belief that a dog has a soul and an afterlife. Interestingly, two out of five believed that humans have a soul and an afterlife. When the same survey questions were put to practising veterinarians in Japan (where Buddhist and Shintoist traditions allow for an afterlife for all living things) every single veterinarian surveyed believed that dogs have a soul which is likely to survive death. Does that sound ridiculous? It doesn't matter. The poet Mark Doty remembers walking in the wood with his now-dead dog Beau, and 'hears' the sound of his paws. He writes,

> *... this is almost a physical sensation, the sound of those paws ... allied to the colour and heat of him, the smell of warm fur, the kinetic life of a being hardly still: what lives in me. And just as I'm feeling intensely grateful for that ... on the autumn path, scents and tones of leather, brass, resin, brandy, tobacco, leaf mold, mushrooms, wet bark – I think* Paradise. *Then I think,* If there's a heaven and he's not there, I'm not going.

My octogenarian father, who delights in Bonnie's company, is convinced that she has a soul. He's in good company, for Elizabeth Barrett Browning wrote, 'If I leave off verse to write in prose, it shall be a dissertation on the Souls of Dogs.' Lord Byron was angry that his dog Boatswain, who saved him from drowning, was 'Denied in Heaven the soul he held on Earth'. Indeed it is hard to imagine any Elysian Fields deserving of the name, without dogs, large, small and middling, bounding through the grass – rewarded for their enthusiasm, joyfulness, readiness, absurdity, intelligence, unconditional acceptance, constancy and devotion by permission to romp for ever in the land of the blessed, a perpetual supply of good food and clear water and chewy treats at hand. It may be foolish, but if we thought it might be true, the promise might help alleviate the terrible grief at the loss of a beloved pet, which Rudyard Kipling warns against, in his anguished poem 'The Power of the Dog':

Brothers and sisters, I bid you beware
Of giving your heart to a dog to tear.

But you can't refuse to love because of the pain which may or may not ensue. New parents usually find themselves overwhelmed by the terrifying mixture of responsibility and adoration which places you for ever on the rack, imagining everything that may – or will – threaten the small humans you love beyond speech. Even when your children have long grown up (like mine) you may still wake at four in the morning, worrying because they are unsettled or unhappy, and dreading future difficulties which life is bound to roll into their path, tripping them when you are no longer there to break the fall. And, loving a dog, you dread the universe of germs and internal growths which could cut short the already short life of the animal who has come to mean so much.

It disappointed me to learn that one of my favourite poets, Rainer Maria Rilke, feared the emotional demands of dog ownership. Committed as he was to his art, he believed (correctly) that to live with a dog would require love and attention he could not give. He was afraid of his inner resources being used up. In a 1912 letter he makes a curious assertion: '... they touch me very closely, these beings who rely on us so utterly and in whom we have helped raise a soul for which there is no heaven.' Is he suggesting that the soul within the dog is a human construct, an imaginative projection, or alternatively a reality 'grown' through the human–canine bond? If the latter, why is he – who believed in angelic power – so very sure there is 'no heaven' for them? Rilke thought of dogs as a 'better' kind of creature than humankind, imagining them as such because they are simpler, more *real* than people. Quite apart from their capacity for devotion, they live closely in touch with the world because they read it through all their senses – which faculties lend a certain superiority ('Who among us can point to a smell?'). What's more, a letter Rilke sent from Spain describes an unsettling encounter with a stray in which he ascribes to the animal an insight (or 'in-seeing' – *einsehen*) equal to his own. He was having coffee when an 'ugly', pregnant bitch came up, pleading for attention. Her eyes 'implored my looking' and in them the poet saw 'into the future or that which passeth understanding'. He gave her a lump of sugar, 'yet the meaning and solemnity and our whole communion were boundless'.

To me, the 'meaning' within that encounter between poet and animal was the same as that I experienced that long ago morning, when I looked at a field full of Hereford cows, on our organic farm. The poet who was so sure there was no heaven for dogs could still ascribe to the animal a spiritual power 'which passeth understanding' and use the religious word 'communion' to convey what happened between them. No wonder the mysterious holy-rolling-gunslinger played by Clint Eastwood in *Pale Rider* described the patch where teenaged Megan buried her murdered Jack Russell as 'holy ground'. So Bonnie continues to teach me that I am a part of a community of animals, neither above nor separate. Sometimes I stare into her jet-bead eyes and wonder what it is she knows, that I do not. At night, when Robin is fast asleep and I am bolt awake, tormented by my usual demons of worry, I reach for her as I used to clutch my teddy bear as a child, curling my body around the ball of her on top of the duvet. Then, at the soft time before daybreak, I will see her eyes shine at me, as if to ask why rest eludes this person she worships? Then I bury my face in her back, inhaling the doggy scent which is sweet to me, and beg her not to go back to sleep, not to leave me 'alone'. But usually this encounter in the silence is itself enough to make me drowsy, as if unconsciously soothed by the beating of that small heart, as a foetus is within the womb.

There's an image in the photographer David Douglas Duncan's book *Picasso & Lump: A Dachshund's Odyssey* which expresses a moment rather like that. An experience of stillness with a small dog which is akin to worship. In the spring of 1957 Douglas paid a visit to his friend and photographic subject, Pablo Picasso, at the artist's home near Cannes. With him was his young dachshund, Lump, which means 'little rascal' in German. On that day Picasso and the small dog fell for each other, and the great man immediately painted his portrait on a plate, writing, 'Pour Lump, Picasso, Cannes 19.4.57' beneath the droll sketch of the sausage dog. Within days 'Lumpito' had established himself as the painter's muse and Jacqueline Roque's companion while her partner was absorbed in his art. Picasso was to immortalize Lump in his series *Las Meninas* – 54 canvases inspired by Velásquez's great work of that name. In the bottom right-hand corner of the original lies a giant hound; in Picasso's variations we see substituted the unmistakable elongated shape of the breed which would later enchant Andy Warhol and David Hockney too.

One day Picasso told Douglas, 'Lump has the best and the worst in us.' In the photograph I love, the artist is staring fixedly at the dog, as if to fathom his mysteries. The bare stone room is lit by two windows. Picasso and Jacqueline sit opposite each other, and with them are four others. The silence is palpable; all six humans are staring intently at Lump, who sits on the floor between them all, doing nothing, not even looking at the photographer but fixing his eyes on the middle distance. The casual composition is anchored by the dog. He is the focus, his trailing lead taking the eye back to the artist's fascinated contemplation and the whole image rendered somehow sacred by the Mediterranean light which gilds Picasso's head, and Lump's as well. 'What was his allure?' asks Douglas and he records that when the artist looked at Lump, 'a sweet gentleness glowed in his eyes'. Who can tell what the artist saw, or why he allowed this particular dog into his world as none before? Dachshund and master both died in 1973. Picasso was

92, and Lump equally venerable at seventeen, but immortalized for ever in art.

One Sunday afternoon in June 2009, Bonnie suddenly began to flip about, squealing like a rabbit wounded by a hunter's bullet, but not yet killed. Nobody was touching her, and this is not a dog who would accidentally ingest poison, since she often has to be persuaded to eat even her expensive small-dog meals. Yet the day before she had been off-colour and we had begun to worry. Now she looked at me piteously and one of her forelegs gave way. I was transfixed at the top of the staircase, so naturally she tried to ascend the first stair, only to fall back, tail low, paws flailing. When I rushed down to scoop her up, the tiny black eyes looked terrified, their whites moongleams of panic. Yet strangely reproachful too. What is this hurting-thing? Why doesn't my mother-goddess make it better? And all the time the high-pitched crying, tearing at the edges of my brain. Her straining ribs were like bird bones beneath my fingers; her heart beat a pitiful tattoo within a chest fragile as paper. I felt helpless.

At that moment I heard the rumble of the motorcycle outside, and Robin returned to take charge, phoning the emergency veterinary service again and again until we could get an appointment. Many times have I been the desperate, worried parent, cradling my child, dreading the worst news – so let nobody rebuke or patronize me with the obvious statement that there can be no comparison, because I *know*. Yet here I was again with all my being concentrated into an unspoken prayer: *Please don't let her die.* At such a moment you remember the grief of friends whose dogs have died, either naturally or after illness, and realize that although you made sympathetic noises, you did not understand. But now your dog is ill and the vet is puzzled and you have that presentiment that, even if this is not destined to be the end, she is halfway through her life – so it is coming. Sooner or later.

At the beginning of 2009, we were fascinated to read about new excavations at Saqqara in Egypt which revealed a burial chamber containing 22 mummies, in sandy niches in the tomb's walls. Amongst the mummies of children, archaeologists found the mummy of a pet dog, surely placed there to follow his owners into the afterlife. This was not uncommon. The dog would be embalmed with all the care given to a human corpse, and after it was wrapped in linen bandages, they would recreate eyes, nose, mouth and ears to make it look as lifelike as possible. What greater mark of value can be imagined? No wonder the long-dead dogs are immortalized on tomb paintings: the rangy basenjis and Dalmatian types with their jewelled collars, and (often under the master's chair) the small dogs with short legs, pricked up ears and curly tails. All acolytes of the dog-headed god Anubis – for eternity.

Other religions have always interested me – after all, I have a Buddhist goddess in my garden and little Hindu sculptures in the house: Ganesh and Lakshmi. Yet in the end I am part of a Christian culture and therefore it matters to me that while there is nothing in the Bible to suggest that any living creature apart from man has a soul, there is also nothing which denies such a premise. I like the Old Testament covenant between man, as steward of the earth and the animal kingdom: ' ... every living creature that is with you, of the fowl, of the cattle, and of every beast of the earth' (Genesis 9:8–7). Jewish law traditionally prohibited cruelty to animals, and promoted active concern for their welfare. The Old Testament is littered with texts containing this message. For example, in the book of Numbers we find the story of Balaam and his ass in which the man is rebuked by an angel for his cruelty to his beast. The rabbinic tradition preached compassion for the welfare of animals at all times. It is the moral requirement expressed by St Francis of Assisi: 'If you have men who will exclude any of God's creatures from the shelter of compassion and pity, you will have men who deal likewise with their fellow men.'

In the New Testament a remark by Jesus is comforting. He tells his disciples, 'Are not two sparrows sold for a farthing? And one of them shall not fall to the ground without your Father' (Matthew 10:29). So the smallest and most insignificant birds – so cheap you get two for next to nothing – are deemed to be so worthy of attention that the most powerful Being in the universe will notice the death of just one of them. With that in mind I see no reason why a person should not conduct a burial ritual for a mourned pet, perhaps using words from St Francis of Assisi, patron saint of ecology and of animals. He believed that we are all one, interrelated Creation, and all – from the smallest insect to the most noble human being, encompassed within the love of the Creator. On his feast day, 4 October, some Catholic and other Christian churches all over the world hold services where animals are blessed. Therefore, if the living creatures can be blessed, why not the dead? For it is a short step from such an honouring of valued animals to feeling that – since we know that dogs too have the capacity to 'love' (the human concept must serve) and since one idea of heaven is a state of pure love – there *could* be a spiritual dimension to our pet dogs about which we know nothing. In truth, I suspect this is not the case, but what does it matter, if believing gives comfort?

Myself, I still lean towards the words of wisdom which emanate from my statue of Kwan Yin, in her garden temple. She is telling me that we must understand that every single thing is in a state of flux; therefore struggling against it is a waste of spirit-energy. Sad we may feel – yet learning to be at peace with a loss begins with understanding that we must live in the moment, knowing that more moments will follow, each one begging to be experienced fully. Clinging to a grief traps the one grieving – and the one grieved for. It is no memorial to a person – or a beloved pet – to be rendered incapable of living because they have gone. Death is just one ending. If it is true that 'what will survive of us is love' then the only way to prove that is to *live.*

I can hear friends who have been plunged into terrible sadness by the deaths of their cherished dogs assuring me that it isn't so easy. At 2.30 p.m. on Wednesday 25 January 2005 (and how she remembers) my dear friend Gaynor's dog was put to sleep, after a long illness and more than one operation. Bentley was a Border terrier and she, a beautiful, vibrant woman, says truly, 'He was the only boy who broke my heart.' She is not making a jest; nor do such levels of grief result from modern sentimentality. Animal cemeteries – like the Cimetière des Chiens in a north-west suburb of Paris, and the one at Molesworth in Cambridgeshire – testify to the seriousness with which our forebears treated the deaths of pets. It was common for the owners of great houses to create pets' burial grounds and commission monumental sculptures of the animals. On a single lichen-covered stone in the woods at Overwater Hall Hotel in Cumbria Robin and I sympathized with a sorrow over a hundred years old, for 'Lyuth – sic a bonnie dog' and 'Brownie – too dearly loved'.

Around 1853 Giuseppe Verdi (whose operas have always thrilled me more than any others) bought a Maltese dog for his mistress (later wife), Giuseppina Strepponi, perhaps anticipating the long hours she would be left alone at their villa, San' Agata, in the province of Piacenza in northern Italy. The former soprano idolized the little dog, who followed her everywhere and slept on her bed. But in August 1862 Verdi wrote to the conductor Mariani: 'A very great misfortune for me has struck us and made us suffer atrociously. Loulou, poor Loulou is dead! Poor creature! The true friend, the faithful inseparable companion of almost six years of life! So affectionate! So beautiful! Poor Loulou. It is difficult to describe the sorrow of Peppina but you can imagine it ... in my house there is desolation.' Giuseppina and Verdi buried the 'faithful and charming' Maltese under a willow in their garden – and visitors to what is now called the Villa Verdi can visit the handsome stone memorial by the lake, inscribed 'All memoria d'un Vero Amico', and see an oval portrait of the blue-ribboned dog, their 'true friend', still hanging in Giuseppina's room.

I find it easy to imagine Guiseppina's grief for Loulou, who looked so like my Bonnie. I understand about Flush and Carlo and reckon Byron's Boatswain did have a soul – because nobody can prove to me that he didn't. Their dogs, like my own, have a purpose. To pause for a moment in the neutral gloom of most days and allow yourself to plug in to the various sorrows of others, past and present, is to be reactivated by an electric current of understanding which can light the world.

The dogs are a way in. They are – in this particular story – the *portal.*

There proved to be nothing seriously wrong with Bonnie that time; anti-inflammatory and antibiotic drugs cleared up whatever it was, and the vets remained mystified. Robin and I were unable to take her out for a week while she recovered, but at last life returned to normal. Each day we take her for the same short walk: across the road, through a road of modern houses (like Wisteria Lane in *Desperate Housewives*), along to the allotments, and round and back through a small park. She likes the walk, but will refuse to come if one of us remains in the house. The whole pack must move as one. One day, when we were admiring the neat rows of cabbages and beans and Robin was saying how good it would be to be self-sufficient, we met a neighbour – a widow. Her steps were slow; she told us her old dog had died. 'The house is so empty,' she said. 'I hate going back there.' Her dog had given her comfort when her husband died suddenly a few years earlier, and through the dark days following. Now the basket was empty, and she found it insupportable. We murmured the right words of sympathy, aware of their inadequacy – knowing too that this is the point at which some people give up, because the pet dog is their last connection to life, or rather, to the will to live.

It's hard to read about the death of Edith Wharton's last dog without being moved. After 11 years together, Linky fell ill on 11 April 1937 and four days later Wharton had to take the decision to have her sick Peke ('the best and last of her race') euthanized. That night she imagined she saw the little dog's ghost by her bed. The day after, her diary says simply, 'Can't remember. Oh, my little dog,' and she tells a friend, 'I wish she could have outlasted me, for I feel, for the very first time in my life, quite utterly alone and lonely.' Then, for several days, Wharton does not mention her pet, but tries to write bravely of other things. At last, on 26 April, comes this cry of anguish: 'Oh, how shall I get used to not seeing Linky any more?' In May she was 'tired and depressed' and noted, 'Cannot forget my Linky.' Then, four months to the day after her dog became ill, Edith Wharton died of a stroke. She must have known that her great novels would give her immortality, but it is easy to understand why the childless woman of 75 had no wish to go on without that little heartbeat at her feet.

Fortunately our neighbour, though in her seventies, proved more robust. A few months later we met her again in the allotments, but this time her face was alight. She couldn't wait to tell us excitedly about her new puppy – a poodle: 'He's making *such* a difference.' Of course. The puppy brought life and movement back into her home. No wonder so many dogs are used successfully in therapeutic work – the best ones trained to respond positively to the most disturbed young people or to men and women suffering from Alzheimer's disease. My father was touched to observe how Bonnie – usually unfriendly to strangers and always restless – somehow knew that she must sit quietly on the lap of his 100-year-old neighbour, giving her such pleasure because she felt herself *liked* by the small dog. One of my readers wrote in response to a letter I published from a woman with multiple problems. Her considered advice? 'The best recipe – making you take long walks and giving you someone to tell everything to – is to get a dog! I've just got my second rescue dog and it really does change your life. Somebody who will love you unconditionally – always.'

Unfortunately it would not do for that to be my own standard response, although I agree that many lonely and depressed people would benefit from what we all call 'the Bonnie effect'.

My favourite evenings are at home, just with Robin and our dog: the pack in a pile on the sofa. Family and friends, though deeply loved, require attention; what's more, sometimes I can no longer face up to the demands of the books I love. After a day wrestling with words and meanings, I like nothing better than to curl up with the pack and watch a movie. But my taste in films becomes worse as I grow older. When J and I were in our twenties we used to queue at an art-house cinema in Chelsea to appreciate Fellini and Bergman. Now in my sixties, I am unashamed to enjoy Jennifer Aniston starring in *Marley and Me* and Sam Neill in *Dean Spanley*. Robin and I share a taste for romantic comedies and any movie which features Hugh Grant playing his own, floppy-haired English self. 'There's nothing wrong with wanting a story to end happily,' Robin says defensively, and although I argue that art does not always afford such a luxury, in my heart I agree. We were talking about Richard Curtis films one day when I pointed that, during the period covered by this book (spring 2002 to summer 2009), I had attended four funerals and a wedding.

'Whose wedding?' he asked, knowing about the funerals.

'Ours, of course!' I said.

I thought I'd not quite reached the age to meet acquaintances in the obituary columns, although, from time to time, there they are – transporting me back to a seventies party, with someone singing Persian love songs or blues to a sweet guitar, as wine flows, joss sticks burn and somebody across the room is falling in love and it will all end with sickness of head and heart. And then, years later, comes the obituary which tolls the knowledge that we are no longer 'Still crazy after all these years' but tired of living and scared of dying. Sometimes.

If imagining the death of your beloved pet puts you into training, it is also a way of avoiding the knowledge that your parents (for example) will die and you will feel bereft. But there was no avoiding those four funerals – and so I pause here to honour my friends, as a way through (yes, another portal) to the next surprising stage of my personal quest, when I'd be accompanied by my small dog alone. You must step with me into these shadows, because similar ones will have fallen across your own path – and there is no avoiding them, not with light-hearted movies nor wine nor sex, nor even laughter at the antics of a cavorting canine companion. The shadows must be embraced.

So, those four people, all of whom I first met in the eighties. First, the writer Bernard Levin died in August 2004. It was time he went, since by then the greatest journalist of his generation had mislaid language within the dense thickets of his mind. We had shared opera, meals and many jokes as well as confidences; I rejoiced in the happiness his last love brought him and, like all those who loved him, watched with despair and horror as Alzheimer's disease pulled him into the pit. We grieved for his lost wit, his bonhomie, his enthusiasms, his passion for wine, women and song, and that great, boundless kindness which piled up glittering Rheingold against the door into the dark. Speaking at his funeral, and then writing his entry for the *Dictionary of National Biography*, were among the hardest things I have ever done, because of the struggle to find words that could leap high enough to reach him.

Then, at the beginning of January 2005 one of Britain's most talented architects, Richard Feilden, died at his home just outside Bath, when a tree he was felling in the woodland he loved crushed him. He was 54 and at the height of his career. The day before his death two of his three adult children were at my home, celebrating my daughter's birthday. Then came the phone call from J, telling me the shocking news. Richard's talent and energy, his idealism, his firm opinions, his quizzical challenges, his hospitality and humour – all gone. He was the one who had once irritated me by teasing my lapdog, but how I wished to hear his banter again. Just a few days before his death the world had been shaken by news of the devastating tsunami which followed the Indian Ocean earthquake, killing over 230,000 people in 11 countries and shattering the existence of their families and communities. Such universal suffering and grief – and yet still one individual death makes the heart contract as you witness the devastation it causes to family and friends. At his funeral, Bath Abbey erupted with Richard's favourite motto, 'Onwards and upwards', and we all took his message of hope out into the cold day.

In November the same year I heard that the editor I had worked with on my children's fiction since 1985 was dead. I had last seen Miriam Hodgson at the end of 2003 when I wept in her arms, telling her about the end of my marriage. After that we had exchanged the odd affectionate note and postcard as usual, but she had retired and I was no longer writing the 'Kitty' stories, so there was no real need to meet. I assumed there would always be a Christmas party where we would slip into our old confidences surrounded by children's authors gossiping and quaffing wine. Now she too was gone. No more little ticks in the margins of a manuscript, no more little pencilled comments like 'Lovely!' and occasional plaintive protests because a character was meaner than she thought strictly necessary. The mournful task of writing Miriam's obituary for *The Times* fell to me and I took it as an honour. The article ended, 'She always said that children "deserve to keep a belief in good defeating evil." That spirit of optimism survives her, both in the books she edited and within those as yet unwritten, where her influence will live.'

A journalist, an architect, a children's book editor … and then another writer. The prolific journalist Miles Kington died in February 2008. Like most people in our trade I had marvelled at his ability to write daily columns which floated above the common run on their airy wit, like cumulus in a summer sky. No wonder people laughed as well as cried at his funeral. An old school friend told the gathering how Miles had been persuaded to judge a dog show during a Highland Games. He knew little about dogs but compensated by dreaming up new categories of canine champion – like 'the most disobedient dog', and the one which looked most like a certain acerbic female television presenter. His wife had to persuade him not to give first prize to the dog which hadn't won any other prizes.

Oh, the poignant humour of non-achieving dogs! No wonder Miles Kington's last book is called *How Shall I Tell the*

Dog? It is a series of witty letters to his agent, putting up increasingly mad ideas for books – because now he is terminally ill he needs a best-seller all the more. Along the way he plays with all sorts of notions, like how to break the news to your dog that now – against all expectations – it will outlive you: 'He might not realize I am going to die, for a start. He doesn't know about death. As I lie expiring ... how do I know that as I open my mouth and prepare to utter my carefully prepared and rehearsed last words, he may not burst in and demand to be taken for a walk? And that my last words, after all that, will turn out to be: "Oh, for God's sake, not now, Berry!"' There was a man who understood the bounding, irrepressible nature of dogs – which could lead him towards jokes, even in the face of his own death.

All the deaths we endure have something to teach us, in the end, and the process is infinite. Thirty-four years on, I have just commissioned the artist and letter-cutter Iain Cotton to create a memorial in slate to the baby son who never drew breath. It will say, 'LOVE'S STILLNESS FOREVER MOVES', acknowledging the permanence of loss, but its transforming power too. And all these thoughts lead me to this point in my story. For how could I ever forget? During those years, the soprano Susan Chilcott died too – and her death was a source of great grief to those who loved her, but a tsunami to J and to me.

One Sunday morning, early in January 2009, I am listening to J talk about her on the radio. The series (on BBC Radio 3) *Private Passions* invites a different well-known person each week to choose music they love and explain why. Presented by the composer Michael Berkeley, the programmes place serious emphasis on the chosen music, as befits the station's remit. I cannot lose my long habit of listening intently when J broadcasts, wishing him to be excellent and admiring when he is, yet at the same time deflated by the realization that it no longer really matters what I think. As the programme's theme tune begins I am guessing what he will pick: some Mozart certainly (probably piano) and definitely some Beethoven (I predict a sonata for piano and violin, the 'Spring'), and of course – I know this – he will select Susan Chilcott singing one of the great arias, even though she recorded but little. I am prepared.

What I am unprepared for is the gradual discovery that the choices form, in a sense, a soundtrack to much of our life together. He does not intend it, but as the programme unfolds, they open gates of memory as not even words can do. He talks about his father, and about his chairmanship of the Bath International Music Festival, and then begins his selection. Benjamin Britten's *St Nicholas* reminds me how, when we were first married, he used to spoof-sing the line 'St Nicholas was born in answer to prayer', telling me how, as a teenager, he loved singing it in his school choir. Every Christmas morning the very first thing we would do was put on his old LP of Britten's *Ceremony of Carols*. He introduced me to such things.

Choosing Beethoven's Seventh he recalls going to Berlin not long after the Wall was torn down, and imagining what it must have been like when the Potsdamer Platz was opened and the Berlin Philharmonic played the mighty Seventh. And I remember his euphoria, his optimism as he brought me home a couple of fragments of the Wall, lurid with graffiti paint. These were *our* times. Then his choice of some wild, mad, hypnotic music from the highlands of Ethiopia rings out harshly on Radio 3, but is no surprise to me because only I know fully how much Ethiopia meant to him, through all the years of making documentaries there. I was the one he came home to, the one he talked to about it all. Does he, in a box in the attic, still have the record *Musiques Ethiopiennes* I bought him?

I was right about the Mozart; he is rueful about his limited skills as a pianist, but says he used to enjoy playing certain slow movements to passable effect – good enough to deceive those who did not know that much about music. As the first bars of the Piano Sonata in A major fill my ears I am transported back to his mother's long, low, beamed drawing room in Cranleigh, Surrey. Polished oak side tables, family photographs in silver frames, deep sofas, blue and gold velvet chairs, little pleated wall lights, a scent of logs and home. It is spring 1968, we are just married, and house-sitting for a week, looking after the Labradors Bill and Ben and catching up with our neglected university studies. J sits at the baby grand piano and plays me this very same sonata – and I lean to watch him, in surroundings more beautiful than any I have ever known, thinking that this man I love playing Mozart (*so* well – to me) is the most exquisite sound I have heard in my 21 years.

His final choice, number six, is introduced with some reflections on the wonders he saw over 30 years as a television reporter and documentary maker – and suddenly a sixth sense makes me say 'Thomaskirche!' to myself. I am right, of course – because I remember what it meant to him to hear the St John Passion in Bach's great church in Leipzig at Easter, when East Germany was still held in the grip of the communist Honneker regime, and the music of Bach was a sublime form of protest. He carefully carried home a simple poster for the concert, which we had framed – rendering due significance to the piece of ephemera. J tells how he sat in the glorious church, thinking how wonderful it would be for that oppressed society to be free, all the while transported (even though he describes himself as 'without faith really') 'by one of the great pieces of Christian art'. Which can transform even the sound of a crowd/chorus calling for the crucifixion of Jesus into a cascade of grace.

I take the lesson. This is a part of the seeking – to realize that the very worst can be so transformed.

But I must retrace, returning to his third music choice, introduced by way of his love of opera. There is Susan Chilcott, between Beethoven and the Ethiopians, between his memories of the Berlin Wall and of famine, bringing the first note of sadness into a programme full of enthusiasm. How could it be helped? How could he not choose her? Michael Berkeley is gracious in his lead-in to this choice, commenting that when events in life are heightened we often say, 'It's like an opera.' J agrees. He says that he always thought his life would go steadily along and that big dramas would happen to other people. But then, 'I fell in love with a glorious singer, the soprano Sue Chilcott, and she with me, and I spent the last three months of her life with her.' He talks about her greatness as a singer, how Placido Domingo described her as a genius, how beautiful she was, how suited for the great, lyric tragic roles – and at last, voice full of controlled emotion, chooses (from a newly released CD, *Susan Chilcott in Brussels*) a piece of music I know very well indeed: Desdemona's poignant final aria, 'Ave Maria'.

When the final 'Amen' has faded, J manages to say, 'You just think when you hear that voice, what the world of music and opera has lost.'

There is no gainsaying it. The beauty of her voice is overwhelming, but so is the message of the words, as the doomed Desdemona prays to Mary for sinner and innocent alike, and for those who are weak and oppressed. She prays for the man who bows beneath injustice and also beneath the blows of cruel destiny. She prays for the powerful man who also grieves. Finally, in her last benediction, Desdemona begs the Virgin to pray for all of us ('*prega per noi!*'), and there, miraculously, in Boito's words and Verdi's music, the separate parts of this whole programme are united into one whole: Beethoven's deafness, Mozart's suffering and early death, the people of East Berlin and of Ethiopia and the other beknighted countries J reported from, Shakespeare's tragedies, all Britten's lost and lonely 'outsiders' – and J himself, a powerful man who also grieves.

'Thy sweet compassion show' ('*tua pieta dimostra*') begs Desdemona.

But what, I think, of *me*?

'I spent the last three months of her life with her,' he said, but there was no mention of that other woman to whom he was married for all those years. Not even in passing. Not even a nod. For a few moments I feel full of sadness and anger, even indignation, because I seem to have become like one of the 'disappeared' of Argentina whose grieving relatives could never discover what had happened to them, or like those airbrushed from history in communist regimes. But the feeling does not last. After all, he made no mention of his new wife either – and I know he would have made such decisions after careful thought, because this programme is about *music*. The music comes first. And Susan Chilcott *is* her music now.

Thus reasoning, I quickly recover – because, in any case, what does it matter? There is permanent solace in what I know: the sharing of a whole, rich life behind the music he chose, the shaping of us both from when we were young, the suitcases packed and unpacked, the phone calls from distant places, the children, the Christmases and anniversaries, the silly names and splendid gifts, the farm, the three dogs and four cats … and so on, even up until the end, and her final, heartbreaking 'Amen'. It was ours – and so it remains. Just as the earlier writing on a palimpsest can always be read by the ones who know it is there, even though new words have been written over it. And just as when, after a note of music ends, its spirit still vibrates within the air.

Without fully understanding why, I bought the new CD J mentioned on the programme, and also the recording of Aaron Copland songs Susan Chilcott recorded with Iain Burnside in September 2002, one month before J first met her at that fateful dinner party. There was something almost furtive about my purchase. I told nobody, but squirrelled the CDs away as if I had done something wrong. Wanting to own them, I nevertheless could not summon the courage to hear them. So a month went by, and I began to write this book with my small dog nestling at my feet. Thinking I might listen in the privacy of my study, I loaded the music on to iTunes on my computer. But each time I went to select one or other – I changed my mind. It was impossible for me to expose myself to that.

Then, one day, a strange thing happened.

When writing, I sometimes have classical music playing quietly all day, relegating (I'm afraid) the glories of Hildegarde of Bingen, Mozart and Haydn to a background accompaniment. I will start somewhere randomly in the category and then just leave it playing. So it is on this particular cold March day, when suddenly I look at my watch and realize I have an appointment at the hairdresser's and must leave immediately. My hair is cut and coloured, then I wander into my favourite clothes shop next to the salon, then into another shop to pick up bracelets and put them down again. At last, after the contented time wasting which I rarely allow myself, I return home. Coat off, gaze critically at the hair in the mirror, make an espresso – and then comes the moment all writers dread. Restarting work that can be put off no longer. I go downstairs to my office, where iTunes has been playing to the empty air all the while.

And – What is *that*? I think.

Wind instruments like birdsong – oboe, flute and clarinet rising and falling cleanly, as if in the stillness of a perfect summer morning.

I stand still, then hear the soprano's first words, 'How beautiful it is!'

The shadowy butterflies fluttering on my screensaver are dispelled as I click to determine what track this is. But perhaps in my heart I already know. Methodically working its way down through the digitized albums, fate has delivered to me, at the precise second I enter my study, Susan Chilcott performing an aria from Britten's *The Turn of the Screw*. It is the very first track on the *Brussels* CD. What would be the odds on such a piece of timing?

She is singing the role of the governess who has arrived at a country house to take care of two seemingly innocent children, Miles and Flora. What she cannot possibly know is that they have been corrupted (in ways unspecified, which adds to the dreadful mystery) by a former valet and governess, Peter Quint and Miss Jessel, who are now dead. Yet they visit the children still. Within moments the mood shifts. In the background you still hear the sweetness of the wind instruments but now they form an ironic, almost cruel contrast to the singer's unease, then fear. She sings: 'Only one thing that I wish/that I could see him …' – but why would you want to see a ghost? The young woman glimpses a man (Quint's evil spirit) and you hear panic rise as she asks, 'Who is it? Who? Who can it be?' in her first intimation of the horror that is to come.

This music is full of ghosts. When the track finishes I press Stop, not wanting to hear her Desdemona and that rending 'Ave Maria'. Or unable to face it.

Do you believe in signs? I asked the question before and still ask. Two weeks after that strange occurrence, the coincidence happened again. This time I had hurried out to the gym, once again leaving the music playing in my study. After exercising I went shopping for food, indulged in more time wasting in clothes shops and at last returned home. Only this time I entered my study in the middle of a track, her voice in full flood once again, asking finally:

Why do they shut me out of heaven?
Did I sing too loud?

The crescendo on the final note seems to defy the forbidding angels ('the gentlemen in white robes') with its defiant volume. This is the recording of songs by Aaron Copland, and happenstance has entered me into track eight of his setting of poems by my beloved Emily Dickinson, who trusted she would be led across into heaven by her dog. There is hardly a pause before the next song begins:

The world feels dusty when we stop to die
We want the dew then
Honours taste dry.

The poem/song tells us what anyone who has been very ill knows: that when you are dying, achievements mean nothing and all you want is a 'fan stirred by a friend's hand' which 'cools like the rain'.

This would be enough – but it is the next song which hits me like a message from another world. (I print this with Dickinson's distinctive punctuation, not the tidied-up version Copland had to work with in 1950):

Heart, we will forget him!
You and I – tonight!
You may forget the warmth he gave –
I will forget the light!

When you have done, pray tell me
That I may straight begin!
Haste! Lest while you're lagging
I remember him!

How can I shut this off? Press the Stop key and return to where I was – before the voice begged me to listen? There is no Pause button for the unfolding of pain. So I will not seek to escape it now – even in the safety of my white room. Because I believe that the random selection of Susan Chilcott singing, out of so many hours of music, not once but twice, has happened for a reason. And I must listen – as an act not of masochism but of meditation. This has little to do with forgiveness, for that is not my prerogative. I am just another flawed soul, muddling along, attempting to understand.

It was impossible to embark upon the next stage of my strange meeting with Susan Chilcott then, not with Robin elsewhere in the house. He would not wish me to do anything which might upset me, and therefore I must keep my intention secret. What's more, I did not want anybody to interrupt and find me out. So I waited. At last, four months after I had listened to *Private Passions*, Robin went away to France and so I could be quite alone, apart from Bonnie, lying in my lap. My room was illuminated only by a candle and the light from the computer screen, where the iTunes visualizer turned the music into magical abstract patterns. With a glass of Sauvignon in my hand I listened to Susan singing Britten (Ellen in *Peter Grimes* as well as the governess in *The Turn of the Screw*), and Verdi, and Strauss and Boesmans. It lasted almost an hour, followed by over an hour of Copland, with more wine. With my dog warming my legs and heart, I heard fear, love, wonder and resignation, as the piano notes were transformed into whirling fragments on my screen, showers of coloured sparks in a night sky. Purple shading to blue to red to green. And in the centre of it all, was the recurring black disc – now large, now small, now bounced away by light, now rolling back to the dark centre – burning on the retina the unmistakable message of mortality.

I thought, How unutterably gorgeous, that voice.

I thought, How could any man resist such beauty?

I thought, How I wish *I* had learned to sing.

But most of all, listening to that glorious sound, encompassing so much universal emotion, I thought of the singer, not the song. Once again, as in 2003, I imagined what it must have been like to know you were going to die at the age of 40, to look at your little son knowing you would never see him grow up and to try to explain that enormity to him. Oh, the pity of it. Glimpsing death, would you not cry out in terror at the spectre, 'Who is it? Who?'? And would you not hold out both hands to grasp those which stretched out in love to help you? Understanding that, I am suddenly filled with an inexpressible serenity, within that dark room. It comes from the knowledge that my husband left me, not to drink champagne with a mistress in a Mediterranean hotel, but to be the friend wielding the cooling fan. To take upon himself the burden of somebody's suffering, in all its ugliness. To face the real human drama – far beyond those artificially heightened emotions of opera – where there can be no resolution, nor catharsis, before the final curtain.

And what if it was bewildering – such an excess of love – to both of us, to our children, to everyone else? No matter. This is the end of this particular quest – just to accept. All I need to know, six years on, is the truth expressed in one of the Copland songs, which now, in the peace of my room and the comforting presence of my dog, I choose to play again and again, loving it more than anything else she sang. It is a setting of a poem by E.E. Cummings – whose work J gave me for Christmas 1968, with a loving inscription of course. There is no irony in such inscriptions. They tell an incontrovertible truth, one which is now echoed in this elegy, which Copland's music renders curiously inconclusive, as if to say, 'Nothing ends, the music continues in silence':

in spite of everything
which breathes and moves,since Doom
(with white longest hands
neatening each crease)
will smooth entirely our minds

— before leaving my room
i turn,and(stooping
through the morning)kiss
this pillow,dear
where our heads lived and were.

That is grace.

So now – since I am the one who is fortunate enough to be alive – I have to ask myself what I will do with the life that is left. This is the question which, as often as possible, I bat outwards too, towards my readers. You who are 30 and you who are 60 – think on it, with me. Each of us will have ways of working it out, but there should be no doubt about the urgency. My way begins with stretching out my foot to the small dog beneath my desk, who patiently waits for any crumb of attention to fall from the preoccupied human companion. Knowing her has taught me that there are more ways of loving than are dreamt of in your romantic novels.

As I grow older I find I detest romance. The Penelope Fitzgerald novel *The Blue Flower*, which sparked thoughts about finding and searching, echoes my mistrust of its blandishments. It tells the true story of how, in eighteenth-century Saxony young Fritz von Hardenberg falls in love with 12-year-old Sophie – an absurdly romantic attachment to a frivolous, ordinary girl he calls his 'true Philosophy' and 'spirit's guide' with no understanding of her real self. The otherworldly Hardenberg will later become the great romantic poet and philosopher 'Novalis', and the Blue Flower was an important symbol for him and for the German Romantic Movement – representing the metaphysical striving for the infinite and unreachable. In one of his novels the hero dreams about blue flowers and becomes obsessed by them, as if they only exist, unattainable, in the world of the mind ...

But wait a minute – in my own garden I see forget-me-nots, cornflowers, hydrangeas, delphiniums, veronicas, wild geraniums. Ordinary blue flowers abound, so why would you search for the Blue Flower? Oh, why does the stupid, agonized romantic perpetually scan the horizon, failing to see the beauty in the lowly, crushed petals at his feet? Why the fevered seeking, without understanding what is already found?

Fritz becomes engaged to Sophie when she is 13, but she falls terminally ill. There are unspeakable operations without anaesthetic; the prognosis is grim. She is destined to die days after her fifteenth birthday, when her fiancé (in the manner of romantics, unable to bear witness) has departed to his own home. But before that, there is a telling moment with the small dogs who run in the margins of the whole novel. Sophie's sickroom is bedlam, full of step-siblings, caged birds and lapdogs, and when the schoolmaster arrives he protests, asking, 'Kindly remove the five dogs, at least, from the room.' The sick girl should be quiet. But other people arrive, witless, blundering, and 'Sophie held her arms out to them all. In the racket her laughter and coughing could scarcely be heard. The little dogs, all desperate to be first, bounded back, with flattened ears, onto the bed to lick her face.'

No one, in the heat and odour of an eighteenth-century room, would have bothered about hygiene. Nor do people nowadays who love their dogs. In any case, the dogs' kisses are healing, even if only temporarily. (I believe Bonnie's licks keep my wrinkles under control.) As the pets bound about on the sick girl's bed, delighting her with their enthusiasm, the old schoolmaster closes his book and thinks, 'After all, these people were born for joy.'

Of course, what happens at the end of that particular story gives the lie to that statement of simple optimism. They loved, were deluded and died young. But the mad, loving licking of the dogs is indiscriminately generous. On a bumper sticker in Charleston, South Carolina, I saw the message 'DON'T POSTPONE JOY'. That is why I offer the lesson of dogs, who are incapable of postponement. Who *must* race, *must* bound, *must* wag, *must* lick, *must* play, *must* be petted – as if their lives, so much shorter than our own, depend on it. They do not seek the Blue Flower, but know instinctively that you have to keep digging in the ordinary little patch that you have, finding new things to sniff at all the time, right here, *now.* The dog says, 'Go for it!'

The messages are everywhere. In steamy Georgia, we stayed at an inn where a miniature Yorkshire terrier ran to greet every guest. Joey was exactly like the two tiny dogs I had met in Amy Tan's San Francisco condo in 2002 – and being reminded of that encounter made me realize how much I had changed. I had learned how to read the beseeching yet frolicsome intelligence in the eyes of the small dog. Cuddling this little stranger on my lap (unfaithful to Bonnie most days in Savannah) I whispered to him that only I of all the guests knew how very busy he was. How meaningful his very small life.

Charles Baudelaire understood. He wrote, 'Where do dogs go? … They go about their business. Business meetings, love meetings. Through fog, through snow, through mud, during biting dog-days, in streaming rain, they go, they come, they trot, they slip under carriages, urged on by fleas, passion, need, or duty. Like us, they get up early in the morning, and they seek out their livelihood or pursue their pleasures.' His contemporary, Alphonse Toussenel, saw further, identifying the point behind most of canine activity: 'In the beginning, God created man, but seeing him so feeble, He gave him the dog.'

Everywhere I see them, and know that they are quietly going about their business of doing good – saving lives as Bonnie saves mine. They tell us to enjoy the simple pleasures of clean water and simple food and a walk and a caress and just sitting right up close to someone you love. They know that to be apart is intolerable. They lead by example – following instincts, loving unconditionally, accepting treats with enthusiasm, being loyal and faithful and quick to forgive. They know that you can show defiance with a short growl, and should have no need to bite. Not able to dissemble, they throw themselves with adoration at the beloved person coming through the door. In their blood runs the knowledge that when you are small, you survive by being lovable – and that is the lesson which matters most of all. It is as if they know that life is but a few pants and wags and therefore all of the above, all those talents, must be crammed in, without stint, in the moments between breakfast, supper and the long dreaming of an eternal chase.

And that is why, determined now to rush at life as Bonnie rushes at the postman's trousers … whilst she can … whilst I can … I listen to the cohorts of small dogs. They tell me I must always 'Go seek it out!' until no longer capable of doing so, because within that urging is promise, adventure, courage. And change. For the process of writing this has led me to another stage, and as I reach the end of one story, I begin a new one.

It sometimes made me uncomfortable that I invariably describe this elegant town house in the city of Bath as 'my' house. Mine. In my name. My children found it for me, it enabled me to make my final escape from the farm and I created it in my own image. Yet how could I have known that I would remarry? One rainy day in August, as we sat talking in the conservatory wondering what happened to summer, and Bonnie snoozed between us, I suddenly realized what Robin had not said, that this perfect home for a writer who likes high heels does not suit a man who longs to grow vegetables and mend fences. To stride over meadows and devise ways of living 'greenly'. To clear undergrowth, chop wood and remake things that have broken down. Sometimes he longs to push out these Regency walls with his elbows and plant a greenhouse in the formal garden. The man brought up on thousands of acres of Kenyan farmland needs space.

And me? I want to slow time down by learning to watch things grow.

It was time to go house-hunting together. As I reach this ending (before yet another beginning) we have fallen in love with a rambling old farmhouse in the countryside outside Bath, a home even older than this one, with beams and crannies, as well as outbuildings which are begging to be restored by a man who can fix anything. We plan to live in a different way, more simply, more peacefully. To listen to stillness at night, broken by the cries of owls and foxes. There will be chickens and perhaps even some sheep. Maybe in time we will rescue another dog – a shaggy mutt who will concede Bonnie's superiority, and tear across those few acres with the lolloping joy of being alive.

As we stood and looked back at the ancient house, frantically doing sums to see if it might be possible, Bonnie leapt through meadow grass and lapped from the river which runs through the garden. Her impractical paws were already muddy; there was a burr stuck to her ear. The lapdog with the jewelled collar looked in her element at the thrilling prospect of coming full circle, and being a country dog again.

EPILOGUE

I am booked for a children's event at the Oundle Literary Festival, to talk about my 'Bonnie' books. Robin, the dog and I make the three-hour drive north-eastwards from Bath to Northamptonshire, a part of England new to us. We're always reluctant to leave our garden, where daffodils and crocuses have already pushed their way through, and the branches of the neighbours' magnificent magnolia, tipped with candles of palest rose, hang over our ancient red-brick wall. After an unusually cold winter, this spring has promise. And I don't much like going away from home.

We are to be given a bed for the night by a generous festival committee member. All over the United Kingdom there are people like this – putting energy into good things and opening their homes to strangers. It reinforces my faith in human nature – sometimes tested by people as well as the news in general. The other week a dear friend predicted 'civil unrest' because of the worsening economy and there are many days when there seems little to celebrate. Yet these small arts festivals all over the land tell a different story. People gather to hear writers and musicians and to talk about ideas. You have to cling to such delights as you notice (and *always* notice) the piercing beauty of flowers or the warmth in somebody's welcome. The wine is sloshing into glasses as we walk through the door. Stuart and Jennifer are going out to a literary dinner but have left supper and tell us their house is ours. The fact that our dog is with us makes us feel at home.

In a way that is hard to explain, she *is* 'home'.

Next morning we have time to explore the area for a while, before the 1.30 p.m. event – and our hostess suggests a visit to Fotheringhay, 'just up the road'. I had not realized (ever too busy to examine a map) that we would be staying so near to the place (surely special to lovers of small dogs?) where Mary Queen of Scots went to her death, accompanied by her hidden Skye terrier. How fitting an accident to find ourselves so near while I am writing this book.

We say our thanks and goodbyes and set off under a lowering sky. The village of Fotheringhay is indeed just five minutes away by car, but there is little to see. Home of a royal line, birthplace of Richard III, the village was of national standing in the fifteen and sixteenth centuries, but now there are just a few attractive houses built from golden stone, a church and the site of the once great castle.

For there is nothing left. The wind blows straight from the Fens in the east, where the river Nene meets the sea. There is nobody around. Church lovers both, we are disconsolate to find St Mary and All Saints closed and even sadder to discover nothing but the green 'motte' where the keep of Fotheringhay once stood, on the broad green banks of the river. A part of my imagination had hoped for picturesque ruins – romantic stones tumbled to earth yet still reminding the visitor of a history which began in 1100. There we might sit and commune with the spirit of the unfortunate queen … But no, that is fanciful, because I knew (from the leaflet our hostess had given me) that it would indeed take much imagination to conjure up an image of the Great Hall where Mary went to the scaffold. But I had hoped for more than what looks like an enormous burial mound on a wide curve of the waterway.

Still, the idea of the burial mound is fitting too, given the desolation of this site beneath the wide, grey sky. They've put shallow wooden steps on one side, to help the visitor climb. I say to Bonnie, 'Come on, you have to honour the spirit of Mary's faithful little dog.' Eternally responsive, she bounds up steps tall to her, until we are standing on the top, looking down over the wide, flat area where the Great Hall would have been. I find I'm humming a poignant tune from distant 1969, the year J and I graduated and began our careers. Sandy Denny of Fairport Convention was inspired by Mary Stuart's story to write the song 'Fotheringay' (an alternative historical spelling) for the LP *What We Did On Our Holidays*. I know the lyrics by heart and can hear those plangent guitar melodies inside my brain:

How often she has gazed from castle windows all
And watched the daylight passing within her captive wall
With no one to heed her call …

Yet I can't help thinking that Denny got it wrong, since Mary was surrounded by servants who adored her, as well as that famous lapdog, the last in a long line of Mary's dogs. They *all* heeded her call, and it's important not to forget the strength of human love and of animal devotion – the contrasting side to a legend of failure, of victimhood, of loss.

As Bonnie races about like a tiny, ruffled cloud I stand still to read the historical leaflet, learning that Mary died with dignity and style, a marked contrast to the churlishness of her judges who withheld from her the last rites and persisted to the end with a battery of puritanical exhortation and abuse. As typical as any was the Earl of Kent, who rebutted Mary's request that her servants could be present at her death.

Aha, I think, but the bastards didn't know about the dog! They would deny the doomed Queen the comfort of people who loved her, but they could not ban her loyal pet. What must it have been like for the doomed woman, to feel his rough coat tickling beneath her shift? I know that he (or she?) would have given Mary courage … 'You're there, *cherie*, you're there.'

Mary Stuart had more soul than those who murdered her. She was a poet who wrote, with both wit and heartbreaking faith, in French, Italian and Latin, and she was writing until the day before she died. A sonnet to her cousin Elizabeth I contains the lines:

One thought that is my torment and my delight
Ebbs and flows bittersweet within my heart

She was begging Elizabeth ('dear sister') to see her, but it was not to be. Mary made so many mistakes in her life; she loved unwisely (like so many) and became a prey to politics and religion and circumstance, yet at the end she conducted herself with absolute dignity. How many people can say that? It is that dignity which remains, when her mighty prison is no more. And the honesty and humility which prompted her to tell her maid, Jane Kennedy, who on her last night read aloud the story of the good thief, 'In truth he was a great sinner, but not so great as I have been.' And at her end she prayed for the forgiveness of sins.

What else is there to pray for?

To be haunted perpetually by one thought, 'bittersweet within my heart' ('*amaro at dolce al mia cor . . .*'), is something I understand. And the absolute necessity for dignity and forgiveness. And the love of a small dog. Standing in that bleak place on top of Mary's tumbled prison, all of this has meaning, and I feel grateful.

The wind attacks me and Bonnie. Robin takes a photograph of 'his girls', capturing a windblown moment of – yes – pilgrimage. I bend to pick up a stone and toss it from hand to hand, fantasizing that this could be a fragment from the castle itself, since stones do remain and huge emotions and great wrongs are imprinted on the earth and nothing is ever finished. But it's time to go, and suddenly I fling the stone down. What is the point in carrying stones away? I am already freighted with too much history.

We are alive and cheerful and have an important job to do.

At 1.30 p.m. around 220 schoolchildren aged six to eight file into the Great Hall of Oundle School, which looks as if it could have been graced by Mary Stuart but was in fact built in 1908 in Renaissance style. I'm waiting at the front with piles of my books – and a bejewelled dog bowl. Hidden beneath the table is Bonnie's bright (embarrassingly so, to Robin) pink dog bag, to be revealed at the right moment.

I have the 'performance' off pat; after all I have been talking to children about my work since my first children's book was published in 1985. With the new series, inspired by Bonnie, Robin and I have devised a little bit of *schtik.* After talking about how writers get their ideas, and asking the children lots of questions, and reading an extract from *Big Dog Bonnie* which tells how my character Harry's mother got the small dog from a rescue home ... at last I ask if they would like to meet 'the real Bonnie', tell them she is shy and doesn't want to come – but say I will call her. So I fish the phone out of her pink bag and call Robin's number. He is, of course, waiting elsewhere with the dog. After the pretend conversation with Bonnie the children are motionless and silent with excitement. Then Robin appears at the back of the hall, puts her on the floor, whispers, 'Go find Mummy' – and the dog races down the middle aisle space, to be swept up, licking and wriggling, by the visiting author, as the children let out collective squeaks and sighs of pleasure.

As any theatre director would see, this works beautifully, and to great effect – a forest of hands in the air, and questions answered, and laughter, and children wanting to ask Bonnie questions (favourite food?) and all the time my dog is in my arms, unbothered by the Great Hall or the children and all their teachers, because she is with me. One little girl has her hand up for ages, frantically waving it for attention. When the teacher finally gestures for her to ask her question she squirms with pleasure and sighs, 'Oh, your dog's so *cute.*'

'She certainly is,' I smile.

Does life get much better than this – with the kids so happy and my dog in my arms and my man smiling at the back of the hall?

When it's over, after the long line of children clutching books to sign has been dispersed, and we walk out past the groups waiting to go back to their respective schools (young voices calling 'Goodbye Bonnie! ...') we head for Stamford. This famous Lincolnshire town is about a 20-minute drive north from Oundle and we'd been told it is worth a visit – 'the finest stone town in England', guidebooks say. Its great house, Burghley, was the home of Sir William Cecil, wily Secretary of State to Elizabeth I and one of the agents of Mary Stuart's downfall.

We should have made a better plan – for the great house is as closed as the church at Fotheringhay. Still, we walk a little in the grounds with Bonnie, looking at a miracle of Tudor architecture. 'We'll come back to this area,' we promise ourselves, for there is Peterborough Cathedral to see, and each year we say we must do a motoring tour of our own country, as John Steinbeck did with his dog, and call it 'Travels with Bonnie'. For now, aware that the journey home beckons, we drive into Stamford, park the car and wander around.

So many churches, so many good buildings, starting from the thirteenth century, and no time to do them justice. That optimistic 'We'll come back' is the promise all of us make to ourselves, in the hope that things won't change too much, that our luck will hold, that our loves will last, that we will walk our lovely, lolloping dogs through plenty more springs yet and go on noticing beauty (in the words of Mary, '*O Seigneur Dieu, recevez ma prière*') until the end.

In the meantime, Stamford's shops are good so I abandon all thoughts of visiting churches and ancient buildings today and spot a scarf in a window. It's cold, which is as good an excuse as any for darting in to buy the two-tone-purple accessory. As I am paying for it, while Robin is waiting patiently with Bonnie, an elderly couple enter the shop. Seeing the dog they coo and fuss – as people generally do.

The husband asks what breed she is.

'A Maltese,' says Robin, and then, after more compliments from the couple, he adds conversationally, 'She's a rescue dog.'

There is a tiny pause; the man looks puzzled. He doesn't understand. 'What does she rescue?' he asks.

Surreal images flash in the mind's eye:

– the small dog plunging into a boiling sea with a rope between her teeth –

– the small dog pinning the villain up against the wall, to protect her police handler –

– the small dog roaming the Alps, a barrel of brandy around her neck –

– the small dog sniffing through earthquake wreckage, looking for survivors –

The moment is too good to miss.

I turn and answer, 'Us!'

ACKNOWLEDGEMENTS

Many friends and colleagues understood why I wanted to write this book, but I must single out my children, Dan and Kitty, who, while not at all enjoying the prospect of old wounds being opened, nevertheless understood their mother's overwhelming need for catharsis, as well as my search for a creative form in which to frame it. My husband Robin gave the usual rock-like support which is central to my life, publisher Jenny Heller is a kindred spirit I am delighted to find, and my agent Patrick Walsh came up with the perfect title – which achievement he has forgotten and denies. The psychologist Linda Blair provided me with invaluable professional bolstering at a time of mini-crisis when I really did not know if I was doing the right thing.

Lastly I wish to thank Jonathan Dimbleby for his forbearance. A person who values privacy more than I do, he is at the same time Chair of that important organisation Index on Censorship, which may perhaps have a small bearing on his dignified silence about what I might or might not write. It is not the only debt I owe him.

Copyright Acknowledgements

The author is most grateful to the editors of the *Daily Mail* and *The Times* for permission to reprint extracts from her articles; also for permission to include the following extracts from copyright material:

'Not Gonna Turn Back' from *The Inside* by Jasmine Cain © Jasmine Cain.

'Late Fragment' from *All of Us: The Collected Poems* by Raymond Carver, published by Harvill Press. Reprinted by permission of The Random House Group Ltd.

'in spite of everything' from *Complete Poems 1904–1962* by E.E. Cummings, edited by George J. Firmage, by permission of W.W. Norton & Company. Copyright © 1991 by the Trustees for the E.E. Cummings Trust and George James Firmage.

'Fotheringay' by Sandy Denny from *What We Did On Our Holidays*, published by Kobalt Music.

'Atlas' from *New and Collected Poems* by U.A. Fanthorpe, published by Enitharmon Press.

'The Housedog's Grave' from *The Collected Poetry of Robinson Jeffers, Volume 3, 1939–1962*, copyright © Jeffers Literary Properties. All rights reserved. Used with the permission of Stanford University Press, www.sup.org.

'An Arundel Tomb' from *Collected Poems* by Philip Larkin, published by Faber & Faber.

'For Becky, Dan and Sarah' from *Collected Poems* by Michael Longley, published by Jonathan Cape. Reprinted by permission of The Random House Group Ltd.

'On Parting with My Wife, Janina' from *New and Collected Poems (1931–2001)* by Czeslaw Milosz, published by Penguin Books Ltd.

Susan Chilcott obituary by Tom Sutcliffe, *Guardian*, 6 September 2003.

'An Attempt at Jealousy' from *Selected Poems* by Marina Tsvetaeva, translated by Elaine Feinstein, published by Carcanet Press Ltd.

'What to Remember when Waking' from *The House of Belonging* by David Whyte, published by Many Rivers Press.

While every effort has been made to trace the owners of copyright material reproduced herein, the author and publishers would like to apologise for any omissions and will be pleased to incorporate missing acknowledgements in any future editions.